To Felix Posen who turned a dream into reality

Yaakov Malkin

Judaism Without God?
Judaism as Culture, Bible as Literature

Translated by Shmuel Gertel

The Library of Secular Judaism

MILAN PRESS

Detroit, USA

Judaism Without God?
Judaism as Culture, Bible as Literature
By Yaakov Malkin
Translated by Shmuel Gertel

Published in 2007 in Israel by *The Library of Secular Judaism*
and *Milan Press*

The Library of Secular Judaism, 11 Uzia, Jerusalem 93143, Israel

Published in Hebrew by *The Library of Secular Judaism,*
Keter Publishing and *Free Judaism* in 2003

ISBN 978-965-91151-0-5

Design and Production: Ikan Maas Media
Cover Painting (detail): Felice Pazner Malkin

Printed in Israel

Contents

Era • Constant Change in Judaism • One Cannot Claim "Judaism says", Just as One Cannot Claim "the Bible says" • Judaism's Many Judaisms • All Judaisms Take Part in the Creation of Judaism as a Culture • What do Israeli and Diaspora Jews Have in Common? • The Main Points of Contention within Judaism Today • Pluralism in Religious Judaism • "Normative Judaism" Exists Only in the Eyes of Those who Believe in it • Debate in Hellenistic and Contemporary Judaism • The Debate over the Existence of a "World to Come" • The Basis of Judaism: Bible or Talmud? • The Multiplicity of Religions and God Concepts in Judaism of the Biblical Era • The Victory of the Golden Calf – a Sign of Pluralism in Yahwist Religion • Sacrifice Culture – an Expression of the Anxiety of Believers in a Personal God • The Synagogue • A Revolutionary Innovation in Jewish History • Foreign Influences on Jewish Culture and Judaism's Contributions to World Culture • The Bible, Monotheism, the Sabbath, the Synagogue • Jewish Contributions to World Culture • The Effects of Mystical Mythology on Jewish Pluralism • Polytheism and Goddesses Enter the Jewish Religion • Belief in God as a Man in Jewish Kabbalistic Mythology • The Bible as a Source of Inspiration for Contemporary Jewish Art and Literature • Atheism Joins Judaism's Many Beliefs • Theogonic Theories in Atheistic Belief since Hellenism • The Principles of Atheism • In Israel, the Bible is Once Again the Basis for Jewish Education • Nationhood, Humanism and Tradition in Judaism Free from Religion • Non-Religious Humanistic Beliefs and Values Reflected in Most Contemporary Jewish Works

Chapter Four

Humanizing and Dehumanizing Education • Education

• Socialisation, Culture and Personal Independence • Recognising Israel's Jewish and Arab Identity • Internalising Equality and Safeguarding the • Rights of Individuals and Society through Education • Nationalistic Education – a Threat to Humanisation • Humanistic Values • Standards for the Evaluation and Criticism of Precepts and Laws • Humanistic Education Depends upon Extensive Study and Social Involvement • Social Involvement • The Role of Classical Literature • What do Classical Literature's Sinful Characters Contribute to Humanistic Education? • Eve and Prometheus • Developing Poetic Sensibility in Humanistic Education • Jewish Education and the Development of Artistic Sensibility • "I-It" and "I-Thou" Relations in Humanistic Education • Education as a Means to Humanization • Teaching Democracy and its Jewish Sources • Developing Linguistic Ability

Conflict between the Victims of Liberation and the Liberators • Moses and his God • The Unique Personalities of Moses and Yahweh as Revealed in their Biographies and in Descriptions of the Roles they Played in Historical Events • Correlation between the Exodus Story and the Historical Background that Arises from Scientific Research.

Part I

Judaism as Culture

Chapter One

Judaism as Culture in Light of Secular Jewish Beliefs

Secular Jews believe in the freedom to choose one's own path in Judaism and in freedom from religious authority, from the obligation to observe religious precepts, and from exclusively religious interpretations of the Bible, holidays, tradition, and all of the works of Jewish literature created within all streams of Judaism.

Prevailing beliefs among secular humanistic Jews support the perception of Judaism as a culture rather than a religion:

• Belief that Jewish national identity is determined by membership in the Jewish People, regardless of a person's religion. Jews are members of the Jewish nation, whether by birth or choice. Their Jewishness is expressed in their awareness of their national identity, just as others are aware of theirs – just as Englishmen or Frenchmen, for example, are aware of their respective national identities – as members of a people and participants in its culture.

• Belief that joining the Jewish People does not require religious conversion. One joins the Jewish People by joining a Jewish family or community, in a personal process, requiring no religious or other ceremony. That is how men and women have joined the Jewish People, from Biblical times to the present.

• Belief in humanistic values in keeping with Hillel's principle: "that which is hateful to you, do not unto others". Such values are essential to our humanity and to the existence of humanising society. Humanistic values are means by which one may evaluate and prefer specific behaviour and laws, and are based on belief in man as the source of authority, creator of commandments and laws, creator of God.

• Belief in humanistic values and humanisation as a supreme

value. It is by these values that secular Jews – free from religion and religious authority – judge all laws, religious precepts, regimes, individual and group behaviour. The morality of an individual – the internalisation of humanistic values – stems from her/his humanisation within society: through family, community and culture.

• Belief that man's humanity is associated with her/his nationality – since the humanisation process occurs within the family, community, society, national language and culture. There is no such thing as a supra-national culture. Every nation lives among a group of nations and cultures, and every national culture is influenced by, and is an integral part of, international culture. Jewish studies should therefore be combined with study of the cultures within which Judaism took shape and within which Jews have lived.

• Belief in the freedom to choose the way in which Jews realise their Jewishness and their Judaism. Jews are not the "chosen people", but they are a "people of choice", inasmuch as they are a people whose members must choose the way in which they wish to realise their Jewishness – in one of Judaism's many Judaisms – and the lifestyle and education that reflect that choice.

• Belief in "Judaism as culture" that includes religion but is not equivalent to it, contrary to the belief that Judaism is exclusively a religion. Belief in Judaism as culture affects one's attitude to democracy and the separation of religion and state, and is a determinant factor in policy, humanistic education and choice of Jewish texts. The culture of the Jewish People includes the Jewish religion in all its forms – Sadducean, Pharisaic, Orthodox, Reform, Conservative, Hassidic, Messianic and others. "Judaism" is not identical to any one of them. Judaism has always included many different Judaisms. Today, these beliefs are widely held in the largest of Judaism's Judaisms – the various streams of non-religious Judaism.

• Belief in God as a literary figure is common to many Jews, who believe that Yahweh, like the gods of all peoples, was created and fashioned by men and women in the ancient literature of the culture of the Jewish People. Like other literary figures in this body of literature – Moses, David, Jeremiah – God/Yahweh is an active force in Jewish culture, and in the consciousness of religious Jews who believed and believe in his existence beyond literature. In secular Jewish culture, God continues to function as a literary figure, in works that evoke an intellectual and emotional response in readers even if they do not believe in an immanent or a transcendent god, or in God as a figure of authority, whose commandments must be obeyed.

• Belief that Jews realise their Jewishness in fulfilling their obligations to society and in participating in the culture of their people runs counter to the belief that Jewishness can be realised only in observance of the halakhic precepts. Many of the prophets believed that social justice was preferable to ritual observance – sacrifice and prayer. There is no equivalence between Jewishness and Jewish religiosity, and most Jews today are "non-religious" as the term is understood in the Jewish religion: they do not observe precepts and prayers, do not belong to a synagogue, do not send their children to religious schools, do not obey the rulings of rabbis, and do not vote for religious parties.

• Belief that the Jewish religion exerts only a marginal influence on the culture and lives of most Jews today. In Israel, religious parties have a significant impact on the character of the country, through participation in government coalitions. The Jewish religion, in all its streams, exerted a decisive influence on the culture of the Jewish People until the nineteenth century – periods in which religion was a powerful force in the lives and cultures of all peoples. The impact of religion on the lives of most Jews has been on the decline ever since the late nineteenth century, and in the early twenty first century it plays only a minor role in their lives.

• Belief that the Bible is the basis of Judaism and the only element common to all Judaisms runs counter to the belief that the Talmud and Halakhah are the source and foundation of Judaism. The biblical anthology comprises a variety of literary, historiographical, legal, philosophical, rhetorical and poetic (religious and non-religious) works, representing the culture of the Jewish People in its formative period. Jewish culture at this early stage, as reflected in the Bible, was rife with tension between clashing religious streams and beliefs, such as the cult of Yahweh as an abstract and exclusive deity, or the cults of the calf, Baal and Ashtoreth.

• Belief that pluralism has characterised Jewish culture throughout history in the spirit of the pluralism we find in biblical Judaism. In every era, Judaism's many streams have produced a variety of philosophical, literary and artistic works – such as mysticism and rationalism in the Middle Ages, Hassidism and Haskalah in the Modern Era, or today's religious and secular streams.

• Belief in the universality of humanistic values, whereby "Yahwistic values" are universal values in Jewish form. Hillel characterised his "meta-value" as "the entire Torah", since it encapsulated the universal humanistic values expressed in the Commandments and the Prophets: the preference of social justice over religious ritual. These values coincide with, and complement those of Kant, who asserted that only a universal value can be considered moral, and that every person is an end and not a means.

• Belief that there have been, and continue to be anti-humanistic, tendencies within Judaism – racism and chauvinism – the sources of which can also be found in the Bible and later Jewish literature. Anti-humanistic principles run counter to the principle of Hillel, inasmuch as they discriminate against women, treat non-Jews with contempt, and advocate the killing of vanquished peoples, including women and children (as in the books of Deuteronomy, Joshua and Samuel).

• Belief in pluralism not only as a characteristic trait of Jewish culture, but as a guiding principle in the development of Jewish thought and Halakhah. The talmudic principle of "both [opinions] are the words of the living God" expresses recognition of the legitimacy of debate, and its indispensability in the search for truth. Every debate encourages and develops the reciprocal criticism that helps define the concepts and issues at hand. Another talmudic concept is that of "teku" – concluding a particular debate with the admission that some questions have no answer, and some debates are irresolvable.

• Belief that Judaism is not an ideology, but a process. Halakhah was never a fixed constitution, but an evolving, dynamic system, shaped by its human creators in a process of constant reform – continuing to this day in those streams that adapt liturgy, ritual, customs and precepts to their beliefs and changing circumstances. Such was the practice of the sages of the Oral Law, contrary to the orthodox religious-sacerdotal Sadducees.

• Belief in the principles of democracy, including decision by majority, and safeguarding minorities and their views. This belief also finds validation in the talmudic culture of majority decision. Since no man can speak in God's name, it was believed, the power of decision was granted to a human majority. Some even went so far as to assert that when a human majority contradicts divine will – it is the human majority that takes precedence (as in the story of Akhnai's oven). At the same time, minority opinions must be preserved, because they might prove right some day (according to Rabbi Judah).

• Belief in human rights and democratic values coincides with the principles declared in Israel's declaration of independence. Israel's Basic Laws – cornerstones of its future constitution – continue to develop Halakhah, in keeping with Jewish tradition's openness to change. Such laws, along with the separation of powers – that together form the basis of democracy in the Jewish state – could bring about a re-examination and abrogation of all anti-humanistic halakhic precepts; precepts that discriminate against the female half of society for example, or against religious minorities such as the Reform or Conservative movements, or others, like the deaf, children of halakhically illicit unions (Mamzerim), or those forbidden to marry.

• Belief in Judaism's openness to the cultural influences of other peoples, which has characterised Judaism in all eras, contrary to the belief in spiritual ghettos, perpetuated by limiting education to traditional halakhic literature. This openness has stimulated the creation of original Jewish works from biblical times to the present, enriched Judaism in each and every period of its history, produced generations of highly educated Jewish intellectuals with a command of many languages and cultures, and enabled Judaism to influence other cultures in turn, through the monotheistic faiths it inspired.

• Belief in the revitalisation of the Sabbath, historical holidays and personal celebrations, as part of the lives of Jews free from the religion of Halakhah. This process of revitalisation and change is one that all Jewish holidays have undergone – from biblical times to the present. Witness the hundreds of new Passover haggadot created within the various religious and secular streams of contemporary Judaism. Religious holidays that developed from sacrificial and nature festivals intended to placate God, are today, in secular Judaism, national and historical holidays without religious significance.

• Belief in the uniqueness of the Jewish People – unique like all other peoples. Peoples are unique not only in their characteristics, but in their very definition. The definition of the Swiss is unlike that of the Welsh, American or Jewish. Just as the biography of an individual defines her/his personality, so the individual history of a people and its culture simultaneously defines it and sets it apart.

• Belief in a single national historical legacy, common to adherents of both religious and areligious beliefs. This consciousness of a common history and heritage, distinguishes Judaism from peoples who share a single religious faith (Catholic, Protestant, Shiite, Sunni. etc.), but come from diverse national-historical backgrounds (French and Italian, Norwegian and German, Egyptian and Iranian etc.). This distinct characteristic allows Jews to continue celebrating historical holidays even after they have lost their religious significance, and to study Judaism as culture and history – including religion – even if they are not religious, but are conscious of their living national culture and heritage.

• Belief that Zionism is the national liberation movement of the Jewish People, and unique among national liberation movements. Zionism strove to liberate Jews from a state of national inferiority – living as tolerated or persecuted minorities – and from the influence of anti-Semitic movements – the moderate to the murderous, past and present. As a fundamentally secular movement, Zionism sought to liberate Jews from the control of Jewish religious leaders, who sought to perpetuate exile, passively awaiting the coming of a divine messiah. Zionism succeeded in its goal of establishing a Jewish state for all Jews who desired – or were forced – to immigrate to it. The foundations for a state had been laid before the Shoah, and the need for it discovered in its wake.

19

• Belief in the peace process as a precondition for the success of Zionism. Peace with the Arab peoples, who tried to destroy the State of Israel and its people before having begun to accept its existence in their midst, is a precondition for the continued success of the national liberation movement of the Jewish People. The failure of this process could bring back dangers with which Zionism and the Jewish state have had to contend in the past.

Chapter Two

Basic Concepts in Judaism as Culture
Definitions are Essential to Dialogue

The definition of a concept is a description of the role we assign to the word that designates it within the context of a particular discussion. A description of the fundamental concepts in secular Jewish discourse and their meanings can facilitate dialogue among secular Jews, and with members of other Jewish streams.

Key concepts in discussions of Judaism include: culture, religion, Judaism, Jewish works, Jewish sources, free Judaism, Jewishness, humanity, humanism, humanisation, humanistic education, Jewish religion, cultural level, values, Jewish values, national culture, national identity, nationalism and racism, pluralism in Judaism, national unity, God as a literary figure, openness to foreign cultures, and chosen/choosing people.

Humpty Dumpty was right of course, that words mean just what we choose them to mean. Wittgenstein was also right however, that without agreement regarding the roles we assign to words in conversation, we would never be able to understand one another, since "meaning" is merely the agreed role played by a word in a given discourse. (Words are like "pieces" in a game, the "meaning" of which we determine when we describe the rules of the game and the roles played by the various pieces – which will assume different meanings, or roles, depending on whether the game is chess or checkers, for example.)

It is thus essential that we define and clarify the meaning of the concepts we employ in a specific discussion, since key concepts can be understood in many different ways.

The following chapters offer definitions – descriptions of the roles and meaning – of concepts, as they are understood by many secular Jews, in discussing their Judaism. Such definitions may play a key role in the promotion of dialogue, based upon a shared meaning of basic concepts, even when the parties hold differing views.

"Definition" also means restriction, placing a fence around the meaning of a word, to keep all other meanings out. Every definition reflects prior assumptions, in accordance with one's beliefs regarding a given topic. The definition of Judaism as culture for example, is at odds with the definition of Judaism exclusively as a religion, because it extends the fence of meaning of the concept of Judaism. Jewish culture is more than a system of religious precepts. It is the sum total of creative works, phenomena and customs – religious and not religious – that together constitutes the spiritual environment in which members of the Jewish people are raised.

Definitions: Culture of a People

We use the term culture in reference to a particular group, including the Jewish People, in the sense of a unique composite of lifestyle, language, founding works of art and literature, common historical and spiritual heritage, shared holidays and symbols, traditions and ongoing development. A cultural composite of this kind can be the mark of a specific community, national society, or group of nations.

Since there are many Judaisms in Judaism, each with its own culture, we distinguish between "national culture" shared by the entire people, and the culture of a specific community (e.g. Yemenite Jewish culture or American Jewish culture) or stream – secular Jewish culture or Haredi Jewish culture, for example.

Israeli Jewish culture is unique among Judaism's cultures: while diaspora Judaisms differ from one another in the extent to which they have integrated into the culture of the lands in which they reside, Israeli Jewish culture develops as an independent national culture, influenced of course by western and eastern cultures, but living within neither. The uniqueness of Israeli Jewish culture stems from the revival of Hebrew as a spoken and creative language, coupled with the encounter between diverse Jewish cultures that developed in dozens of lands and cultures.

Every national culture bears an affinity to the culture of a particular group of nations: western or eastern culture, for example. Familiarity with the culture of a given people would thus also entail familiarity with the cultures that have influenced it in the past and the present. Religion is one of many aspects of culture. Its influence often dominates all areas of cultural activity, as was the case in Jewish culture prior to the 18th century; and sometimes its influence is very minor, as in the case of 20th century Judaism.

We distinguish between "culture" and "civilisation", or in the words of Buber (*Penei Adam*): Civilisation is the intellectual shaping of scientific, practical and utilitarian order, and the concrete realisation of that order through government and other instruments. Culture is the movement of the human soul for the sake of its expression, desire, and attempt to give form to its essence. Before this movement, all things are merely substance without form. Its creations are the ephemeral symbols perceived as the soul's truth. Unlike civilisation, culture cannot be accumulated, it must be created anew in each generation, its products not a means to an end, but an end in themselves, their own meaning, with which they imbue life. Culture provides the forms with which man shapes himself, employing the materials and traditions afforded by the society in which he lives.

In the masterpieces that represent a given culture we find expression of the isolation and uniqueness of their creators and of man in general.

Creativity and tradition are the two faces of culture. It is only together that they possess cultural value.

Judaism

The term Judaism describes the pluralistic and evolving culture of the Jewish People, including its religion and various streams, and is not synonymous with Jewish religion in any of its forms. The history of Judaism is the history of the culture of the Jewish People, including the development of its religious and secular streams, and the religious and secular works of art and literature it has produced in all eras.

In the twentieth century, a majority of the Jewish People resided among the peoples of Europe and America, whose cultures underwent processes of extreme secularisation. Rapid secularisation rendered the greater part of Judaism a "secular culture" – free from the religion of Halakhah. Most Jewish works – "Jewish sources" – created over the past century, are products of non-religious Judaism.

Zionism and the development of the Israeli cultural and political entity were a turning point in twentieth century Jewish history and culture, even before the establishment of the State of Israel. The development of Judaism in Israel began to exert an influence on all of Judaism's Judaisms. Late twentieth – early twenty first century "Judaism" differs in both essence and character from biblical Judaism (from the period of wanderings to the return from exile in Persian times), Hellenistic Judaism (from the conquests of Alexander and the Maccabean wars to the completion of the Bible and the Mishnah), Byzantine and mediaeval Judaism, Judaism of the Renaissance and the Enlightenment, Judaism in the age of emancipation and the ninteenth and twentieth centuries. The most significant differences between late twentieth – early twenty first century Judaism and past Judaisms pertain to changing attitudes toward religion and national identity and the relationship between the two, the disbanding of traditional communities, and attitudes to the spiritual and cultural centre developing in Israel.

As early as the ninteenth century, Judaism began to be perceived as the culture of a people, rather than a religion. In western Europe, the "Wissenschaft des Judentums" ("Science of Judaism") developed in Jewish intellectual circles, with the objective of studying the culture of the Jewish People. From that time until the present, images of the historical circumstances of past Judaisms have undergone constant change. The scholarship, thought and creative work produced during this period, free from the religion of Halakhah, have cast past Judaism in a new light.

Israeli Judaism, secular for the most part, produces an unprecedented wealth of art and literature, engages in intensive Jewish educational activity encompassing the majority of Jewish youth in the world today, and possesses the largest number of Jewish institutions of higher learning, the greatest concentration of research institutions and scholarship, Jewish publishing houses, Jewish theatres, Jewish film and television production companies. As this development gains momentum, and the experience and sheer quantity of works produced in Israel grows, so does the impact of secular Israeli Judaism on all Judaism throughout the world.

Jewish Works

Jewish works are works that are influenced by the Jewishness of their creators or join the body of works that play a role in the Jewish cultural life of a particular period or stream within the Jewish People.

The culture of a people is represented in its unique works, sometimes adopted by other peoples as part of their own body of classical works (for example: the Iliad, Oedipus Rex, the Bible, Shakespeare).

Selections of Jewish works constitute "Jewish sources",

representing specific periods in Jewish history. The selection of works included in the biblical anthology are a sample, representing the culture of the Jewish People in its formative period, and its history – as reflected in its collective consciousness and memory.

Since religion was the dominant element in the culture of ancient Israel – as in other cultures of the time – most works in the biblical anthology attest to the religious beliefs of their authors. In the process of the Bible's compilation and redaction, secular works such as Song of Songs and Esther – in which the authors make no reference to God – were also included.

The Jewish works of the Bible – mostly in Hebrew, with certain passages in Aramaic – reflect the prevailing cultural and religious pluralism within the Jewish People at that time. Its historiography, oratory, narrative and drama, poetry and philosophy, laws and jurisprudence, represent a broad range of streams and trends in Jewish culture, in the realms of religious ritual, art and literature, holidays and ceremonies, beliefs and opinions.

Similar anthologies could represent the totality of Jewish culture in any given period. Contemporary Judaism is represented in Jewish poetry and narrative, drama and screenwriting, philosophy and academic research, historiography, jurisprudence, painting and sculpture, music, theatre and film – in all of the languages of the countries in which it is produced.

Religion

Religion is one form of culture: an aggregate of rituals, precepts and beliefs. Religion generally includes belief in either an immanent or a transcendent supernatural deity, who is the source of authority and author of religious precepts – both moral and immoral. Most religions credit God with the ability to punish or reward as he sees fit, or in keeping with the instructions of those who purport to speak in his name. Members of most religious communities believe in those who speak in God's name, as if invested by them to serve as God's representatives, and to mediate between them and the divine – figures such as priests, clerics, prophets, etc. Most religions require members to show loyalty to their institutions and leaders, provide for their financial support, obey all of their commands, and defend them and their authority against all who oppose them.

Obedience to religious leaders often assumes extreme forms – like obedience to the Pope, whom many Catholics believe infallible; or obedience to rabbis, on the part of political leaders or democratically elected parliamentarians. Obedience to a religious leader or rabbi, who acts independently of those chosen by the public to be its legislators, undermines the democratic principle by virtue of which they were elected.

Religion generally encourages fear of punishment or expectation of reward in the hereafter, or of supernatural beings and unexpected phenomena, present beyond the perceptible world. At the same time, most religions cultivate a sense of superiority to members of other faiths, and to those they consider irreligious.

Religious leaders often believe they have the right or duty to impose the laws of their religion upon those who are not religious, members of other religions, or those who merely espouse beliefs different from their own.

Jewish Religion

The Jewish religion comprises many different streams that, in one fashion or another, observe the halakhic precepts. These streams, such as the Conservative and Reform majority and the Orthodox minority, contrast and clash with one another. What all Jewish religious streams have in common is the observance (according to various approaches) of the halakhic precepts, prayer and blessings to God, study of ancient Jewish religious texts, belief in a common heritage contained in the Bible, and in most cases – synagogue membership or attendance, within the respective streams.

The Jewish religion exerted a significant influence on the culture of the Jewish People and most of its works until about two hundred years ago. Constant change and numerous streams and tendencies – from the Mosaic and Aaronic currents to present-day divisions – have been characteristic of the Jewish religion throughout its history. Since the completion of the Bible and the Talmud, many have tried to cast the Jewish religion as monolithic – based on a permanent system of halakhic precepts, according to the majority rulings found in the Talmud.

Most Jewish religious communities accepted the principle of observance of the halakhic precepts and prayer, although differences in customs and rites were often significant (for example: the prohibition or permission of polygamy, liturgical variations, differing attitudes to magic, to the Oral Law, to the Shulhan Arukh and its commentaries). The Jewish religion as the religion of practical precepts does not require belief in a specific divine phenomenon.

In the seventeenth and eighteenth centuries, Judaism and the Jewish religion underwent a series of revolutionary changes, under the influence of radical agents such as: Kabbalah and messianism, Spinoza and Jewish philosophy, Hassidism and Mitnagdism, Reform, Neo-Orthodoxy, Haskalah, moderate Conservatism, radical and anti-Zionist conservatism, secular nationalist and religious-Zionist movements.

In light of these changes, the influence of the religion of Halakhah, fixed in hallowed tradition, diminished. In the ninteenth century, emancipation and spiritual auto-emancipation led to widespread secularisation among Jews, as among non-Jewish Europeans.

Mass immigration and the collapse of many shtetl communities in the late ninteenth century, and the concentration of Jewish population in the capital cities of western culture, changed the face of religion and accelerated the secularisation process in Judaism.

The Jewish religion and the halakhic precepts underwent far-reaching change in most Jewish religious communities in the western diaspora. Most communities eliminated the women's gallery in the synagogue, with some allowing women to serve as rabbis, cantors, religious judges and halakhic authorities. Many effected liturgical and ritual change. Members of most religious communities ceased observing the halakhic precepts in most aspects of their lives.

Most Jews in Israel and the diaspora are not "religious", in the sense that they do not observe the precepts of Halakhah, are not synagogue members, are not guided by rabbis, and do not send their children to religious schools.

In Israel, Orthodox religion has once again become a significant force, due to the division of non-religious Judaism into two camps – on the basis of attitudes toward the Arabs, war and peace – and the need of both camps to win the support of the small religious minority in order to hold power in Israeli democracy. However, even in Israel only about 20 percent of the population belong to religious communities – a percentage that has remained unchanged since the state's establishment.

Free Judaism

Free Judaism is Judaism that is free from the religion of Halakhah. It is the Judaism of secular Jews, just as Haredi Judaism is the Judaism of the ultra-Orthodox, and Religious-Zionist Judaism is the Judaism of the Israeli neo-Orthodox – including some who have moved closer to the haredim, and others who have remained moderate.

Free Judaism is the largest and least structured of all Judaisms. It consists primarily of "congregants", without congregations. Most Jews in the world live according to its principles and share its beliefs, but few belong to organised communities (with the exception of the more than 200 communities of the secular Kibbutz Movement in Israel, and some 60 secular congregations in America).

The lives of free Jews reflect their beliefs regarding the ethical principles of human rights and obligations toward the society in which they live and the people to which they belong. They reflect the prerogative of humanised man to criticise, change and revitalise tradition and shape values, which forms the basis on which to evaluate and choose or reject laws and customs. Guided by these beliefs, secular Jews are free from halakhic precepts of which they do not approve, but are able to adopt customs, traditions or precepts that pass the test of humanistic criticism; the test of ethical values that promote the quality of life of the individual, family and community.

Secular Jews observe the Jewish traditions they find beneficial and pleasurable, such as: Sabbath and holiday meals in the company of family and friends, sometimes including traditional songs and texts, modified to suit their tastes and beliefs, like the new Passover haggadot, or haggadot for Tu Beshvat and Israel Independence Day.

Free Judaism is the Judaism of most Jews and Jewish writers and artists in the world today. Most contemporary Jewish works are produced within free Judaism, and become part of its culture. Some of these works are used in its educational institutions, and the best among them become points of reference in the discourse of Jewishly educated secular Jews in Israel – for example, the works of Heine, Bialik, Tchernichowsky, Alterman, Sholem Aleichem, Agnon, Yizhar, Buber, Brenner, Chagall, Danziger, Mahler, Bernstein and others.

Free Jewish education must strive to impart to students, the culture of their own and surrounding peoples. Education within the context of free Judaism will provide students with a thorough introduction to Judaism and world culture, and to humanism as a system of culture and universal and Jewish ethical values.

Jewish Sources

As a constantly evolving culture, Judaism's sources can be found in Jewish works representing every period, stream and movement. In the course of Jewish cultural development, works produced centuries ago are employed alongside contemporary works.

In order to get to know Judaism's sources, one must look beyond the "Jewish bookcase"; a term that has become synonymous with talmudic and midrashic literature, purported to represent the essence of Judaism.

Judaism's new and ancient sources reflect Jewish culture as it has been expressed in every artistic medium. Such works were produced in the fields of literature and philosophy, frescoes and mosaics in ancient synagogues, painting and sculpture from the time of the first three temples to Yahweh and the Hellenistic period to the present, music and theatre, film and television.

In the twentieth century, the culture of the Jewish People was enriched with more works than in all of the previous three millennia. This wealth can be seen in the variety of works produced in various languages and diverse Jewish cultures throughout the world, and in their sheer quantity.

Jewish education in all Judaisms strives to impart the customs, values, literature and art that best represent its culture in the present. Through these things, students become acquainted with the Jewish culture in which they are being raised. As they grow up, and to the extent to which they are afforded the freedom to do so, they may explore other streams of Judaism, as well as other cultures.

Judaism free from the religion of Halakhah must do the same. All study units and subjects should include selected Jewish works produced over the past two hundred years, through which students may become acquainted with the culture of the secular society in which they live, and the way in which it illuminates Jewish sources of other streams and periods that act upon and influence contemporary Judaism.

Jewishness – Who is a Jew

"Jewishness" is a term that denotes membership in the Jewish People. A person is Jewish because s/he was born into a Jewish family or community and raised a Jew, or because s/he joined the Jewish People by joining a Jewish family or community. One may be Jewish or join the Jewish People regardless of one's religion, or the religious or secular stream to which one subscribes. Joining the Jewish People is therefore not contingent upon any process of conversion.

Since the Jewish People is – like all peoples – unique not only in its characteristics, but in its very definition, Jewishness is also unique. Since the Roman Empire granted citizenship to members of different nations, and since nation-states began to grant citizenship, or "nationality" to their residents, the concepts of "nationality" and "citizenship" have become practically synonymous.

In Israel, for example, there are today over five million citizens who are "Israeli Jews" – alongside a million non-Jewish citizens, including "Israeli Palestinians", "Israeli Druse" and "Israeli Christians". The national identity of Jews and Palestinians is in no way compromised by their being "Israeli", just as Welsh national identity is not affected by UK citizenship, and the national identity of French-Quebecois is not affected by the fact that they are "Canadians".

National identity, including "Jewishness", is usually not a

matter of desire or choice. It is determined by family origin and the process of education in national society. Only in exceptional cases is it the result of a conscious decision – generally the decision to join a specific family or community.

Humanity, Humanisation

Humanity is the potential within every human being; manifested in a range of characteristics acquired by those raised in human society – just as "wolfishness" is the quality acquired by one raised in a wolf pack (including a human child lost among wolves).

"Humanity" is also the realisation of man's unique potential, through humanising education in national society and the society of nations. Man's humanity is thus contingent upon education in national society, because there are no supra-national societies. Humanisation entails nationalisation of the individual.

Education in national culture also entails awareness of and openness toward the cultures of neighbouring peoples, because all peoples live among other peoples and all cultures are influenced by other cultures. Exceptions to the rule are isolated groups, like the Papuan tribes discovered in Fiji.

Humanity is the sum total of characteristics acquired by man through the process of humanisation – socialisation and acculturation – including the internalisation of the humanistic values that ensure the continued existence of humanising society and constant improvement in the quality of human life.

Humanisation

Humanisation becomes the standard for the evaluation and preference of values, education, customs and traditions, laws and precepts.

Protagoras' assertion that "man is the measure of all things" can be said to represent humanism, only when its subject is humanistic man, i.e. one who adheres to humanistic values. A racist or a chauvinist cannot be a measure for ethical evaluation and preference, since the values s/he espouses ignore man's duty toward the other and the universal, and result in the dehumanisation of persecutor and persecuted, subjugator and subjugated alike. The subjugation of women results in their dehumanisation and in the dehumanisation of those who subjugate them; discrimination against members of another people, and their enslavement leads to the dehumanisation of both occupier and occupied.

Dehumanisation is the loss of the ability to distinguish between good and evil – termed psychopathy in the fields of psychology and criminology. Dehumanisation is manifested in unbridled selfishness, undermining society's ability to function as a humanising force, so that most individuals are prevented from realising their unique human potential.

In the long term, the dehumanisation of rulers and ruled, within a family, people or group of peoples, will result in the disintegration of society, its economic and political sustainability. Such has been the case in societies – such as Nazi Germany, the USSR, Cambodia and Iraq – controlled by selfish and psychopathic tyrants.

Humanistic Values

Values are the standard for the evaluation and preference of behaviour and laws. They can therefore be either humanistic or anti-humanistic.

Humanistic values are those that comply with the "meta-values" of Hillel, "that which is hateful to you, do not unto others", and Kant, "treat man always as an end and never as a means only; a law cannot be moral unless it is universally valid". These three principles are meta-values (on the basis of which other values

34

are judged and preferred or rejected), and are compatible with one another.

Humanistic values thus include equality between the sexes and between peoples, freedom of expression and personal autonomy, the duties of the individual toward society and the rights of every individual within society, the obligations of society toward the individual, and democracy as the best possible form of government.

The standard for evaluation and preference of values is the humanisation process itself – since only values that promote humanisation are worthy of approval and preference, and those that cause dehumanisation should be rejected.

Humanism is the belief in humanistic values and the authority of man to establish such values and rules, in order to safeguard the rights of all people, and create the social and educational conditions for individual humanisation.

Jewish Values

Jewish values are universal values in Jewish form, like Hillel's meta-value that is, in his opinion, the essence of "the entire Torah". These values are the common element underlying Moses' Commandments, the Prophets' preference for social justice over ritual and prayer, Abraham's protest against the injustice of collective punishment, and Job's outcry against those who ascribe sin to one struck with misfortune – justifying God even when he is in collusion with Satan.

Universal humanistic values, that promote humanisation and quality of life, are shared by many peoples – religious and secular Jews included. Anti-humanistic values that give rise to dehumanisation may also be shared by religious and secular Jews.

Jewish historical and literary tradition laid the foundation for values of freedom, equality and justice in making the epic of liberation from slavery in Egypt the founding story of the Jewish People, and the foremost justification for laws of justice (e.g. "And if a stranger sojourn with thee in your land, ye shall not do him any wrong... [he] be unto you as the home-born among you, and thou shalt love him as thyself for ye were strangers in the land of Egypt." – Lev. 19).

Erich Fromm, who viewed humanism as the aspiration toward the unity and freedom of man, saw in the exodus myth and its centrality to Jewish culture, the basis of humanistic values in Judaism.

Humanistic Jewish values clash with anti-humanistic and racist Jewish values; values that sanction a sense of Jewish superiority over members of other peoples; of men over women; or the right of Jews to murder or drive conquered peoples from their land – as described in the book of Joshua, and advocated by some contemporary secular and religious Jewish political parties and individuals.

Anti-humanistic values lay behind the mass murder of worshipers at the Tomb of the Patriarchs and Matriarchs of the Jewish nation at the hands of a murderous doctor from Kiryat Arba, later glorified by rabbis and others. The same values led rabbis to decree Yitzhak Rabin a "rodef" (a halakhic term for one who poses a mortal threat to others) for having furthered the peace process – thereby sanctioning his murder at the hands of a religious Jewish assassin.

Values vs. Precepts

Humanistic Jewish education must bring students to internalise humanistic "Jewish values" – identical to universal humanistic values – and inoculate them against anti-humanistic, nationalistic and chauvinistic Jewish values.

"Laws" and "precepts" differ inherently from "values", since laws are rules that permit or prohibit certain specific behaviour, whereas values are standards for evaluation and preference. or rejection of laws, precepts and behaviour.

Values are shaped by humanistic or anti-humanistic belief. Laws or precepts are enacted by a ruling legislator or majority decision, i.e. by human beings, under specific circumstances, and therefore require re-examination with every change in circumstances or beliefs.

The precepts pertaining to the sacrificial cult for example, were enacted, according to Maimonides, at a time when the Jewish People worshiped the gods of other peoples, who believed that their deities required nourishment and the "sweet savour" of burnt flesh. In Maimonides' opinion, these precepts remained in force after the religious revolution of Moses, only because of the difficulty in eliminating any customary practice – even one based on a discredited belief. These practices – which would have been meaningless to believers in an incorporeal God with no need or desire for the slaughter and incineration of living creatures – could only be eliminated gradually. Maimonides offers an example, indicative of his approach to the precepts in general: had the Israelites at the time been told to stop bringing sacrifices, they would have been astounded; it would have been as if Jews today had been told to stop praying or observing Halakhah.

This approach underscores the difference between values and precepts. Values stem from the beliefs of rational and intuitive man. The commandments of human legislators (who sometimes purport to speak in God's name) on the other hand, must only be obeyed as long as required by custom or democratic law.

The halakhic precepts sustained by religious authorities – like state laws – cannot be considered values or "Jewish values". Giving precepts precedence over values entails rejecting the humanistic essence of Judaism as perceived by Hillel, because one who observes precepts that are incompatible with such values, will continue for example, to insult half of humanity, when he thanks God in his prayers, for not having made him a woman.

One who discriminates against women, adhering to Halakhah and traditions he believes to be sacred – in divorce, marriage, or the appointment of religious court judges, rabbis and community leaders – acts in a fashion that runs counter to Jewish values; identical to universal, humanistic values – including the principle of equality between all human beings, male and female. One who banishes women to a "women's court", far from the men and the Torah scroll (although the "Women's Court" in the Temple in Jerusalem was an inner courtyard, open to both men and women), behaves as a male chauvinist, contrary to the value of equality, and without halakhic justification. If the intention were merely to separate men from women, for reasons of menstrual impurity, the men could just as easily have sat in what is now the "women's gallery", leaving the women to stand near the Torah and the cantor's podium.

The prevailing belief among those free from the religion of Halakhah, that values take precedence over halakhic precepts, is diametrically opposed to the prevailing belief among adherents to halakhic Judaisms. The latter place the precepts of Halakhah above humanistic values, including those adopted by Judaism.

This contrast between belief in the supremacy of values and belief in the supremacy of religious precepts, lies at the heart of the unbridgeable gap between secular and religious Judaism; the gap between democracy – whose laws and statutes are subject to the scrutiny of the supreme court, on the basis of humanistic values – and halakhic-religious Judaism that observes sacred precepts and obeys the rulings of rabbis not elected by the democratic system. Yeshayahu Leibowitz therefore rightly claimed that he does not consider himself a humanist, because he sanctifies all of the precepts, even those that are racist and murderous, such as the commandment to murder the entire people of Amalek, including women and children.

Culture, Humanity and Their Influence on Quality of Life

The level of humanity and culture one enjoys is proportionate to the extent to which one realises one's human potential, engages in spiritual activity, internalises humanistic values, and participates in national and international culture. Most people today are exposed to a profusion of media and information, symbols and works common to various cultures, alongside the works, events and phenomena that represent the national culture in which they live.

When people devote all of their time and efforts to their narrow field of expertise – whether in science, technology or business – their spiritual potential remains dormant. The more they engage in spiritual and artistic activity that allows them to take part in, and appreciate the living culture of their own and surrounding peoples, the more of their spiritual and emotional potential they will realise. Their spiritual world will be enriched with experiences and challenges, acquaintances and topics for discussion – connecting them to society, from which they are separated by their limited field of professional activity.

A higher level of culture ensures greater quality of life in the context of family, friends and community. The greater awareness people have of the representative works of their culture; the greater their involvement in spiritual, social and educational activities, the richer and more varied their lives. Consequently, they have access to a greater variety of emotional and spiritual enjoyment, enriching conversation with friends and family and increasing their sources of interest and experiences – including those that are independent of health or financial means, as explained by Aristotle in the Nicomachean Ethics.

Aristotle was the first to point out an association between ethics and quality of life. People who relate to themselves and to others on the basis of rules deriving from their humanistic values; people who strive to realise their spiritual, domestic and social potential, enrich their lives with pleasurable and challenging activity, even when they are poor in material goods.

Quality of life is contingent upon spiritual and social activity, possible only when experts look beyond their specific field of expertise, and join the rest of society in shared cultural activity.

Active involvement in Jewish life, as a living, evolving culture, within the larger context of world culture, will foster the type of enrichment that raises the level of culture and improves quality of life. Education that familiarises people with the totality of their culture and its sources will provide the means for active involvement in the spiritual life of their community.

Nationality, Identity and Self-Identification

Nationality is the socialisation of an individual within a people, comprising both national identity and involvement in national culture. While national identity in itself is a fact over which individuals generally have no control, national self-identification entails a range of social, spiritual and educational activities, through which the individual may become acquainted with the culture of the nation, its problems, and the various approaches to their resolution. National self-identification requires that one be acquainted with the requirements and duties of solidarity toward members of the national society, and with the rights afforded by membership in that society.

An individual's level of culture shapes the content of her/his nationality: awareness and involvement in national and international cultural life, familiarity with the representative works, the ability to participate in the education – within national culture – of her/his children and those of the community, and the ability to impart the moral values that sustain national and international society, and their expression in national cultural heritage.

Although a person's nationality is determined by causes beyond her/his control, it provides the potential and impetus for cultural, social and political activity.

Many had believed that nationality, as a significant factor, was disappearing from the lives of individuals and society, due to economic and technological tendencies toward internationalisation, and the need for a stronger international community, with a concomitant weakening of nation states. In recent years however, we have seen a strengthening of nationality – in the aspirations of small nations to greater political independence; in a growing of awareness of the sources and distinct character of national cultures; and in the promotion, through education, of national self-identification in cultural and spiritual life.

Alongside ever-increasing exposure to international media and works of entertainment enjoyed by people of different nationalities, there has been a bourgeoning of national cultures, including a growing interest in their roots and sources.

The rebirth of Hebrew language and culture in Israel – home to Jews from dozens of countries and cultures, who have taught their children to identify with the culture of the Jewish People – is one of the most striking examples of national revival in the twentieth century. Exploring the meaning of "Jewish identity", in an era in which "Jewishness" has lost its religious character for most Jews, is one of the ways in which Israeli and diaspora Jews engage in national self-identification. The passage from national identity to national self-identification requires a corresponding passage from cultural passivity to activity, involving exposure to a broad range of Jewish cultural works of all kinds within Israeli Judaism – stimulating and affecting creative and scholarly activities in the diaspora.

Jewish Humanistic Education

Humanistic education, Jewish humanistic education included, operates on two seemingly contradictory planes:

1. It strives to humanise individuals, acculturating them to society, bringing them to internalise its prevailing humanistic values, and acquainting them with its representative works, as well as their own obligations and rights, in accordance with its laws.

2. It strives to promote spiritual independence and develop each individual's unique personality, by cultivating creativity and a critical approach to society's conventions, to the classical works that represent its culture, to its traditions, religious and cultural heritage, and the laws and precepts by which it is governed.

In fact however, these two tendencies are not contradictory at all. Like Aristotle, many humanistic educators believe that they must help students realise their own potential: the potential that will allow each of them to make a unique contribution to society.

In fostering critical ability and creativity, society encourages development and enriches its culture, engendering greater openness to new ideas, as well as the constant re-examination of laws and conventions, in light of changing circumstances.

Erasmus saw knowledge as a prerequisite for human freedom – since the more a person knows, the more s/he is aware of the reality in which s/he lives, the potential and choices it offers, the changes it undergoes and the ways in which to deal with them.

Imparting knowledge is a necessary but not a sufficient condition for humanistic education. Without the internalisation of moral values that are the standard for evaluation and preference, knowledge can be detrimental to a person's humanisation, inasmuch as it provides tools that can enhance her/his ability to act in a racist or chauvinist fashion.

Jewish humanistic education, like all western humanistic education, strives to achieve its goals through a variety of social activities, engaging students in creative pursuits, study and discussion, while acquainting them with contemporary culture and the cultural legacy of their own and other peoples.

Works of art, literature and philosophy play a central role in humanistic education, not only as a way of introducing students to the cultural legacy of their society, but also as models of innovative and unprecedented creativity, coupled with social and moral criticism.

The protagonists of classical works of art and literature are not paragons of virtue. Their lives are filled with transgressions, judging by humanistic standards. Abraham and such literary figures as God, Jacob, David, Medea, Oedipus, Macbeth, Lear and Faust – are all guilty of terrible sins, in terms of humanistic values.

The educational value of the works that fashion such protagonists, lies in the way in which they are portrayed – offering readers not only unique, emotionally and aesthetically moving forms of expression, but also timeless human and moral dilemmas, involving clashes between individuals and society, individuals and themselves and their values, between their minds and their hearts.

A culture's classical works play a crucial and twofold role in humanistic education. They introduce students to the common elements of the culture in which they live, and encourage critical thought and deliberation with regard to the dilemmas they present.

Works that represent the culture of the people and peoples, within which the students live, comprise not only timeless classical works (considered superior over the course of many generations) but many contemporary works as well.

Humanistic education is an ongoing process of discovery, through encounters with works of philosophy and art, produced and presented today – as in the past – in all areas and all media. In Judaism, such education exposes students to the wealth of Jewish culture present and past in the context of its surrounding cultures.

Pluralism in Judaism

Judaism's pluralism is reflected in the numerous streams, beliefs and views it has boasted throughout history; in the pluralistic principles that have guided Jewish thought and discourse since the days of the Talmud; in the recognition of the legitimacy and value of debate in the search for truth, and an approach to conflict that treats "both [opinions]" as "the words of the living God".

Pluralism in Jewish culture during the period of the First Temple to Yahweh in Jerusalem and the temples to Yahweh in Beth-El and Dan is reflected in the biblical stories that represent and describe the multiplicity of religions, beliefs and cults to many gods, which prevailed among Jews at the time. The concept of God as an abstract being clashed with the conception of the God of Israel as a golden calf. God's inherent justice, as presented in the Prophets, clashed with opposing views – like those found in the stories of Abraham, Job and Ecclesiastes (Koheleth).

Judaism of the Hellenistic period saw the rise of various independent movements and sects: Hellenistic Jews and their opponents, Sadducees, Pharisees, Hassideans, Essenes, Jewish Christians, Zealots and their opponents. The growth of the Jewish diaspora in Africa, Asia and Europe, also resulted in greater decentralisation of Judaism. In Palestine, opposition to the Sadducean religious-sacerdotal establishment arose, and at the time of the Maccabees, civil war again erupted, between those who had adopted western culture and their opponents.

The Sadducean religious establishment adopted a western lifestyle, believed in the Written Law, and opposed all reform. The Pharisee reformers objected both to the Sadducees' Hellenistic tendencies and to their religious conservatism, seeking rather, to pursue further development of the Jewish religion, Halakhah and belief, by means of the Oral Law.

At the time of the war against Rome, there were also factions opposed to the revolt – figures such as Yohanan ben Zakai and his students, or the Jewish military commander and historian Joseph ben Matityahu (Josephus Flavius) – who went over to the Roman side, greeting the commander of the Roman forces and winning his protection for the continued development of Jewish culture under Roman rule. The war factions split, and began to fight among themselves, leading the Judean commonwealth to ruin.

"Both [opinions] are the words of the living God" is a talmudic principle that symbolises the passage of pluralism from a Jewish trait to a guiding principle in Jewish thought.

It expresses the belief that anyone can speak in God's name, and that all sides of a debate are therefore worthy of attention; that minority opinions must be preserved – for they might someday become majority opinions and thus binding as law; or that some debates cannot be resolved, and must be declared "teku" (a draw, literally "let it stand", i.e. remain undecided). This is a revolutionary concept in the history of religion and theology.

Halakhah thus appears as a process rather than a constitution; an ongoing progression (*halikhah* in Hebrew) toward truth and justice.

Since the Middle Ages and the Renaissance, Jewish pluralism has increased, with the development of numerous communities on different continents, within many different cultures, in addition to the proliferation of various religious and philosophical streams: rationalists and mystics, messianics, *Hassidim* and *Mitnagdim*, *Maskilim* and assimilationists, apostates and forced converts. In

45

the Modern Era, Jewish pluralism has developed at an ever greater pace, as it has split into secular and religious factions, each with its attendant streams, and far-flung diaspora communities. The democratic system in Israel has strengthened relations between the various factions within pluralistic Judaism, due to the increased interdependence between Jewish communities, ethnicities and religious streams – each of which has the ability to influence policy, government coalitions, the economy, and security of all Israelis.

Unity is contingent upon a lack of uniformity, upon the multiplicity of ways in which one can realise one's Jewishness without cutting oneself off from Judaism as a whole.

Pluralism is not Relativism

Pluralism is the recognition of the multiplicity of beliefs and views, streams, lifestyles and religions that exist within the culture of the Jewish People. Pluralism has been a distinctive feature of Judaism since its conception in biblical times. Since the days of the Talmud, it has also been one of Judaism's guiding principles.

Pluralism is not relativism, which ascribes equal value to every belief and opinion, humanistic and anti-humanistic.

Jewish pluralism encourages debate between those who hold different opinions, each believing their view to be superior to that of their opponents, and striving to prove they are right – with vehemence, confidence, determination and tenacity – like the schools of Hillel and Shamai, and like Jewish disputants ever since.

Relativism today implies renunciation of belief in the preferability of one position over another, in the existence of absolute values, vital to society. Relativism demands tolerance even toward racism and nationalism.

Nationalism and racism are types of selfish arrogance that view one's own nationality, race, gender or religion, as superior and deserving of greater rights than other human groups – like the "Aryan" Nazis, or male chauvinists. Nationalism and racism have been shown to cause dehumanisation and social disintegration, on the basis of values that ignore the rights of members of society who do not belong to one's own gender, nationality or race, or do not share one's beliefs.

Racist values, such as anti-Semitism, are thus absolute – and not relative – evil. No relativistic approach can justify them, even if those who believe in them have been inculcated by parents, teachers and their cultural heritage.

Racists and chauvinists – like the Taliban in Afghanistan, the Khmer Rouge in Cambodia, or the Nazis in Germany – pose a threat to the quality of life of every family and community. The more that racists shun the culture and society of those whom they reject, so their spiritual and emotional lives are impoverished, and their humanity is threatened with the danger of psycopathy.

The cultural relativism that Herder began to develop in the ninteenth century, in the belief that there are no inferior or superior cultures, regained currency in the late twentieth century, on the fringes of multiculturalist and postmodernist theory. Those who espouse cultural relativism and compare cannibal culture to the culture of open, western society, renounce their belief in humanistic values as a standard for the evaluation of worthy and unworthy, good and evil.

The struggle against racism and its theoretical apologists is vital to humanistic education, which therefore strives not for compromise between beliefs, but for dialogue between their adherents.

National Unity – One History, Many Beliefs

In Judaism as culture, all streams have always shared a belief in a common national history – one that has co-existed with various and often contradictory beliefs in the religious and other realms. Cultures that have developed under the influence of Christianity and Islam on the other hand, have boasted common religious beliefs alongside beliefs in diverse national histories.

In every period of Jewish history, Jews have espoused conflicting beliefs regarding: God, his exclusivity, essence and existence; Judaism as a binding religion or evolving culture; Jewishness, its definition and the conditions for becoming Jewish; the halakhic precepts and the supremacy of humanistic values over Halakhah; openness to external cultural and religious influences; Jewish education, its goals and its content. Judaism's multiplicity of beliefs and streams has never shaken the belief shared by all Jews, in a common national history, in the Bible as the basis of Judaism and its ancient historical record.

Jewish unity is expressed in the issues on which Jews fail to agree. All of Judaism's Judaisms debates the same issues, and the bond that exists between opposing sides in a common dispute, makes the dispute itself a source of unity.

Such issues include: the form and content of Sabbath and holiday observance in Israel; the Bible or the Talmud as the basis of Jewish education; "who is a Jew" and the Law of Return as positive discrimination, or an expression of a sacred right to the Land of Israel; relations between religion and state; the right to reform Halakhah (like the sages of the Oral Law and Reform Judaism today), or freedom from all of its precepts.

Debates between adherents of various Jewish beliefs, take on a political hue in Israel, demanding the attention and involvement of all participants in Israeli democracy – secular and religious alike. In Israel, these and all debates concerning Judaism increase contact and interaction between the various Jewish streams, deepening their consciousness of belonging to a single people.

Judaism's Openness to the Cultural Influences of Other Peoples

Judaism has been exposed to, and influenced by the cultures of other peoples, throughout its history. Its art and literature and the distinctive features of its religion and culture – from the Bible to the present – show clear traces of the influences of Mesopotamian, Canaanite, Phoenician, Egyptian, Greek, Islamic, Christian, Indian, Persian, Slavic and secular European and American cultures.

In every period of Jewish history, these influences have favoured the creation of original Jewish works. "Biblical criticism" has demonstrated the originality of the works of the Bible, in comparing them to the works and mythology of the Ancient Near Eastern cultures that influenced them. Naturally, the works of the Bible – like all cultural works – were influenced by older and neighbouring cultures. It is specifically in comparison to the products of these cultures however, that the Bible's originality in form and content, religious and philosophical messages, stands out. One example of this is the biblical creation story, which in fact comprises two contradictory versions. Elements of polytheistic Mesopotamian mythology were incorporated by the authors-redactors in a work that is both the basis of monotheism and of humanistic belief in equality between the sexes – Adam having initially been created both male and female, in the image of her/his God.

This constant openness to external cultural influences can be seen today in the development of Judaism within secular Israeli culture – influenced by all of the cultures with which it comes into contact on a daily basis, while producing its own original works.

In the past, this combination of receptiveness and originality, created cultural bridges between Judaism and other peoples. The national memory preserved in the Bible credits Solomon with a pluralistic approach to culture in the capital of the Jewish kingdom. In Jerusalem, he built temples to all the neighbouring peoples' religions and cultures, marrying their daughters, and turning Jerusalem into not only the world's first monotheistic capital, but its first multireligious city as well. (There is of course no proof of the historical truth of these accounts. It is significant however, that national memory ascribes such things to Solomon, while at the same time considering him the ideal king of Judaism's golden era.)

Thanks to its openness to external influences and its own originality, Judaism has managed to preserve its continuity and distinctive character, while maintaining contacts with other cultures and religions. The influence that Judaism has exerted on the religions and cultures of all peoples, who have come under the sway of Christianity and Islam, began under the Roman Empire, in the early first millennium.

Jewish Contributions to World Culture

In the part of the world united within the single political entity of the Roman Empire, various forms of Jewish belief proliferated among the "God-fearers" – those who accepted the principles of Jewish ethical monotheism, but not the yoke of the halakhic precepts.

"God-fearing" communities, scattered throughout the Empire – alongside Jewish communities – were particularly receptive to Christian versions of Judaism. Paul's approach, whereby the duty to believe supersedes the duty to observe the precepts, naturally appealed to those who already tended toward ethical monotheism but had little interest in observing the precepts of Halakhah.

This form of monotheism, with its commitment to justice and charity, and belief in the promise of redemption, was one of Judaism's contributions to the peoples who adopted it through

Christian Judaism. The new myth – in which Jesus, charismatic rabbi to Jewish disciples from Nazareth, becomes the son of God, and a human sacrifice to atone for the sins of all who believe it to be so – facilitated the spread of the new religion created by Paul, which incorporated many polytheistic elements in its mythology.

The new Christian faith, based on the Jewish Scriptures, disseminated them throughout the Roman Empire. When Christianity became the state religion of the Empire, and as such spread to the three continents that surround the Mediterranean, it also brought with it institutions created by Judaism: the synagogue as opposed to the temple, the Sabbath, prayer instead of sacrifice, and the study for its own sake of the Holy Scriptures and their commentaries.

Christianity preserved and disseminated not only the canonical books of the Tanakh, but other Jewish works as well, excluded from Jewish tradition by Rabbinical Judaism and reclaimed only in modern times – over 1,500 years later. Such works include: the books of the New Testament, the Apocrypha and Pseudepigrapha – including the books of the Maccabees – philosophical works such as those of Philo of Alexandria, Jewish historiography and books such as those of Josephus Flavius, written to combat anti-Semitism.

The Sabbath went from a uniquely Jewish institution to a universal one, expressing a new approach to time: human time, divided into work-weeks, ending with a compulsory day of rest. This day of rest was unprecedentedly egalitarian, extending the right and duty to rest to all people – masters and slaves, parents and children, men and women – and humanely stipulating that beasts of burden must also be allowed to rest.

The Sabbath was intended to free men from the burden of earning a livelihood, in order to afford them a day of leisure. Over the years, so many prohibitions were added to the religious Sabbath laws, that today, most Jews no longer observe them –

and have thus restored the Sabbath to its original state, as a holiday of rest and leisure, entertainment and enjoyment.

God as a Literary Figure

God was created and fashioned by human beings in their art and literature, and in their beliefs, which have constantly changed his form, essence and meaning. In the minds and hearts of believers in his existence as an active force within nature or beyond its infinite confines, God is generally perceived not only as a creator, but also as a governor, who commands, supervises and metes out arbitrary and unexpected punishment. He therefore inspires fear in believers, and hence a desire to placate him with sacrifices or observance of his commandments.

In the spiritual lives of those who do not believe in God as an existing, creating, governing or supervising being, "God" is fashioned as a literary figure, created by the authors of ancient myths or the literary and artistic works that have given the gods their respective forms and roles in various cultures. These divine protagonists live in such works of art and literature, alongside other literary figures, often in human or animal form.

The Jewish literature of the Bible, and subsequently all streams of the Jewish religion, view God as having no past, no existence prior to the one portrayed in the various biblical stories regarding human beings who took notice of him. Unlike the gods of other religions, the biblical God has no family history or personal biography.

Both religious and secular Jews perceive and relate to God in a variety of ways. The Jewish religion does not require any specific belief in God, although many attempts (rejected by most Jewish streams) have been made to imitate Catholicism and establish a binding Jewish "credo".

Moses once saw God's face and back, but at their fateful meeting, before the fire that did not consume, Moses saw God as devoid of all shape or form, as: "I will be that which I will be"; "is" that will be all becoming; existence that cannot be defined in terms of the present, but only in terms of future potential. (This concept is similar to Aristotle's Prime Mover, adopted in various forms by mediaeval Muslim and Christian philosophers, torn between "two truths" – the truth of religion and the truth of reason – since they were convinced, like Abelard, that one can only believe in that which can be attained through reason.)

Contrary to Moses' conception of God, stands that of the author of Genesis: God in man's image, walking in his garden in the cool of the day, enjoying Abraham's hospitality, or struggling with Jacob at the Jabbok ford. Aaron and most of the people with him at the time saw God as a golden calf. Elijah saw him as the voice of silence. In the new mythology, developed in the mystical literature of talmudic and especially mediaeval times, God appeared as an emperor sitting on his royal throne, surrounded by ministers and angels; as Shekhinah.

In philosophical thought, like that of Maimonides, God is devoid not only of corporeality, but of any concept within human grasp. Spinoza's God is nature, and to the atheists influenced by Spinoza – God has no existence beyond the literature and thought devoted to him.

Even religious thinkers like Maimonides, viewed the biblical stories in which God is described in human terms, as allegories, the product of human imagination. Hence the God of biblical narrative, according to this approach, is merely a literary invention, the true significance of which can only be understood by a select few.

Since works of art and literature breathe independent life into the invented characters they portray, God continues to live as a literary figure even among those who ascribe no existence to him, beyond these works.

This view of God as a literary figure is typical of the "Bible as literature" school (Auerbach, Daiches, Kermode, Alter, Bloom, Miles, Talmon, Zakovitch, Hoffman, Peri and many others). The "Bible as narrative art and poetry" approach also considers God a literary figure.

The creation of God by human beings, in their own image, is an expression of the human desire to understand the transcendent, just as it is an expression of man's megalomania: the desire to resemble a force capable of creating nature and all life within it – to rule over it, or destroy it.

In the 1960s, graffiti on a wall in Paris asserted that "God is Dead – Nietzsche", beneath which someone added: "Nietzsche is Dead – God". God is not dead. He continues to live in the consciousness and experiences of those who believe he exists only in literature and art.

Humanistic Atheism in Judaism

Humanistic-atheism is the belief in humanised man as the source of authority and values that ensure society's continued existence, as well as the happiness and quality of life of each individual and of the social unit as a whole. Atheism sees man as the creator of God, and therefore does not believe in the observance of religious precepts, also created by man.

Humanistic atheism teaches critical evaluation not obedience, consideration of others, not sacred laws that cause them harm, and recognition of the cultural and philosophical value of classical works that are born anew in every generation, and reveal the potential within man and its perpetual realisation.

The essence of humanistic atheism is the belief in responsibility for one's own actions, the ability to choose one's own path on the basis of moral values, to shape one's life, and to create a spiritual reality, through culture – including the creation of God as a literary figure. Atheists like Bertrand Russell see belief in God not only as something unnecessary for understanding the universe, but as something harmful, inasmuch as it prefers the divine interest to the human.

There are also anti-humanistic atheistic beliefs, just as there are both humanistic and anti-humanistic religious beliefs.

Many Jewish atheists and agnostics continue to observe some of the halakhic precepts, without any rational or moral justification, but simply out of respect for tradition, and in the belief that they contribute to the unity of the Jewish People. Most Jewish atheists circumcise their sons, some give their children traditional bar/bat-mitzvah ceremonies in the synagogue (even when it is their first and last time at services), are married by a rabbi, and sign a ridiculous contract (ketubah) written in a language they do not understand (Aramaic), in which they promise to provide compensation in case of divorce. None of these things contradict their humanistic-atheistic beliefs, as long as they derive satisfaction from them, and cause no harm to others.

Those who believe in God as the source of binding precepts, consider atheists "heretics", who should – according to some (e.g. Plato and Maimonides) – be put to death. Such hostility to atheism attests to its prevalence in ancient times, in both Jewish and non-Jewish societies. A number of documents point to the existence of atheistic beliefs beginning in the third millennium BCE.

Humanistic atheists believe that democratic laws should be upheld, and should adhere to moral values. Atheistic and religious humanists thus strive to abrogate precepts that contradict humanistic principles, such as religious laws that discriminate against the female half of humanity, or violate the rights and dignity of members of minority groups, homosexuals, or those forbidden to marry according to Halakhah.

Religious and Ideological Fanaticism

Fanaticism is a belief – religious or secular – that repudiates all moral values, the supremacy of life over death (like the fanaticism of those who took their own lives "for the sake of freedom" at Massada), and the right to hold and disseminate divergent opinions. Examples include: supporters of the religious tyrants in Iran or Afghanistan, or of the secular tyrants in Nazi Germany or Bolshevik Russia, who imprisoned, exiled or killed those the fanatics considered to be "heretics".

"And slay every man his brother, and every man his companion, and every man his neighbour ...and there fell of the people that day about three thousand men. For Moses had said, consecrate yourselves today to the Lord, even every man upon his son, and upon his brother; that he may bestow upon you a blessing this day."

These are the words that the biblical author placed in the mouth of Moses (Ex. 32:27-29) when he led the civil war against those who believed, like Aaron, that God-Yahweh could be represented by the image of a calf. The 3,000 believers in Aaron's version of the Torah were killed by the soldiers of Moses, the man to whom ethical monotheism and the commandments that establish the rules of universal morality – including the injunction against murder – are attributed elsewhere in the biblical anthology.

Murderous fanaticism would thus appear to exist in the human spirit alongside lofty ideals – religious and secular alike.

The fanatic's beliefs bring about her/his own dehumanisation as a result of her/his dehumanisation of others. Dehumanisation occurs in the mind of a fanatic, when the other, who does not share her/his beliefs or fails to live up to them, ceases to be human in her/his eyes.

The secularisation process did not reduce the dangers of fanaticism. From the French revolution to the Nazi and Bolshevik revolutions, the murderous force of secular ideological fanaticism became apparent. The combination of political and religious fanaticism has been one of the most dangerous in history – as demonstrated by the Zealots who brought about the destruction of Jerusalem at the dawn of the first millennium CE; or the modern-day zealots who sought to cause the deaths of large numbers of Arabs on the Temple Mount, and murdered a Jewish Prime Minister of Israel – as a sign of their future intentions.

Making loyalty to a leader or to an idea – religious or secular – a supreme value, denies believers the ability to distinguish between good and evil, as if returning them to the Eden of psychopaths, where there is no conscience, no sense of shame or guilt, as if they had not yet tasted from the fruit of the tree of knowledge.

The dehumanisation of the fanatic and of her/his victims is common to all types of fanaticism – religious, ideological, nationalistic, racialist, classist or cultural. In this sense, those who murder gynaecologists for performing legal abortions resemble those who believe the image of the calf represents Yahweh. In this sense, those who murdered and incited to murder an Israeli Prime Minister for having furthered the peace process and neared its completion, resemble the anti-Semitic murderers of Europe.

Fanaticism usually entails blind loyalty to a leader who purports to speak in the name of God or in the name an idea, often supported by "scientific evidence" (racist or classist), detached from universal human values, and rejecting the validity of Kant's dictum, whereby a principle cannot be considered moral unless applied universally.

Streams in Judaism

A stream in Judaism is a social, religious or cultural movement within the Jewish People, differing completely or partially from other movements, for example: the majority stream is "Judaism free from the religion of Halakhah"; while the streams of the religious minority include "Haredi Judaism", "religious-Zionist Judaism", "American neo-Orthodox Judaism", "Reform Judaism", "Conservative Judaism", "Reconstructionist Judaism", "Karaite Judaism", "Samaritan Judaism", etc.

In the eighteenth century, Orthodoxy began to develop within the various streams of Haredi Judaism. Its goal was to perpetuate Halakhah and the Shulhan Arukh, as interpreted by its own rabbis, in keeping with the prevailing beliefs in the hassidic and mitnagdic sub-streams of Haredi Judaism. "Orthodox" Haredi Judaism revived the Sadducean-Karaite resistance to innovation – or in the words of the dictum cited by the nineteenth century Orthodox leader Moses Sofer ("Hatam Sofer"): "new (produce) is forbidden by the Torah". Jewish Orthodoxy developed as a reaction to the renewal movements – Haskalah and Reform – that began to appear in religious Judaism and in Judaism free from the religion of Halakhah, in the cultures of the Jewish communities of Europe, America, Africa and Asia.

New streams began to develop within secular Judaism as well, such as the anti-Zionist Yiddishist movement in pre-Holocaust eastern Europe, and Zionist Hebrew culture in Palestine.

This diversity is an expression of the pluralism that has prevailed in Jewish culture throughout history. Together, these streams form the dynamic mosaic of many Judaisms with a single Judaism.

Chosen/Choosing People

The Jewish People is a "people of choice" in the sense that its members choose the manner in which they express their Jewishness and their Judaism, the stream to which they belong, and the body of art and literature that represents Jewish culture in their eyes. In the 20th century, a majority of the Jewish People, concentrated in Europe and the Americas, chose to abandon the Haredi stream of Judaism in favour of Judaism free from the religion of Halakhah, and immediately faced a choice between its various sub-streams. Most of the Jews in Israel/Palestine also chose Judaism free from the religion of Halakhah, and created the new Hebrew culture that had developed within it. A tiny minority within the Jewish People chose and continues to choose eastern European Haredi Jewish culture: speaking Yiddish, wearing mediaeval Polish dress – sanctified in their minds as Jewish attire – studying the Talmud exclusively, and doing their best to ignore twentieth -twenty first century culture.

The religious belief that the Jewish People is a people of choice – in the sense of a people chosen by the god of the universe, and therefore superior to all other peoples – poses a threat to the sanity and humanisation of its members, as a belief that leads to the dehumanisation of the non-Jewish other that is the rest of humanity. The belief that one's people was chosen by the god of the entire universe to lead the world to redemption, is inevitably accompanied by religious and political fanaticism.

The multiplicity of Judaisms in Judaism and the multiplicity of streams within each of these Judaisms, present every Jew with the choice of living within one, leaving and joining another, or creating a path of her/his own in which to express her/his Jewishness. Since most Jews in Israel and the world have chosen Judaism free from the religion of Halakhah, most have also rejected the misleading and dangerous concept of "chosenness", believing instead in their freedom of choice in their lives as Jews and in the Jewish stream in which they choose to educate their children.

Most Jewish parents in Israel (two-thirds) have chosen to send their children to non-religious schools, thereby choosing the non-religious stream in which they wish to educate their children. Most Jewish parents in the diaspora – religious parents who belong to synagogues affiliated with the majority streams, and secular parents who do not belong to a synagogue – have chosen to educate their children outside Judaism, in non-Jewish schools that do not teach the culture of the Jewish People, including the classic literature of the Bible. Some Jewish parents in the diaspora (about a third) have chosen to send their children (until age 13) to supplementary Jewish education (a few hours a week) in a synagogue. For the most part however, such supplementary education does not introduce its students to living and evolving Jewish culture, making do with a few biblical or liturgical texts and some words of Hebrew. As a result of this choice, most Jews raised in the diaspora are familiar with the culture of the country in which they live (e.g. English, French or American culture), but not the culture of the Jewish People – religious or secular.

Jews, who seek to assimilate and ignore their Jewishness, also make a choice. As long as they are aware of the fact that they are Jewish and that those around them see them as such, they must choose a way in which to live Jewish lives, or ignore their Jewishness and deny or hide it from their environment and their children, as did many parents following the Shoah, and as do many parents in the West, products of second or third generation mixed – Jewish and non-Jewish – marriages.

Among assimilated Jews, and even Jewish converts to Christianity, there are those who choose to preserve certain customs linking them to their Jewish past, as did many of the, Conversos in Spain – often called anusim or forced converts, although in most cases they were given a choice between conversion and emigration. Those who chose to become Christians gained entry to a wide variety of professions, many attaining high office in government and the Catholic Inquisition, arousing jealousy and religious zeal among the "Old Christians", who rejected the "New Christians", and thereby laid the foundations of racism in Europe. In the nineteenth century, many European Jews, like Heine and Mahler, converted to Christianity, because as Jews they could not earn a doctoral degree or aspire to high office in western Europe, even after the Emancipation.

In Israel, Jews are aware of their Jewishness, as their national, linguistic, cultural, social and political identity. They do not face the choice of Jewishness and assimilation: they can only assimilate with other Jews.

Even in Israel however, Jews must choose. In choosing a school for their children, they choose the stream of Israeli Judaism in which they wish to express their Jewishness. They must choose a religious or secular lifestyle, and a position regarding the issue of "who is a Jew", determining their attitude to the Law of Return and the character of the Jewish state.

The Secular Stream in Judaism

The secular stream in Judaism shares most of the characteristics of the other Jewish streams. In the nineteenth century, centres of secular Judaism developed mainly in the large cities of Europe, to which Jews flocked from the small towns where the majority of the Jewish population had previously resided. In the twentieth century, secular Judaism developed rapidly in the large Jewish concentrations in Europe and the Americas – home to a majority of world Jewry. Its influence spread throughout the Jewish communities of Asia and North Africa, as a result of the work of the Alliance Israelite Universelle educational movement and its network of schools.

Mass immigration from Europe to the Americas, South Africa and Palestine led to the establishment of new centres of secular

Judaism. Palestine was to become secular Judaism's most prolific centre, with the rebirth of Hebrew culture in the first half of the twentieth century. Since the establishment of the Jewish state, Israel has become a spiritual and cultural point of reference for all other Jewish centres throughout the world.

Secular Judaism has produced most of contemporary Judaism's works of art and literature, as well as most of the new social and political movements that have reshaped the lives of Jews in Israel and the diaspora. Secular Judaism, free from the religion of Halakhah, is also the author of an unprecedented development in Jewish history: the establishment of non-religious Jewish educational systems in Israel, from pre-school to university. The curricula offered at these schools combine science and the humanities with world and Jewish culture. The main language of instruction in secular Judaism is Hebrew. In the diaspora such systems existed up to the Second World War.

Within secular Judaism there have been conflicting streams and ideologies with hundreds of thousands of members, such as: the Bund and the communists, Yiddishists and anti-Zionists, Zionists, and the Israeli secular movement that re-established Hebrew as the spoken and creative language of the Jewish People.

International Jewish organisations were established without any religious basis – organisations such as the Zionist Organisation, the World Jewish Congress, and trans-national secular Jewish parties.

The establishment of a Jewish entity in Israel/Palestine and the revival of Hebrew culture have been secular Judaism's greatest and most enduring achievements. Although this stream comprised only about five percent of the Jewish People prior to World War II, it soon began to exert a significant influence upon the Jews of the world, their culture, and political and educational movements.

Most of the Jews of Palestine on the eve of the Second World

War belonged to the secular stream of Judaism. It was under its leadership that Jewish autonomy developed under British rule – before the establishment of the Jewish state: Jewish education system, universities, colleges, schools and pre-schools, independent cultural institutions and organisations, the Academy of the Hebrew Language, theatres, an art academy, museums, publishing houses, associations for the advancement of secular Israeli culture (e.g. the teachers', painters' and writers' associations), daily newspapers, Hebrew publications, a Hebrew radio station, and a film studio. The first ever secular cultural communities were established within the kibbutz movement, developing new ways in which to celebrate the holidays and the Sabbath, and new rituals for bat/bar-mitzvah, weddings and mourning – free from the religion of Halakhah.

Democratically-elected institutions, both local and national, acted to establish an independent system of collection and taxation, an underground army of 100,000 male and female soldiers, and a police force under British command, but staffed in most areas of Jewish settlement by Jewish officers and men, some under orders from the elected institutions of the secular Jewish autonomy. The religious Zionist factions – a minority of the Jewish population – also supported the institutions of the secular Jewish autonomy, although they were boycotted for the most part by the haredim.

The centres of most Jewish streams, including those of secular Judaism – the stream to which most Jews in eastern, western, central and southern Europe belonged – were destroyed in the Shoah. The following years witnessed the breakdown of secular Jewish movements and their educational systems even in the United States. Most suspended activity, and their large daily press ceased publication.

In Palestine, the Jewish stream free from the religion of

Halakhah created a vigorous and independent Jewish entity, establishing the groundwork for the first secular, democratic Jewish state in history. Today, Israel is home to more than half of the Jewish People, and a majority of Jewish youth under age 18.

Secular Judaism's Inherent Weakness

Unlike other Jewish streams, secular Judaism has no leadership representing its interests as a distinct stream in Jewish culture and education, and no clearly formulated educational doctrines accepted by most of its teachers. Only a few have actually articulated the beliefs by which they live and teach. In the secular stream, there are few organised cultural communities that provide for the distinct spiritual, educational and social needs of their members.

The few organised secular communities that do exist (on kibbutzim, in secular congregations in the United States, and some independent havurot in the diaspora) cannot serve as paradigms. Most of those who follow a secular Jewish lifestyle do not belong to any organised social-cultural community. To the extent that they do have community centres, these are generally geared toward physical fitness and recreation, rather than the educational-spiritual needs of a secular community.

The secular stream lacks institutions for the training of "popular teachers" (which Buber sought to develop), capable of creating and sustaining Jewish cultural communities. Consequently, the secular stream lacks the professional secular leadership such cultural and educational communities require – like the religious streams' numerous rabbis, or the handful of secular educators and rabbis at work in the secular stream.

Secular Judaism's organisational and political weakness has resulted in the fact that Israel's non-religious school system – serving the vast majority of the Jewish population – is the only one without its own autonomous educational authority. While each of the Jewish religious streams in Israel enjoys educational autonomy, funded by the taxpayers, and run by representatives of the various religious and political streams (Shas, Agudat Yisrael, Degel Hatorah and the National Religious Party), the non-religious stream has no authority over its schools – run for years by government-appointed education ministers representing or influenced by the religious parties.

Kulturkampf

The war of culture in Judaism is a struggle between streams that espouse different or opposing views. The leaders of these streams generally strive to impart their principles and Jewish lifestyles to the members of the other Jewish streams. Ideological, religious, economic and political factors lie behind the clashes between streams that differ from one another culturally and socially. In the Jewish state, it is these clashes that constitute the country's "kulturkampf".

The differences between Judaism's various streams are often more than just a matter of lifestyle. They encompass ritual and holiday-celebration, ideological positions regarding Jewish history and God concepts, beliefs regarding the existence or non-existence of the hereafter, roles assigned to the Jewish state, and the degree of openness toward other cultures. They also differ in their perceptions of the future and the role of the messiah, as well their attitudes toward Halakhah – advocating its immutability or recognising the changes it has undergone – and what is more, regarding the extent to which its religious precepts take precedence over the laws of a democratic society. The differences may even include modes of dress and spoken language (e.g. the differences between the haredim and other Jewish streams).

Culture wars have been a part of Jewish history from the very beginning. Since Judaism is inherently a culture characterised by a belief in a common history, alongside a variety of different or opposing beliefs, its wars of culture pose no threat to the unity of the Jewish People. They threaten Jewish unity only on the rare occasions when they become violent and deteriorate into civil war.

For most of Jewish history, these culture wars have been non-violent. Communities that have joined different Jewish streams have lived apart from one another, even within the same town. Passage from the centralised rule of the religious sacerdotal establishment and the Sanhedrin to the extreme decentralisation of Jewish dispersal and the independence of individual communities, rabbis and leaders, has allowed, and continues to allow, the peaceful co-existence of divergent streams engaged in culture wars.

Proponents of radically opposing views, such as the haredi, secular, Reform and Conservative communities in the United States, live separately and avert clashes with one another because they have no interests that require them to meet.

In Israel, the common and opposing interests of the various streams are on the rise, and consequently so is friction between them. The contrasting beliefs and positions of the leaders and members of the different streams colour their constant interaction in parliament, government, local authorities and the judicial system.

The kulturkampf between the religious minority and the secular majority in Israel is therefore intensifying. It assumes the form of a partisan struggle, in which some of the religious streams are represented by political parties. These parties obey the rulings of rabbis who are not elected, but have the ability to influence Knesset and government decisions, through their appointed representatives. Isolated outbursts of violence at demonstrations, destruction of property, and violent attacks on individuals – reflect the extent of the unbridged gap between the prevailing beliefs in the divergent streams of Israeli Judaism.

At the heart of this culture war lies the debate between the majority of Israeli Jews and non-Jews, who believe in the supremacy of democratic law over halakhic precepts; and the representatives of the religious streams, who believe in the supremacy of Halakhah over democracy and all its institutions.

All other conflicts between the religious and secular streams in Israel stem from this one – conflicts concerning the supremacy of humanistic values over the precepts of Halakhah, equality between the sexes, Jewish humanistic education, the Law of Return, conversion laws, the definition of Jewishness, the status of rabbinical courts and who may serve as a rabbinical court judge (women and representatives of all secular and religious streams in Judaism), the obligation to serve in the armed forces charged with defending the country's citizens, the obligation to obey one's rabbi or one's commanding officer, the Sabbath laws and other religious laws governing secular behaviour, etc.

In the collective national memory, culture wars have been a part of Judaism ever since its founding at Mount Sinai. With the settlement of the Israelite tribes in the Land of Israel, began a war of culture between monotheistic Jews, and polytheistic Jews – who worshiped Baal, Ashtoreth and Moloch.

Wars of culture persisted in Hellenistic times: between Judaism that had opened up to the influences of western culture and insular Judaism; between those who believed in the existence of a single world and those who believed in life after death and the world to come; between the many different sects arising within a growing Jewish population in Israel and in the diaspora.

The culture wars took on a variety of new forms in the Middle Ages. Violent outbreaks decreased, since Jews were scattered in small communities and lacked the means to wage actual war. Non-violent culture wars raged between rationalists and mystics, and between messianists and their opponents. Even these conflicts however, erupted in violence from time to time, as in the burning of Maimonides' works in the streets of Paris (according to the thirteenth century testimony of the Hassid of Verona).

In the Renaissance and Age of Enlightenment, the gaps between the various streams of Judaism increased. In the West, there was a growing openness toward other cultures, their philosophy and the rationalism behind it; while the East saw the rise of Hassidism, disseminating Kabbalah and Jewish mysticism within religious Judaism. The culture wars between *Hassidim* and *Mitnagdim*, *Haredim* and *Maskilim*, intensified – coming to a head with the growth of secularism and the appearance of the Zionist and anti-Zionist movements in the twentieth century.

The wars of culture do not preclude a sense of Jewish unity, reflected in identification with other Jews, and in a sense of national identity based on a common past. Only rarely do the wars of culture incur violence – the terrible assassination of Prime Minister Yitzhak Rabin, for example.

The twentieth century witnessed a small number of violent outbursts related to the culture wars, for example: the disturbances caused by fanatic defenders of the Hebrew language ("ivri daber ivrit") at the Mograbi Cinema in Tel Aviv, when Yiddish films were screened; haredi slander of Eliezer Ben-Yehuda, for his role in the revival of the Hebrew language – resulting in his arrest by Ottoman authorities; attacks against young women in Jerusalem, by haredim who disapproved of their attire; haredi damage to property during the course of demonstrations over Sabbath observance in Jerusalem; secular damage to religious schools illegally established in secular neighbourhoods.

In most places and at most times, throughout the Jewish culture wars – from the Age of Enlightenment to the present – the struggles between the various streams have been characterised by ideological debate and attempts to secure positions of power within the community, society or country. Violent clashes have been infrequent and short-lived, compared to Europe's large-scale, destructive and lengthy civil wars, which also stemmed from wars of culture and religion. With the establishment of the State of Israel, when power and resources passed into Jewish hands, the war of culture between the religious and secular streams gradually intensified. Since Israel's wars of culture are a product of the contrast between belief in the supremacy of Halakhah over democracy and the conviction that democracy and humanistic values must take precedence over religious precepts, the two positions can never be reconciled.

All that remains is to engage in dialogue, with the aim of achieving peaceful co-existence between all who accept the majority decisions of Israeli democracy. At the same time, maximum educational and cultural autonomy should be encouraged within each of the streams, on condition that all agree to fulfil their obligations to society, and provide their students with knowledge of democratic values and the necessary skills to lead productive lives in today's economy and society.

Chapter Three

Pluralism Characterises Judaism throughout the Ages

Changing attitudes to Judaism today have highlighted the pluralism that has characterised it throughout its history – reflected in a multiplicity of opinions, religions, beliefs and streams.

Changing attitudes to the history of Judaism as the culture of the Jewish People can be seen in the diversity of subjects, literary works, testimonies and documents, considered "Jewish sources".

History begins with the Present

Proust claimed that every reader comes to know the characters of fiction, by recalling the people s/he has encountered in life. Historians and readers of history also recount the past in relation to the present and its formative events.

The present has changed the image of Judaism's past, through scholarship, archaeology, new ideas, beliefs and interpretations we ascribe to ancient texts. Perceptions of Judaism's past in the early twenty first century are quite unlike those of two or three centuries ago. The background and sources of the holiday of Hanukah in the minds of those who were ignorant of the Books of the Maccabees because they had been removed from Judaism are quite different from the images of the holiday and its sources in the minds of those who have read them.

We, who live within the history of Judaism and take part in its making, face conflicts rooted in memory of the past and the manner in which we reshape it. This new awareness affects the political positions of Jews in Israel, their attitudes to the peace process and to decisions regarding the country's borders. Some sanctify every place that can be linked to a historical event. Others see the constantly shifting borders of the Jewish kingdoms and areas of settlement in the past as justification for territorial compromise for the sake of peace. Both groups draw upon the past, as perceived in the eyes of the present.

All Judaisms educate children and adults in the Jewish cultural heritage unique to the Judaism in which they live. Such is the case with Haredi Judaism, religious-Zionist Judaism, the various types of Reform Judaism, or secular Judaism free from the religion of Halakhah and its interpretations of ancient texts.

Difficulties and disputes relevant to our lives in the present become a point of departure for the study of Judaism and its past. Perceptions of the past affect the nature of today's conflicts, e.g. the Sabbath laws – eternal or changing – the status of women within the community and within the state, etc.

The culture of the Jewish People has been marked by pluralism since its inception, and clashes between religious streams have been a part of its experience since its very first war of culture. Such clashes between the various religious streams continued throughout the Middle Ages, Renaissance and Enlightenment.

Pluralism is the recognition of the variegation within Judaism, as a characteristic element of Jewish culture throughout all eras. The pluralism that became the guiding principle in Jewish thought in talmudic times, today affords legitimacy to all streams, opinions and beliefs within Judaism. None of these represents "normative Judaism" and none represents a deviation from the norm. Judaism is not equivalent to any of the Judaisms it comprises, but is rather their sum total.

On the basis of this approach, one may study and become acquainted with each of the streams in Judaism, its characteristics, prevailing beliefs and customs, their roots in the history of Judaism as culture, and the similarities and differences between them and the dominant streams of the past.

Since pluralism is not relativism, this approach to Judaism also entails value judgment – evaluation of the religious laws and precepts, customs and traditions that currently prevail in the various streams, or have done so in the past – on the basis of contemporary humanistic values.

Judaism as culture studies thus address not only the similarities and differences between the Jewish streams, but also encourage students to adopt a critical approach toward the various beliefs, and positive and negative precepts – some of which are enshrined in tradition and harm neither men nor women, and some of which appear to violate the rights of men and/or women to dignity, liberty, equality, and the opportunity to develop the unique human potential that lies within each and every one of us.

In Jewish studies, one's personal beliefs will affect the way in which one approaches the body of works representing the variety of streams in a given period of Jewish history. Nevertheless, the search for "historical truth" can be shared by adherents to different beliefs, on condition that they disregard all taboos and prohibitions with regard to sources and documents that may be consulted, and recognise each and every stream within Judaism as an integral part of it, although they may reject its specific precepts and customs.

A Brief History of Jewish Pluralism

From Judaism's inception to the proliferation of the movements free from the religion of Halakhah, pluralism has been in evidence in every era of Jewish cultural development, in a broad range of literature, historiography, art and design, liturgy, philosophy and scholarship. The numerous and conflicting streams that have characterised Judaism in every period, have all belonged to a single Judaism – the culture of the Jewish People – developed and enriched by its internal diversity and contrasts, for at least three thousand years.

In the formative period of its split into two kingdoms, Judaism witnessed clashes between adherents of an abstract God and those who believed in God as represented by the image of a golden calf; a dispute that raged throughout the period of the two kingdoms, with golden calves installed at centres of the Yahweh cult in the kingdom of the ten tribes.

From the days of Israelite settlement in the land of Canaan, Canaanite religious beliefs and practices – particularly the cults of Ashtoreth and Asherah, Baal and Moloch – spread within Judaism. These polytheistic religions coexisted with, and sometimes even supplanted, monotheistic religion in both kingdoms, as in the period in which the cult of Baal and Ashtoreth became the official state religion in the kingdom of the ten tribes.

Solomon was the first king to recognise the possibility of peaceful co-existence between the cults of many deities within Jewish culture. In constructing temples to many gods in the capital of the first Jewish kingdom, he made Jerusalem not only monotheism's first capital, but also the first polytheistic capital to boast a monotheistic temple. It was part of a process of ensuring peace with the peoples and powers that lay beyond the borders of the new state. Internal opposition to his rule – due to the corvée he had imposed – set the stage for the opposition voiced by the prophets of Yahweh to the many temples he had built, and to the openness he displayed toward the cultural and religious influences of neighbouring peoples. A prophet of Yahweh appointed Jeroboam the son of Nebat to head a rebellion against Solomon, assuring him that it was God's will.

Opposition to such polytheistic tendencies was mounted by the relatively small faction of the prophets of Yahweh, who continued to believe in the exclusivity of the God of Israel and to combat all manifestations of "idol worship". Religious pluralism

73

in Judaism was encouraged by the political establishment, with the full support of the Jewish priests and prophets in the employ of the royal court of Israel. The biblical redactors too opposed this religious and cultural pluralism, as evidenced by their textual glosses (e.g. in the books of Judges and Kings). Their staunch opposition to such pluralism did not prevent them from including detailed descriptions of the many gods and religious rites that prevailed in the Judaism of their day in the biblical texts. The contrast between belief in a single historical legacy and a multiplicity of religious and ethical traditions in Judaism becomes tangible in the age of the first three temples to Yahweh – in Jerusalem, Beth-El and Dan – known as the First Temple Period.

The Split in Judaism in the Hellenistic and Second Temple Periods

During the Second Temple Period, Judaism split into Hellenistic Judaism and Rabbinical Judaism, Palestinian Judaism and eastern and western diaspora Judaism. Jewish communities at the time witnessed the development of opposing streams and sects that clashed with and condemned one another, in the name of the single Judaism to which they all belonged. Sadducees and Pharisees, Essenes and Jewish Christians, Jews receptive to western culture – called "Hellenists" by their opponents – and Jews who isolated themselves from Hellenistic culture, but were in the end, influenced by it (as evidenced by mosaics and synagogue frescoes, or elements of a polis on the Temple Mount – with a gymnasium and hippodrome; see also S. Lieberman on the influences of Greek culture on the sages of the Talmud).

Following the destruction of the Second Temple in Jerusalem and the dissolution of the Jewish kingdom, the royal and priestly establishment collapsed, to be replaced by synagogues, communities, rabbinical and local leadership, both in Palestine and in the Greek, Latin- and Aramaic-speaking diasporas.

Throughout the first millennium of the Common Era, the Hellenistic-Byzantine period of Jewish history, the sages of the Oral Law continued to reform Jewish religion and beliefs, precepts and practice, institutions and holidays. Their deliberations and rulings have been preserved in the Mishnah and the Gemara, and their accompanying literature. In these discussions and majority decisions, the sages developed and shaped Halakhah, and created a wealth of legends, including a mythical world-to-come, the hereafter, the heavenly royal court of the King of Kings, inhabited by angelic and divine beings, an Eden transposed from the beginning of history to its end, and Gehenna as a place of eternal sadistic torture.

The Hellenistic period witnessed the development of a broad range of Jewish literature, reflecting the various Judaisms of the time: Hellenistic Jewish literature (including Philo, Josephus, Ezekiel the Dramaturge, the authors of the books of the Maccabees, and other poets and writers), Rabbinical Jewish literature (the Mishnah, the Talmuds, the Midrash), Christian Jewish literature (parts of the New Testament, before Christianity broke away from Judaism), and the literature of the desert sects (the Dead Sea Scrolls).

Types of Pluralism in Mediaeval Judaism

In the Middle Ages, differences between Jewish communities on three continents – Africa, Asia and Europe – increased. In isolated areas on each of these continents, unique Judaisms developed, such as Benei Israel Judaism of southern India; Yemenite Judaism; Chinese Judaism; Ethiopian Judaism; Caucasus Judaism and its links with the kingdom of the Khazars; – European Judaism, created at a crossroads of Jewish immigration from Germany,

75

Slavic and Khazar lands; Spanish and Portuguese Judaism, etc.

In addition to the geographical and cultural divide, the Middle Ages saw the development of a religious-philosophical divide: extreme rationalism (like that of Maimonides in the Guide of the Perplexed) based on belief in an exclusive and abstract God, alongside the growing influence of kabbalah and mysticism within widespread movements, such as Hassidism. Various messianic movements – David Reuveni, Shabbetai Zevi, Jacob Frank – underscored the distinction between ethnicity and the religion of Halakhah, laying the foundations for anti-messianic Zionist thought. Alongside the tendency to confine Halakhah to a fixed system of laws and precepts, (from Maimonides' Mishneh Torah to Joseph Karo's Shulkhan Arukh and the glosses by Moses Isserles), many (e.g. Judah Loew of Prague) continued to believe in the talmudic principle of "both [opinions] are the words of the living God" and the ongoing development of Halakhah. Kabbalistic (Lurianic) beliefs in the function of the religious precepts in "repairing the world" and furthering redemption, were accompanied by a growing belief in magic, astrology, and God's corporeality and "stature" (*Shiur Komah*).

Integration into other Cultures during the Renaissance and Enlightenment

The processes of liberation from the yoke of religious precepts and rabbinical domination unfolded at times and in places where Jews lived within the culture of the Renaissance and European Enlightenment. During the Renaissance – centuries before their emancipation, at the hands of Napoleon, from communal authority – the Jews of Italy (of all extractions) integrated into the culture of their neighbours, while preserving their own Jewish identity. In the Low Countries, communities of "new Christians" (forced converts from Spain and Portugal) newly returned to Judaism, grappled with a new approach to Judaism (Spinoza and pantheism) – one that departed from conservative tradition and its belief in the divine authorship of the Bible and God as a unique entity, distinct from nature.

The processes of secularisation were reflected in new currents of philosophy and belief, which arose in both eastern and western Judaism in the eighteenth and ninteenth centuries – during the period of enlightenment and large-scale migration to the large cities of Europe and America. By the ninteenth century, atheistic beliefs and a Judaism free from the religion of Halakhah were the primary sources of inspiration for Jewish creativity in all fields. At the same time, there arose orthodox religious streams that – like the Sadducees and Karaites before them – eschewed change, believing (as Moses Sofer) that "[all that is] new is forbidden by the Torah".

Movements for the reformation of the Jewish religion also developed – "Reform" and later "Conservative" Judaism, in Europe and America.

Over the course of the twentieth century, Judaism – both religious and secular – became progressively more pluralistic, defining itself as the culture of a people rather than its religion. American Judaism began to take on the distinct character of a Jewish "community" in its own right – the newest and largest such community. Israeli Judaism quickly developed as a point of encounter between Jews of all traditions, continents and streams – religious and secular: a spiritual, cultural and educational centre for the entire Jewish People (today, a majority of world Jewish youth under the age of 18 attend Israeli educational institutions).

Israeli Judaism is the product of secular Zionism and the revival of Hebrew as the language of speech and artistic communication in all media. It has become increasingly representative of Judaism as a whole, as a result of the decreasing number of Jews in the diaspora, and the role it has come to play in Jewish education. Judaism is not religious in the sense that Jewish religion is defined by Orthodox religious Jews: most Jews do not observe the religious precepts, do not belong to or regularly attend synagogues, do not recite blessings or pray to God, and do not educate their children in accordance with the Jewish religion. There is however a growing variety of religious movements in Judaism that, together with the secular Jewish streams, further underscore its pluralistic character.

A Variety of Works Represent Each Cultural Era

The selection of works that constitute the Bible presents a variety of views and beliefs, and describes a broad range of lifestyles, rituals and religious approaches characteristic of the Jewish masses, leaders and kings, priests and prophets.

The biblical anthology includes all of the genres recognised in western literature today – prose, epic and lyric poetry, drama, poetical philosophical treatises, historiography, works of law and prophetic rhetoric, as well as descriptions of customs and rituals, daily life, festivals, figurative art in sanctuaries and public places, palaces and temples.

The beliefs and approaches represented in the Bible express both theodicy and its rejection, belief in the exclusive divinity of Yahweh and rejection of such exclusivity, opposing views on the relationship between sin and punishment, on the preference of social justice over religious observance, on discrimination against women in Jewish society, on the powers of Jewish rulers over their subjects, and on the essence of the covenant between God and his people. The biblical anthology as a whole represents the first historical-cultural era in the history of the Jewish People:

78

from its origins as a single family joined by a mixed multitude of members of other peoples, to the destruction of the three temples to Yahweh and the two co-existent Jewish kingdoms, exile and the return of a small minority from Mesopotamia to Judea under the aegis of the Persian Empire, and the formation of an independent Jewish entity in Jerusalem and its environs, alongside a Jewish-Samaritan entity in Nablus and its environs.

Despite the small number of books it contains, the biblical anthology affords a glimpse of cultural life during the periods it treats: the opposing streams, prevailing religions, artistic endeavours, influences of other cultures on daily and creative life, and the radical changes the Jewish People underwent during the course of the centuries to which the works of the Bible relate.

In light of modern scholarship and archaeological discoveries, it is clear that the books of the Bible should not be taken as authentic historical records of actual events that occurred at the time and place noted by the biblical authors. Like all bodies of literature, the works of the Bible reflect the historical reality from which their various elements are drawn; a historical reality fashioned in the collective memory of the Jewish People, yet exerting a real influence on its cultural, social and political life. In all of these senses, the Bible can – as suggested by Bialik – serve as an excellent model for similar anthologies, representing other periods of Jewish cultural history. Each period would be represented by a collection of Jewish works in all literary genres, reflecting all of the Jewish streams, traditions, diasporas, sects and movements of the era.

Constant Change in Judaism

Jewish beliefs, rituals, customs and traditions, holiday and life-cycle rites, are recreated in every era, as are approaches to classic works and their sanctity, Jewish and foreign languages and their role in Judaism, and the protagonists of Jewish history and literature – including God. Such new forms and content are incorporated into Jewish culture, but do not always supplant older traditions, often hallowed in the hearts and minds of some. When Rabbeinu Gershom banned polygamy, over a thousand years ago, the practice continued within many Jewish communities, as if the very concept of family had not undergone a revolutionary change. When women rabbis and cantors began to officiate in the synagogues of the majority Conservative and Reform religious movements, and secular Judaism began to appoint women to the judicial bench at all levels, Orthodox communities continued to bar women from serving as rabbis, cantors and religious court judges. When Jewish philosophers such as Maimonides declared their belief in an abstract God, not only incorporeal but entirely beyond human conception, others continued to believe in an anthropomorphic God, seated on a throne, having "stature" (*Shiur Komah*) and measurable limbs.

Everything changes in Judaism. Innovations however, accumulate alongside that which is retained – new beliefs and customs coexist with older traditions. It is this combination that forms the basis of the prevailing pluralism in the culture of the Jewish People. Precepts, laws, customs and beliefs have never been the be-all and end-all of Judaism. Every law and custom, institution, lifestyle and ritual in Judaism has undergone and continues to undergo far-reaching change within Jewish culture and its component religious streams.

The changes in Judaism have occurred at various times, within various groups, and at various paces. The changes in Judaism were accelerated, when the Jewish religion passed from temple and sacrificial cult to one of synagogue and prayer. This transformation led to extreme decentralisation, and encouraged further change that transpired in some communities but not in others – influenced by the different surroundings in which Jews lived and created.

In the collective memory of the People preserved in the Bible, such changes begin to appear as early as the years of wandering in the desert. Aaron's Tabernacle and idols differed fundamentally from Moses' Tent of Meeting, in which there were no altars, sacrifices or priests. The temple to Yahweh constructed by Solomon, with its winged human-faced figures in the Holy of Holies, differed from the temples to Yahweh in Beth-El and Dan, which were dominated by images of the golden calf. The Second Temple in Jerusalem differed from its predecessors, and underwent far-reaching changes when reconstructed by Herod. The variety of forms and original artistic creations increased with the proliferation of synagogues throughout Palestine and the diaspora, as clearly evidenced by the difference between the frescoes of the synagogue at Dura Europos – including the depiction of a nude figure pulling Moses from the Nile – and the prevalence of stylised designs, zodiacal symbols and Greek mythological elements in the decorative art found in synagogues in Palestine.

The synagogues themselves underwent radical change, arousing considerable controversy. Initially, there was no separation of men and women in these synagogues, and they lacked a "women's court" (as in the Temple). Centuries later, women's courts began to appear in some synagogues, only to disappear within a few centuries from most synagogues around the world. Today there are synagogues in which men and women sit, sing and dance together, in which services are accompanied by musical instruments on the Sabbath and holidays (in the tradition of the Temple); and conversely, synagogues in which women are seated behind walls that separate them from the main part of the sanctuary, in which all who are called to the Torah and lead prayers are male, in which prayers are recited without musical accompaniment, and in which there are no paintings or other works of art.

Today, there are once again increasingly varied works of figurative and abstract art in synagogues and Jewish meeting places in Israel and throughout the world. On the Sabbath, in Israel, thousands flock to such meeting places in hundreds of museums, to enjoy Jewish and other works of art, as if no prohibition against the depiction of human figures had ever existed among certain Jewish groups.

The nature of the Jewish streams in conflict with one another has changed, in the variety of beliefs that have developed in almost every aspect of Jewish culture and religion, including: the biblical belief in the exclusive existence of this world, the Messiah, Providence, the nature of God, the desirability of a halakhic state, the necessity of religious observance, and the ways in which the holidays are celebrated.

Many religious and secular streams have developed within the culture of the Jewish People, each of which represents Judaism in its own way, just like Maimonides' extreme rationalism, Nahmanides mysticism, or Spinoza's pantheism.

The swiftest and most far-reaching changes began to reshape Judaism itself, with the spread of secular humanism, agnosticism and atheism, which would become an integral part of Jewish culture, alongside the religious streams.

Radical changes in Jewish education caused most Jewish youth to abandon religious schools in favour of non-religious educational systems – Jewish in Israel, and non-Jewish in the diaspora.

Pioneers in education free from the religion of Halakhah – such as the "Alliance Israelite Universelle" in the Mediterranean region, the Hebrew-language "Tarbut" and Yiddish "CYShO" schools in Europe, and primarily, the secular education system in Palestine and later the State of Israel, currently attended by a majority of Jewish youth in the world – facilitated and accelerated the process of change. Jewish intellectuals in Arab lands, from Iraq to Morocco, swelled the ranks of Jewish writers and artists whose work lay beyond the boundaries of religious culture, some joining the secular Jewish intelligentsia throughout the world, who spoke and wrote in European languages, were acquainted with world classics, and educated their children in a spirit of openness toward western culture. Secular Jewish writers from Arabic-speaking countries took an active role in European culture, alongside Jewish writers and artists from eastern and western Europe and America.

At the same time, Jewish religious educational systems perpetuated the forms and content of study enshrined in centuries-old tradition, ignoring the changes that Judaism had undergone in the modern era. Today, Haredi Judaism continues to educate boys and young men in yeshivot, which have flourished in secular Israel as never before in the history of Jewish education. By virtue of the pressure they have exerted on the secular political parties, the Haredi minority in Israel has obtained stipends and exemptions from military service for all its yeshivah teachers and students, despite their being a tiny minority within the Jewish people. Non-religious Jewish education in Hebrew, Yiddish, German and English has brought the ideas of the Haskalah to thousands, increasing the secularisation of Jewish culture, building bridges between Jewish and western cultures, and accelerating the processes of change in Israeli and world Judaism.

One Cannot Claim "Judaism says",
Just as One Cannot Claim "the Bible says"

In Judaism, as in the Bible, a variety of beliefs clash with, or even utterly reject one another. The assertion "Judaism says" is therefore incorrect, as is the statement "the Bible says". One should rather say: "in Judaism it is said" or "it is said in the Bible".

Judaism is a pluralistic culture, not a monolithic ideology. It is thus impossible to attribute a particular position on a given subject to Judaism as a whole or to the entire Jewish People, just as one cannot ascribe a specific opinion to the Bible as a whole.

Those who perceive Judaism as the evolving culture of a people do not attach ideological or religious significance to Jewish history – as if it were fulfilling some messianic or divine purpose. Jewish history, according to this approach, represents only itself. Like the history of any other people, all of its developments have causes and reasons, but lack a predetermined goal. The history of the Jewish People has shaped it in a unique fashion, just as an individual is shaped in a unique fashion by her/his personal biography.

Contemporary Jewish historiography strives to paint a picture of what actually occurred, rather than what should have occurred. Henri Bergson once said of Pujet: "He was a wonderful man. He never let an idea of any kind stand between him and reality". Jewish history is not the fulfilment or expression of an idea, but a process comprising events and artefacts, that together constitute the pluralistic and multifarious culture in which Jews have lived for over 3,000 years. Attempts to describe "what really happened" rely on the cross-checking of evidence, on the works of art and literature that serve as post factum historical documents, and help construct a historical picture. By means of such images, one can observe the plurality that emerges in the culture of the Jewish People, rather than any one of its expressions as its entire essence.

Judaism's Many Judaisms

Judaism comprises many different Judaisms: ethnic, geographical, religious and ideological.

The creative works of all of Judaism's Judaisms together form the whole of Jewish culture. The various Judaisms exist side by side, at times – on opposite sides.

Judaisms with religious and ideological tendencies exert an influence on the lifestyles and religious observance of their adherents, often including mode of dress, speech, sexuality and family life, education and political socialisation. Such differences can be observed in the gaps that exist between haredi, secular, religious-Zionist, religious-Reform, Karaite, Samaritan and Reconstructionist Judaism, etc. There are also ethnic-geographical Judaisms, distinctive in culture, lifestyle and often spoken language, liturgy and ritual, as well as their attitudes to other Judaisms and to their surrounding culture: e.g. American, Moroccan, Polish or Israeli Judaism.

The totality of the culture of the Jewish People, created at the juncture between all of Judaism's Judaisms, comprises the entire range of works representing the various Judaisms. Polish and eastern European Jewish culture constitutes only a part of Judaism, differing greatly from the culture of the Jewish communities of the Mediterranean, the Arabian Peninsula, India, East Africa or North America. And each of these differs completely from the Jewish culture developing in Israel as a result of the encounter between diverse communities and traditions within a single national state.

The Palestinian minority in Israel – about one fifth of the population – lives under the influence of the Arab culture of the region, and does not affect Jewish Israeli culture, at least not in the same way that American culture influences American

Jewish culture, or French culture influences the culture of the Jews of France.

The American Jewish community, the largest in the world, developed its own unique identity only in the twentieth century. Its characteristic traits however, set it apart from all other Jewish communities. Despite its size and influence, most school curricula fail to address the culture and distinct features of this community. Although hundreds of thousands of Israelis live in America, most Israelis are ignorant of the vast body of religious and secular works produced by American Judaism; works in Yiddish and English, in theatre, art, music and film, religious and secular-humanistic thought, Jewish institutions of higher learning, communal projects and large creative bodies established as a result of Jewish integration into the culture of the United States – together constituting one of Judaism's greatest cultural phenomena. Acquaintance with these achievements is essential to understanding contemporary Jewish culture as a whole.

Israelis are familiar with only a small part of North African Judaism (and even that is virtually unknown in the diaspora). In order to be acquainted with the spiritual and creative world of North African Judaism – from Egypt to Libya, Tunisia, Algeria and Morocco – one must be acquainted with a selection of its creative works from the beginning of the second millennium to the present. Throughout its history, North African Judaism has produced philosophers, historians, poets, sages and kabbalists, and today – writers and scholars celebrated in Jewish and other cultures. The works that represent North African Judaism include the writings of Philo, Maimonides, the Septuagint and Jason's Maccabees (an epitomised version of which is extant), Albert Memmi, and many other members of the North African Jewish intelligentsia, who were educated in Jewish French culture, contributed and continue to contribute to scholarship, literature and philosophy, art and society, in Israel and in France.

North African Judaism should not be viewed only in terms of the sermons of rabbis who preside over political parties, culinary and other popular traditions associated with the Mimouna festival, stories of demons, sacred tombs, or rabbi-saints and their disciples. All of these things belong to the popular culture of the Jewish communities of North Africa, but fail to represent the culture as a whole, just as the customs, foods and hassidic tales of the eastern European shtetl (that disintegrated in the second half of the nineteenth century), its demons, miracle-workers and sacred tombs, are hardly representative of the rich culture – literary, philosophical and artistic – of eastern European Judaism.

Most of the works that represent the various regional Judaisms of the 20th century are free from the religion of Halakhah – i.e. created beyond the confines of the Jewish religion. It is therefore doubtful whether they can be considered representative of the ancient traditions of the communities in which they were produced. Nevertheless, culture is not linear: the ancient and the modern commingle to form the whole of living culture – the culture to which people are in fact exposed.

Through a selection of works representing the creative variety within each of these Judaisms, one may become acquainted with them – their distinctive features, as well as the things they share with Judaism's other Judaisms.

All Judaisms Take Part in the Creation
of Judaism as a Culture

Everything created within one particular Judaism is created within Judaism as a whole: a single culture shared by the entire Jewish People. The works and customs created in one of the various Judaisms, at first appear to belong only to that Judaism. Over time however, the best of these become part of the unique culture of the Jewish People: the Oral Law created by Iraqi Judaism, Maimonides' works written in Egypt, the Kabbalistic works of Provence, Spain and Safed, the Haskalah literature of Germany and Russia, Yiddish works composed in Alsace, Italy, Bohemia, Poland, Ukraine and the Baltic lands, Ladino works of the Mediterranean basin, Jewish literature written in German and English in western Europe and America, twentieth century Jewish art and literature produced in Palestine and the State of Israel. Together, they constitute a single Jewish culture, common to all Judaisms, and a select few influence and shape the culture of the entire Jewish People.

All of Judaism's Judaisms – whether ethnic, religious or free from the religion of Halakhah – take part in the process whereby the culture of the Jewish People is created. Familiarity with Judaism is familiarity with this process.

There is no contradiction between "Israeli" and "Jewish" culture, since Judaism includes Israeli culture in all its forms, just as it includes German and Yemenite Jewish culture, or Babylonian-talmudic and Hellenistic Judaism. The works of Maimonides, Spinoza, Shneur Zalman of Lyady, the Gaon of Vilna, Y.L. Gordon, Heine, Bialik, Alterman, Sholem Aleichem, Woody Allen, Chagall, Soutine, Danziger, Mahler, Bernstein, Schoenberg, A.B. Yehoshua, Amos Oz, David Grossman, Amichai, Ben-Haim, biblical pop songs like those of Danny Sanderson, and Israeli film and television productions – all take part in the creation of Judaism as the culture of the Jewish People.

What do Israeli and Diaspora Jews Have in Common?

What do religious and secular Jews have in common? What do Yemenite and Californian Jews have in common? What do Jews in all lands and Judaisms have in common, and what sets them apart from members of other peoples?

What Jews – secular and religious – share, is the belief in a common history, an affinity with the classical literature of the Bible, the national language, evolving national cultural heritage, Eretz Yisrael as the homeland of the Jewish People and its national state, national holidays, and recognition of the need to deal with the ever-present threat of actual or potential anti-Semitism.

• Belief in a common history is also shared by those who believe that the image projected by the ancient Jewish sources does not correspond to historical reality, and should be reconstructed, on the basis of evidence and documentation – including these same ancient sources.

• The cultural affinity with the Bible, as the only element common to all of Judaism's Judaisms – religious and secular – is also shared by those who see the Bible as a religious document or an anthology of classical literature that is a collection of historical documents as well, and by those who see it as the "portable homeland of the Jewish People", as characterised by Heine.

• Affinity with Hebrew as the national language – an ancient language in continuous use by Jews for at least 3,000 years, and which has once again become a spoken and creative language, the official language of the Jewish state, and the language of education of the majority of Jewish youth in the world.

• The cultural heritage of the Jewish People includes Jewish works – i.e. works that have been influenced by the Jewishness of their creators, or have themselves played a role in Judaism.

Jewish works have been created in many Jewish languages (languages spoken only by Jews – such as Yiddish, Ladino, Maghrebian in Morocco, Tat in the Caucasus, Jewish-Italian, Jewish-Yemenite, etc.). Many Jewish works of literature and philosophy have been written in the languages of the peoples in whose midst their authors lived (such as Aramaic, Greek, Arabic, German, English, French, Russian, etc.). Jewish works in the plastic and performing arts have been produced in every era, and today include Jewish theatre, film and television productions.

• Eretz Yisrael is perceived by the Jews of the world as their common birthplace and national homeland, and today, once again, as a political and spiritual centre of the Jewish People; the only country in the world in which the Jewish population is growing, and its cultural works are ever more numerous and diverse than all of the Jewish works produced throughout the rest of the world.

• National holidays that were transformed, in Judaism's religious eras, from natural and historical festivals to religious holidays, are again becoming historical, personal, and social holidays, without religious significance, as the number of Jews who celebrate them increasingly belong to a Judaism free from religion.

• Recognising the threat posed by anti-Semitism – in both its moderate and violent forms – and the need to defend against it, is also shared by most Jews in the world, and is a source of the Jewish solidarity that makes it incumbent upon every community and every individual to act in times of danger – as has in fact happened in each of the twenty centuries of Jewish history since the destruction of the Second Temple. This recognition is also linked to another:

• Recognition of the common fate shared by all Jews, as Jews, and of the obligations of Jewish solidarity, in addition to those imposed by solidarity with all human beings. This type of recognition, like most of the characteristics listed here, is internalised, and becomes a part of the Jewish national consciousness of the individual, through the education s/he receives from family, community and society as a whole. These characteristics are shared by Jews of all religious, cultural and geographic traditions. None are contingent upon observance of the halakhic precepts, or the positions one takes with regard to the many debates within Judaism. The characteristics Jews have in common are what set them apart from other peoples, pertain only to them, adopted by those who join the Jewish People, and generally remain present (at least in the first generation) even in those who leave the Jewish People through conversion to another faith or social and cultural assimilation.

The Main Points of Contention within Judaism Today

Contemporary Judaism is witness to ever more vociferous clashes between religious and secular Judaisms, particularly in Israel, in which the democratic system has strengthened religious minorities, and increased the dependence of all of the parties – religious and secular – upon one another.

The debates and clashes between the various streams of Judaism have stimulated its development throughout history. The rifts between the streams and factions have always appeared unbridgeable, and have spurred members of all streams to action and creativity, in order to strengthen their own unique form of Judaism. Some of the works they produced would eventually become part of the general canon of Jewish culture, demonstrating the value of debate.

At the heart of the kulturkampf raging in Israel today, lies the debate between the majority of the Jewish population, which believes in the supremacy of democratic law, and the religious camp that believes in the supremacy of Halakhah. All other disputes between religious Jews and Jews who are free from the religion of Halakhah, derive from this basic dispute: between those who believe in the supremacy of humanistic values over halakhic precepts, and those who believe in the supremacy of the precepts of Halakhah over all other values or laws, including the democratic laws and decisions of the Knesset and the Supreme Court.

• The conflict between those who believe in full equality between men and women and those who see women as inferior, who recite the daily blessing "blessed is He who has not made me a woman".

• The conflict between educators who believe in being a part of world culture, and teaching the classic works of other cultures, as the basis of humanistic and Jewish education; and those who believe in insularity and intentionally eschew world culture and its spiritual and artistic treasures.

• The conflict over the law of return: Should it apply only to those born to Jewish mothers, or should it be extended to anyone who joins the Jewish People in some other fashion? Is national identity determined by a person's race and religion, or by the social and culture life they lead as part of the people they have joined?

• The conflict over the conversion laws: between those who believe that joining the Jewish People does not require conversion to the Jewish religion, since Judaism is a culture that includes but is not limited to religion; and those who believe that only the conversion rites of the minority Orthodox stream in Judaism should be recognised by the Jewish state, or that the conversion of the majority Jewish religious streams – Conservative and Reform – should be recognised as well.

• The conflict over conscription to the army: between those who believe that it should apply to post-high-school students, and those who believe that only secular students should be conscripted in order to defend those who choose to pursue yeshiva studies, and are therefore exempted from service, and the dangers it entails.

• The conflict over a soldier's duty to obey rabbis or military commanders in units headed by both rabbis and officers.

• The conflict over freedom of and from religion, reflected for example in the debate over the Sabbath, dietary laws, burial, marriage, circumcision, Passover, fasts, and other religious laws imposed on secular Jews – whom the religious themselves call "free", but whose freedom they refuse to recognise.

These conflicts cannot be resolved through compromise, primarily because they reflect the contrast between the principle of the supremacy of Halakhah over any man-made democratic law or constitution, and the principle of the supremacy of universal humanistic values and their expression in democracy, above the precepts of all religious streams or the rulings of rabbis, even when these purport to speak in God's name.

Pluralism in Religious Judaism

When Rabbi Shach, one of the most extreme leaders of Jewish Orthodoxy, asked "what is the closest religion to Judaism?" he replied, "the Habad religion of the Lubavitcher [Rebbe]". He believed that the Judaism of the followers of the Messiah of Brooklyn – who believe they are following in the footsteps of the Ba'al Shem Tov and Rabbi Shneur Zalman of Lyady (author of the Tanya) – is not the same as the religion that he and his fellow *Mitnagdim* – who believe they are the successors of the Gaon of Vilna – espouse.

At the same time, albeit far-removed from Haredi Judaism, religious Judaism also includes American neo-Orthodoxy and its Israeli satellites, and religious-Zionist Judaism in its moderate and extreme forms, as well as Reform and Conservative Judaism – the majority of religious Judaism in the world today. All of these streams belong to the religious "camp" in Judaism, which has been shrinking rapidly since the early twentieth century, with the growth of Judaism free from the religion of Halakhah – in both its "secular" and "traditionalist" forms. In the messianic Habad movement, which migrated to Brooklyn in the early twentieth century, there are those who believe that their Rabbi, Schneerson, is the messiah – even after his death. There was a sect that developed in the synagogue of James, brother of Jesus, in Jerusalem of the first century, the adherents of which believed their rabbi of Nazareth was the messiah, and that his death would not prevent his second coming, that would bring redemption to his people and the world.

Haredi Judaism, in all of its many factions and hassidic courts, as well as many of the other Orthodox Judaisms, view the Reform and Conservative movements as wholly un-Jewish. The Haredi minority does not recognise the rabbis of the majority of religious Judaism in the world, their rulings, or the weddings and conversions they perform.

Religious Judaism of the Hellenistic period experienced similar schisms. At the time of the Second Temple, and following its destruction, deep and irreconcilable differences arose between the Hassideans – the Hasmoneans' earliest supporters – and Jewish Hellenists; and later, between Sadducees, Pharisees, Essenes, desert sects, Zealots, etc. When Rabbinical Judaism denounced the Hellenistic Jews as "Hellenisers" and idol-worshipers, it set itself apart from a large part of the Jewish People, both in Palestine and the diaspora, who had integrated into culture. The Pharisees rose up against the Jewish king Alexander Yanai, because he followed the customs of the Hellenistic kings of neighbouring kingdoms, and did not accept the authority of Rabbinical Judaism.

"Normative Judaism" Exists Only in the Eyes of Those who Believe in it

The prevailing pluralism in Judaism of the Hellenistic and Byzantine periods is reflected not only in the differences and clashes between Pharisees and Sadducees, but in the rich mosaic of Judaisms, sects and communities of various streams, living on different continents, influencing and influenced by different cultures. None of the Judaisms of the Hellenistic period can be presented as definitive "Judaism", just as no contemporary Jewish stream represents Judaism in its entirety. At that time, as in the present, "normative Judaism" existed only in the eyes of those who believed in the exclusive Jewishness of their own stream. Many Jewish Christians believed that they were the true Israel, and that all of the other streams had betrayed the spirit and future of Judaism. Rabbinical Jews believed that they alone represented true Judaism, which was betrayed both by the Sadducean priesthood and the Hasmonean court. Sadducees and Karaites believed faithfulness to the letter of biblical Halakhah to be the only true Judaism, and the Oral Law's interpretations and life after death to be deviations from, and perversions of Judaism. Samaritan Jews believed that all of the other sects and streams were not authentic forms of Judaism, theirs being the only continuous Jewish tradition to have been preserved in the Land of Israel, within the realm of the ten tribes. The Hellenistic period of Jewish history cannot be called the "talmudic period", just as talmudic Judaism today cannot be considered normative Judaism. The importance of a given stream or sect, in terms of its contribution to Jewish creativity, spirituality, beliefs and ideas, is not determined by the number of its adherents. The works and institutions through which a particular stream becomes known and through which it exerts an influence on the development of Judaism as a whole, are far more important than its actual size.

The few prophets of Yahweh whose words are cited in the Bible, are portrayed by the biblical authors as representing a minority (often of one), that stood up to the authorities and the majority of the people. The lyrical-rhetorical works of these prophets, their revolutionary ideas – valuing justice above ritual – would go on to have a far greater spiritual impact than the ideas expressed by representatives of the rulers and the majority of the Jewish People in biblical times.

The ideas of Spinoza and those who followed in his footsteps would, for many years, be considered the opinions of an insignificant and outcast minority, until they eventually came to form the basis of the philosophy espoused by a majority of the Jewish People – free from the religion of Halakhah and belief in a personal God.

The exponents of Zionism were an insignificant minority among Jews in the ninteenth and early twentieth centuries – opposed or ignored by most of the large secular, Orthodox and Reform movements. Two generations later, secular Zionism would come to represent the Jewish People as a whole; its ideas and beliefs a source of inspiration for national liberation and the cultural revolution sparked by the revival of Hebrew as a spoken and creative language.

In the Middle Ages, Rabbinic-talmudic-halakhic Judaism was considered "normative Judaism" in many Jewish communities throughout the world. Today, it is the province of an Orthodox minority with little or no influence over the spiritual and cultural lives of most Jews, and is no longer representative of Judaism as a culture.

In biblical times – the formative period of Jewish culture – only the prophets of Yahweh saw their beliefs as normative Judaism. According to their own testimony, the majority of the Jewish People did not share their views.

Debate in Hellenistic and Contemporary Judaism

The conflicts that developed between the various streams of Judaism in the Hellenistic era – in the late first millennium BCE and the early first millennium CE – are reminiscent of the clashes between Judaism's different streams today.

The sages of the Oral Law carried out sweeping reforms during the Second Temple Period, and in the aftermath of the destruction of the Temple. In accelerating the constant process of change in Jewish culture and religion, they ensured Judaism's continued existence as a living, evolving culture, capable of adapting to changing circumstances.

At the same time, Jews who lived in and were integrated into Hellenistic culture, brought about a cultural revolution, by opening Judaism to western culture, Greek classics and philosophy; reflected in the Talmud (as demonstrated by Lieberman), and in the works of Hellenistic Jewish philosophers and writers such as Aristobulus of Paneas, Philo, and Josephus Flavius. The structure of the Greek-Jewish polis (in the diaspora – particularly in Egypt; and on the Temple Mount) had an impact on the future development of the independent Jewish community. In the arts, Greek painting and sculpture influenced synagogue mosaics and frescoes, theatres in cities with Jewish communities boasted Jewish actors and playwrights (such as Ezekiel the Dramaturge), statues were erected in public places (e.g. in the synagogue of Nehardea and the bathhouse of Acre), many Jews attended gymnasia (such as the one on the Temple Mount), and the Jewish High Priest sent a delegation of Jewish athletes to take part in international Hellenistic sporting events.

Such trends, led by the Jews of large urban centres – aroused considerable opposition among the Hassideans and other opponents of the influences exerted by the Hellenists on Jewish life. When the Hasmonean royal court increasingly came to resemble the courts of Hellenistic kings, the cultural struggle between the two factions became a political one – as reflected in the rebellion and civil war instigated by the Pharisees against the Jewish monarchy. The cultural revolution and reforms of the sages of the Oral Law were sharply opposed by the "Orthodox" of the day – the Sadducees, and their successors, the Karaites. The religious establishment and priestly aristocracy belonged to the Sadducean stream, and resisted the Pharisees' attempts to change biblical Halakhah. Like today's Orthodox, the Sadducees and Karaites sought to freeze Halakhah, adhering to views that prevailed in biblical times – believing in the existence of a single world, and sharply opposing the Pharisees' invention of a "world to come" and life after death. Like Judaism today, Jewish culture in the Hellenistic era was a mosaic of different Judaisms that clashed with one another, and enriched Judaism as a whole.

The works produced during this rich and varied cultural period reflect multifaceted historical developments: Hellenistic Judaism, the Hassideans and the Hasmoneans and the civil and cultural war they waged both against the Jewish Hellenists, and against the religious coercion of the Syrian Empire; the third Jewish kingdom – founded by the Hasmoneans, which was to last until the first century CE, and in which Judaism of the Oral Law continued to develop; the debate between the Sadducean religious establishment and its Pharisee opponents, as well as conflicts between other Jewish sects and streams – Essenes, Christians, desert sects and zealots; the development of the synagogue and its works of Jewish figurative art; the large centres of Hellenistic Judaism – in Egypt and Libya – and of talmudic scholarship in Palestine and Babylonia; the formation of the Bible – from holy scripture, recognised as such by the early Hellenistic era, to the completion of the biblical canon toward the second century CE; the process of gathering and editing the works of the Oral Law, until the completion of the Mishnah in the second century, following the destruction of the Temple, brought about by the failure of the Trajanic and Bar Kokhba Revolts.

This prolific era in the cultural history of the Jewish People can be discovered through the works it produced: later works of the Bible, the Mishnah and the New Testament, tannaic Midrash and discussion, the philosophical works of Philo, the historiography of Josephus and the authors of the Books of the Maccabees, the Apocrypha and Pseudepigrapha – excluded from the Tanakh and included in the Christian canon – the Dead Sea Scrolls, Judeo-Greek and Judeo-Aramaic poetical and exegetical works, drama and liturgy, plastic arts in synagogues, descriptions of lifestyles, laws and disputes, reflecting the period's various and conflicting streams of thought and belief.

It was in the Hellenistic era that rifts began to appear between a Judaism open to western culture, and one determined to keep it out; between a conservative Judaism that sanctified written Halakhah, and a reform-Pharisean Judaism that sought to adapt to changing circumstances; between a Judaism that clung to the biblical belief in the existence of a single world, and a Judaism that espoused belief in a hereafter. The very same rifts can be found in contemporary Judaism – making Jewish culture of that time of special interest to us today.

The Debate over the Existence of a "World to Come"

Like most of the authors and redactors of the Bible, the Sadducees believed that death is the end of life, and that there is no world but the physical one in which we live. Judaism of the Hellenistic era, like Judaism today, harboured these two, conflicting beliefs: belief in the existence of a single world and the finality of death, and belief in a hereafter and the resurrection of the dead.

Belief in resurrection of the dead in the hereafter was widespread in the cultures and religions of the ancient Near East (Egypt and Mesopotamia), and would therefore probably have appeared to the biblical authors as expressions of idol worship. With the proliferation of Mosaic monotheism and its renunciation of the hereafter and the belief that death marks the beginning of a new life, Jewish believers parted ways with the cultures of their neighbours. This was in fact one of the unique elements of the ancient Jewish monotheistic faith, expressed in the works of the Bible.

This unique feature of Mosaic belief is also reflected in the work of the biblical redactors – who placed the Garden of Eden at the beginning of time rather than at its end. Belief in the existence of a single world also lay at the heart of the prophets' demand that justice be done here and now. This belief in a single world brings biblical literature closer to the mentality of today's Jews who are free from religion.

Following the destruction of the Temple, the Karaites were one of the largest Judaisms to clash with Rabbinical Judaism. They followed in the footsteps of the Sadducees, recognising only the authority of biblical Halakhah. The Rabbanites followed in the path of the sages of the Oral Law, in their innovative and imaginative hermeneutical and homiletic interpretations – that changed the meaning of Scripture and served as the basis for the new halakhic rulings of the Talmud and the literature associated with it. Clashes between these two approaches – petrifying conservatism and animating reform – have been at the heart of Judaism's culture wars ever since.

The approach of the Sadducees and the Karaites, like that of today's Haredim, was doomed to failure, since it led – and continues to lead – to cultural stagnation. Throughout Jewish history, those who have tried to freeze Halakhah, groups or streams that have failed to take part in the constant development and change in Judaism as a culture – have suffered decline and spiritual sterility. There are only a few tens of thousands of Karaites left in the world today (in Lithuania, Crimea and Israel), and the Haredim – although a majority in the nineteenth century – today account for only about five percent of the Jewish People.

Toynbee's mistaken characterisation of Judaism as a "fossil" civilisation, was the result of his having limited his field of observation to conservative Haredi-religious Judaism – of minor significance in terms of contemporary Jewish cultural development.

The Basis of Judaism: Bible or Talmud?

The debate between those who consider the Bible to be the basis of Judaism as a culture, and those who view the Talmud and the literature associated with it as the basis of Judaism as a religion, lies at the heart of all debate regarding the nature of Judaism today.

Those who perceive Judaism as the religion of Halakhah, view all of the hermeneutical and homiletic literature from the Oral law forward, as Judaism's primary source and main subject of study. On the other hand, those who perceive Judaism as the culture of the Jewish People, view the classic literature of the Bible as the foundation of that culture – a point of reference for all Jewish literature, the Talmud included.

Jews free from the religion of Halakhah see the Bible as the sole core element common to all of Judaism's Judaisms; the point of departure for the development of all its various streams – including the talmudic stream. Jewish literature in all its forms includes numerous references to the Bible: in the Apocrypha and Pseudepigrapha, Christian Jewish literature, mystical and kabbalistic works, philosophy, religious and secular poetry, prose and drama produced in all eras – Hellenistic, mediaeval, Renaissance and contemporary.

Those who perceive Judaism as a pluralistic and evolving culture cannot accept the assertion that the Talmud is the "source of all Judaism", above all other bodies of Jewish literature, the sum total of all Jewish wisdom, repository of all of Judaism's important sources.

The Modern Era, with the advent of emancipation and secularisation, saw the rapid development of "western" Judaism: open to western influence, and actively seeking integration into western cultures.

Large centres developed in the nineteenth century, primarily in eastern and central Europe, Palestine and the Americas – but including many intellectuals and writers in and from Arab and Islamic lands a well. All of these countries also saw the development of reactionary movements – Sadducean and Karaite in their approach to sacred texts – adopting an insular approach to other cultures, and isolating themselves from the majority of the Jewish People, that continues to develop and integrate into western culture in the early twenty first century.

These reactionary Judaisms saw in the Talmud, the basis for their conservatism – despite its characteristic open discussion and debate (often unresolved) – by means of which it in fact developed and elaborated Halakhah, rather than ossifying it. This is one of Judaism's great cultural paradoxes: reactionary Judaism bases itself upon the Talmud – although the Talmud itself views pluralism as a guiding principle, debate as the path to truth, constant change as a guarantee of the vitality of Jewish culture, and Halakhah (from the Hebrew root h-l-kh – to walk) as constantly moving forward. Judaism free from the religion of unchanging Halakhah on the other hand, sees the Bible as the foundation of Judaism, although its authors and redactors believed that human beings can make divine pronouncements in God's name, or conversely, revoke them by majority decision.

As the Haredi camp decreases, and its fears for its own survival grow; as the rate of Jewish integration into western culture increases, and secular Israeli culture develops – based on the Hebrew language and the classical literature of the Jewish People – the greater the gap and sharper the contrast between a Judaism in which the exclusive objects of study are the Talmud and its accompanying literature, and a Judaism that sees all Jewish literature as representing Judaism.

The Multiplicity of Religions and God Concepts in Judaism of the Biblical Era

"Both [opinions] are the words of the living God" guided the redactors of the Bible and was reflected in their inclusion of texts of contradictory ideologies. In the biblical era, like today, Judaism as culture and Judaism as religion were not identical. The works of the Bible describe and reflect a Jewish culture that encompassed opposing tendencies both within Yahwistic religion, and between the cult of Yahweh, and those of other gods.

Sharp divisions arose between those who believed exclusively in the God of Israel, and those that believed in the existence of other gods (living and providential) as well. The attacks launched by the prophets of Yahweh were directed at the masses, and at the hundreds of prophets of the Israelite royal court, who worshiped Baal and Ashtoreth. The Yahwist prophets' denunciations of Jewish polytheists attest to the extent of the phenomenon in biblical times – from King Solomon, who built temples in Jerusalem to Yahweh and neighbouring gods, to the common people. There were Jewish parents who sacrificed their children on the altars of Moloch in Jerusalem. There were times (like those of Elijah) in which the prophets of Yahweh, fearing for their lives, were forced to hide in caves, go into exile, or flee to the desert, as a result of their persecution within the Israelite kingdom. The cults of Baal and Ashtoreth played central roles in the lives of Jews and their popular culture – in the images they erected "on every high hill, and under every verdant tree", in the orgiastic rituals in the temples of the Canaanite gods – including copulation with sacred prostitutes (even in Jerusalem, there were quarters for sacred prostitutes, perhaps in the period in which a statue of Asherah – mother of the Canaanite gods – stood in the Temple of Yahweh). Ashtoreth figurines could be found in private homes, and the religion of Ashtoreth and Baal was the state religion in the kingdom of the ten tribes, at the height of its economic and political power, under the rule of Ahab. All of this attests to the centrality of the religions of the Canaanite gods in Judaism of the biblical era – i.e. in the cultural life of the Jewish People in the Land of Israel from the period of conquest and settlement to the destruction of the three temples to Yahweh: in Dan, Beth-El and Jerusalem.

The battles of the prophets of Yahweh against the polytheistic streams in Judaism at times resulted in acts of violence – like the slaughter of the prophets of Baal following their defeat at the hands of Elijah in the fire-making contest on the altars near Muhraka on Mount Carmel. Such temporary victories, like the removal of pagan idols from the Temple in Jerusalem and the destruction of the image of Asherah that stood there, or Hezekiah's crushing of "the brazen serpent that Moses had made", failed to diminish the variety of religions that existed within biblical Judaism. Elijah – who dared not attack the prophets of Ashtoreth – was forced, after his temporary victory over the prophets of Baal, to flee to the desert for fear of the Israelite monarchy's wrath. In his solitude, he discovered that God is not to be found in wind, earthquake or fire, but "in the sound of delicate silence."

The image of Asherah removed from the Temple in Jerusalem, was restored to its place a number of years later. Despite attempts at its permanent removal, the Asherah remained in the Temple of Yahweh in Jerusalem for two-thirds of its existence. Perhaps that is why the artist who depicted "Yahweh and his Asherah" on a pottery shard discovered in the Negev, considered the mother of the Canaanite gods to be "the Asherah of Yahweh".

Even in the final days of the Temple in Jerusalem, Jeremiah recounts that the Jews continued to sacrifice their children to the Moloch, on altars they erected at the foot of Mount Zion, in the apparent belief that Moloch, like all other gods, desires sacrifices dear and precious to his supplicants, that he might show them his grace.

The biblical historians – authors and redactors of the books of Kings – reinforce the view of the prophets, that most of the Jewish People worshiped the gods of the Canaanites, either alongside or instead of Yahweh, God of Israel. Although the prophets, historiographers and biblical redactors all condemn the phenomenon of polytheism in Judaism, as one of the causes of the misfortunes that befall the Jewish People, they repeatedly attest to its widespread existence within Jewish culture – the same culture that produced ethical monotheism, later adopted by other peoples as well.

The Victory of the Golden Calf – a Sign of Pluralism in Yahwist Religion

During the course of the brief civil war at the foot of Mount Sinai, thousands of those who had followed Aaron – the first high priest – and worshiped the golden calf, were slaughtered, and the image itself was destroyed and ground to powder. A few centuries later however, it was resurrected by Jeroboam, king of ten of the twelve tribes of Israel – and its worship established in his Northern Kingdom. The Jewish king declared the golden calf to be the God of Israel who had brought the People out of Egypt – the very words used by Aaron at his inauguration of the first golden calf. The victory of the cult of Yahweh the golden calf is manifest – clearly documented in the Holy Scriptures of the Jewish People.

The story of the golden calf is characteristic of the culture of the Jewish People – constantly evolving, and pluralistic in every era. Numerous conceptions of Yahweh, the God of Israel liberator from Egypt have arisen within the Jewish religion. Belief in the great and distinctive myth of a people freed from slavery is common to all Jewish factions – worshipers of the calf and their opponents, adherents to the religion of Halakhah and those who are free from religion. Belief in a common historical legacy is consistent with various and opposing beliefs, in ancient and modern Judaism alike. This common belief in a historical legacy has been accompanied, throughout Jewish history, by a variety of beliefs regarding the attributes of God – liberator and creator, who rewards good and punishes evil; or merely a fictional character. Debate between various forms of belief and ritual in ancient times has been preserved in the collective memory as a characteristic element of Judaism, from its very beginnings. The God of Moses is presented by the authors of his biography, as existence that embodies all future existence – who says of himself "I will be that which I will be" – i.e. "I will be all that will be". Existence of this kind, wholly potential, is the same as the Prime Mover of Aristotelian philosophy, and as such, cannot be represented by a statue or mask, like other gods. The figurative representation of Yahweh distorts God's essence as perceived by Moses, according to the authors who shaped that essence in their works.

Aaron, as in the dialogue in the second act of Schoenberg's opera, *Moses and Aaron,* knows that the People is not ready to worship an abstract God. He therefore encourages them to bring gold, that an image of their god might be fashioned – which many will see as God himself, and will believe the words of the high priest that this – i.e. the god in the image – is the God who freed them from slavery and brought them up out of Egypt.

Following his victory over the first gold calf, Moses leaves the Israelite camp and establishes an alternative place in which to meet with his god. The Tent of Meeting is a place of communion with the spirit of God – a place where there are no sacrifices, no priests, no images, and no libidinous festivals. It is simply a place in which the individual can commune with his God, who is the Place (Hamakom), every place.

In the centre of the camp, the Israelites built a temple and a new altar, on which the priests brought sacrifices to Yahweh, in keeping with traditional practice in all of the pagan temples (as explained by Maimonides). In the inner sanctum of the Tabernacle that the Israelites had erected to their god, stood two statues – not of calves, but of cherubim, probably resembling the Mesopotamian karibu, with human faces and the giant wings of a mythological bird. Statues also stood in the Holy of Holies of the First and Second Temples in Jerusalem, and Philo saw them as representing the dual essence of God – masculine and feminine, justice and wisdom, punishment and loving-kindness. In the Temple of Jerusalem, there also stood twelve statues of the golden calf, bearing the brazen sea on their backs. There is no indication that they were intended as representations of the God of Israel, but they would probably have reminded many of the divine image of the calf only a short distance away – in Beth-El.

In the temples of Yahweh in the kingdom of the majority of the

Jewish People, the calf triumphed over its opponents, and in the eyes of its adherents would have been a symbol of the power and glory of the God of Israel – although destroyed and ground to a powder, it arises again to be the object of veneration of believers in the national god.

From that time to the present, religion in Judaism has been divided into many streams and diverse god concepts. The authors of *Shiur Komah* perceived God (probably as early as talmudic times) as a giant larger than the universe, the size of whose limbs – nostrils and fingers, for example – can be calculated. Maimonides considered all who conceive of God in human form to be heretics, whose beliefs run counter to those of the Jewish religion. The authors of the Hekhalot and Merkabah literature saw God as an emperor seated on a throne and surrounded by thousands of ministering angels and other celestial officers, as befits the king of all the world's kings. Those who followed in Maimonides' footsteps perceived God not only as devoid of corporeality, but beyond all human comprehension. Mediaeval mystics saw God as an entity permeating all existence that contracted in order to create a void in which the world might come into being; others saw God as copulating with the Shekhinah and Lilith; while a religious man such as Spinoza saw God as identical with nature and the universe.

These sharply contrasting god concepts within Judaism are marks of the pluralism that has characterised Judaism since its founding at Mount Sinai, and in all stages of its development to the present day.

All who see Judaism as culture know that its numerous religious streams are all part of the Jewish religion, and fulfil roles in the cultural development of the Jewish People and in the lives of individual Jews who profess one of the many and contrasting beliefs – religious and secular – it comprises.

Sacrifice Culture – an Expression of the Anxiety of Believers in a Personal God

Sacrifices – intended to placate or nourish God, were the focus of religious life in biblical Jewish culture, as in neighbouring cultures. Sacrificial religion expresses a belief in the power of God to do harm; in the need and possibility of averting such harm by providing him with living sacrifices. Ritual sacrifice and slaughter of humans or animals were common to many religious cults, on all continents. Why did Jews continue to bring sacrifices to Yahweh, even after the proliferation of the Mosaic belief in an abstract God, who derives no nourishment or any other benefit from sacrifices?

According to Maimonides, this strange phenomenon can be explained by the fact that the Israelites were idol-worshipers before they came to know the Torah of Moses, and were thus accustomed to bringing sacrifices – a practice from which they were gradually weaned, over many centuries, since human beings are incapable of giving up their habits overnight. This rational explanation of a historical process of weaning from a religious custom that would have been meaningless to believers in an abstract God such as that of Moses, casts new light on all religious customs. Many of these are meaningless in terms of the beliefs of those who practise them, yet they continue to cling to them out of force of habit, because that is human nature. Had the sacrifice-bringers been approached and urged to cease such practices, because they lack all meaning or purpose in the relationship between man and the God of the universe, they would have been shocked at the very thought. By way of analogy, Maimonides writes that it would be like someone suggesting that we cease praying or observing the commandments.

This analogy at the end of Maimonides' psycho-historical explanation of the custom of sacrifice left many religious Jews perplexed. It would seem to imply that all ritual customs – such as prayer and precept-observance – are merely traditions to which people adhere out of habit, and from which they could be weaned over time, for they too can be of no significance whatsoever to an abstract God, devoid of all positive attributes. Others saw such an explanation, in and of itself, as dangerous heresy, like other ideas presented by Maimonides.

The story of the binding of Isaac – one of the greatest and most shocking in all of Jewish literature – attests to the willingness (or collective memory of a time when such willingness existed) of religious Jewish parents to sacrifice not only their domestic animals, but also their children to their god; not only in the religion of Moloch, but in the religion of Yahweh as well. This kind of religious belief expresses fear of the capricious and vindictive behaviour of the gods. The gods, it was believed, could do anything they pleased, and man could protect himself against his fate, as a victim of divine arbitrariness, by placating his gods with sacrifices. Sacrifice is one of the more pathetic expressions of the sense of helplessness behind man's attempts to deal with the unknown.

Judaism's culture of sacrifice was abandoned in the wake of the religious and cultural revolution that accompanied the passage from Temple to synagogue – from the sacrifices of "God's house", to structures devoted to communal gatherings, celebration, study and prayer. This cultural revolution spread throughout the world through institutions similar to the synagogue, established by the monotheistic religions influenced by and stemming from Judaism.

The Synagogue – A Revolutionary Innovation in Jewish History

A revolutionary change came about in the synagogue: the abolishment of sacrifice in a communal house that is not the house of God. Communal "assembly-houses" (synagogues) were apparently first established in the eastern (Babylonia) and western (Egypt) diasporas, following the destruction of the Temple of Yahweh. The synagogue as a place of communal assembly reflected and brought about a cultural revolution in Jewish history, and in the cultures of many other peoples influenced by it.

The synagogue is the antithesis of the Temple in many ways: the Temple was the house of God – the synagogue, the house of a human community; the Temple a place of sacrificial cult – the synagogue, a communal centre for study and education, reading and interpreting sacred texts, housing courts of law, public libraries (*beit midrash*) and communal institutions, a place in which holidays and life-cycle events are celebrated, and personal and public prayer conducted. The synagogue played an active role in the founding, organising and strengthening of the cultural community that supplanted the tribe. Following the destruction of the Jewish national and religious centre, the synagogues facilitated the processes of decentralisation and pluralism in Judaism. Independent Jewish communities developed distinctive characteristics, affinity for the culture of the lands and societies in which they lived, original works and unique traditions, with some communities or groups of communities founding new streams in Judaism (such as Hassidism).

It is thanks to the synagogue communities that Judaism and its religion continued to exist and evolve. In the absence of a Jewish state, the continued existence of Judaism as a culture was contingent upon the existence of synagogue communities. In places where such communities disintegrated – as in the first waves of immigration to America – Judaism and Jewish religion gradually disappeared.

After the destruction of the Second Temple, the synagogue as an institution began to appear everywhere that Jews or Christians lived. When Christianity became the religion of the Roman Empire, synagogues (churches) replaced temples throughout the pagan world. Islam, which was influenced by Judaism and Christianity, continued to spread the synagogue (mosque) throughout the communities of its faithful – in the west and the east.

Remnants of Jewish synagogues from the third century BCE in Egypt attest to the existence of such communal centres among Greek-speaking Jews at the beginning of the Hellenistic era. The synagogue and its customs of public reading and study created the need for a Greek translation of the Torah, that the congregants might understand the readings. Aramaic translations of the Torah served a similar purpose among synagogue-goers in Mesopotamia and the Land of Israel.

Jewish plastic arts (mosaics and frescoes) developed in the synagogue, as did Jewish education for both children and adults, the custom of reading from classical Jewish literature and the art of homily that accompanied it, study for its own sake and the creative hermeneutics that produced the midrashic literature, regional conferences to discuss matters of Halakhah, centres of learning (*yeshivot*), and biannual periods of study for laymen (*yarhei kalah*).

Synagogues gradually developed a culture of prayer and a liturgy, to replace outmoded sacrifice rituals. During the Second Temple Period, the synagogue continued to develop, alongside the sacrificial cult in the Temple in Jerusalem, as an alternative path within Jewish religious culture. There was in fact, a synagogue on the Temple Mount itself, near the Temple.

Figurative art also offered its own interpretations of the biblical myths (see Goodenough on the Dura Europos paintings). Prayer and benediction supplanted sacrifices in national-religious festivals and personal celebrations. Divine worship no longer depended upon slaughter and the taking of human or animal life.

When Christianity parted from Judaism, it continued the culture of prayer and the synagogue, but included symbolic human sacrifice in its rituals: representing the consumption of the flesh and blood of the son of God. In Judaism, there are few remnants of the sacrificial cult – apart from the study and discussion of the laws governing the Temple rites (and the custom of sacrificing chickens and roosters on the eve of Yom Kippur).

Synagogues proliferated with the growth of the Jewish diaspora on the various continents, and among diverse peoples and cultures. Synagogues fulfilled similar functions in all diaspora communities – both as multi-purpose community centres and as centres of religious worship, halakhic study and discussion. The large number of synagogues, and loose ties between them, facilitated the development of different streams within Judaism, diverse liturgies, different interpretations of Scripture and Halakhah, and a variety of holiday, marriage and mourning customs. In this sense, the synagogue fostered pluralism in Judaism as a culture and as a religion. Groups of synagogues within the same country over time came to belong to different streams within Judaism – such as Ashkenazi and Sephardi synagogues in Europe and Italy, hassidic and mitnagdic synagogues in Europe and Israel, and Orthodox and Reform synagogues throughout the world today.

There are often great differences between synagogues, even on the same street. At the Friday night services of the Conservative Congregation B'nai Jeshurun, on 86th Street and West End Avenue in New York, men, women and children sing and dance together, accompanied by a piano. At the same time, only a few minutes' walk away, women are seated behind a high barrier, and services are conducted in the Orthodox Ashkenazi rite, without musical accompaniment, without singing or dancing, with most of the liturgy recited by prayer leaders rather than by the congregation.

These Sabbath eve services – like all holiday services at religious synagogues of all kinds – bear little resemblance to the holiday and Sabbath services at the secular synagogues in Detroit or Chicago, conducted by the community's ritual committee, with the participation of a secular rabbi, or rabbinical students at the International Institute for Secular Humanistic Judaism. In their rich and varied services, there are no prayers or benedictions, only singing and discussion related to the holiday and its significance to those free from religion, to the obligations that stem from the humanistic values in which they believe, and to tradition and the roles it has played, and continues to play, in the culture of the Jewish People.

These communal assembly-houses, with their religious and other activities, distinctive architecture, works of art they have produced, documents they have preserved, and unique traditions – have played an important role in the development of Judaism as a pluralistic culture, from their inception to the present.

To this day, wherever there are Jews, communal synagogues continue to function – mostly as religious institutions, in the tradition of one of Judaism's religious streams. Judaism's vast experience in the use of synagogues as cultural community centres has shown that in order to survive, they must: provide fixed structures for spiritual and educational activities, and holiday celebrations at fixed times; be led by popular teachers ("rabbis"), versed in Judaism and general culture, trained or skilled in community leadership. Martin Buber's attempt to establish a college for adult education teachers, and attempts by the Movement for Secular Humanistic Judaism in the United States to train leaders (*madrikhim*) and rabbis for its dozens of communities – strive to address the spiritual and communal needs common to most people; needs that cannot be satisfied without a framework for communal activity, like the synagogues/ assembly-houses that developed within Judaism.

Foreign Influences on Jewish Culture and Judaism's Contributions to World Culture

Foreign influences on Jewish art, literature, religion and culture, can be found in every period of Jewish history. Mesopotamian, Egyptian, Canaanite, Greek, Muslim, and – beginning in the eighteenth century – European and American influences, are all clearly evident in the development of Jewish culture and the works it has produced.

Foreign cultural influences can also be found in original Jewish works – like original works in all cultures. Contrary to previous tendencies in the field of biblical criticism, which stressed the similarity between Near-Eastern and biblical myths, the differences between the original Jewish works and those that influenced them are manifest today. Current knowledge of Mesopotamian creation and "Garden of Eden" myths highlights the originality of the biblical narrative: the story of Yahweh's original sin in withholding knowledge and morality from the man and woman he had created, woman's subsequent rebellion and victory – granting mankind knowledge and morality in spite of the creator's desire to withhold them, just as Prometheus gave man fire, in defiance of Zeus' will.

There is no national culture that has not been influenced by other national cultures. Any study of the body of cultural works produced by one people thus becomes the study of that culture's affinities and relationships with the cultures of other peoples.

Such combined studies of Judaism and other cultures will also reveal the influences exerted by Judaism – through Christianity and Islam – on other peoples, in the realm of religion, philosophy, literature and the arts, society and community, synagogues and sabbath, holidays and the relationship between religion and state.

Forms of celebration such as the Greek symposium were cast into original festive structures, like the Passover Seder, shaped during the Hellenistic era, and bearing clear marks of the symposium – such as reclining, four cups of wine, and the combination of food and drink with discussion and reading.

The pattern of open discussion, questions, premises, and summaries, characteristic of talmudic literature, was also influenced by Greek dialogue, as found in the works of Plato. The original talmudic dialogues served as a basis for the development of Halakhah, a culture of discussion, hermeneutical and narrative literature, deviating both from its original subjects and from the great bodies of work representing the culture of the Jewish People in the Hellenistic era. The influences of Greek culture enriched these works, without detracting from their originality.

The influence of Greek art can be found in the art that developed in the synagogues – the mosaics and frescoes that helped to establish a tradition of Jewish art; a subject addressed at length by Cecil Roth and Bezalel Narkiss. These works were also the first stages, and sources of inspiration of art in the early church – the forerunner of mediaeval Christian painting.

The principles of democracy and decision by majority, first established by the Greeks, also exerted a profound influence on Judaism. Whereas in the biblical period, many believed in the exclusive authority of those who spoke in God's name, the sages of the Talmud believed that to no longer be the case, and consequently that human beings, in their discussions and democratic decisions, are the sole arbiters of halakhic change. These democratic principles have fostered Jewish pluralism. Religious communities in many Jewish streams today, effect liturgical and halakhic change by means of elected committees.

The influences of ancient eastern mythology – Sumerian, Canaanite, Hindu – are apparent in Jewish mystical mythology, and in the figures and exploits of the Hebrew goddesses; as demonstrated by Raphael Patai. Hindu influences on Kabbalah was first suggested by Scholem. Further study however, revealed many similarities between the Jewish goddesses – Shekhinah and Lilith – and the Hindu goddesses, and their relations with men and male divinities. Here too, external influences served as sources of inspiration for original Jewish works – such as the Zohar, the most extensive anthology (over a million words) of Jewish mysticism, including many new mythological elements that influenced the development of religious Judaism, and stood in sharp contrast to the rationalistic trends developing simultaneously within Jewish culture.

From the Renaissance and Enlightenment to the present, Jewish culture has experienced increasing western cultural influences, and Jewish artists and writers have, in turn, exerted an influence on western cultures. In the ninteenth and twentieth centuries, Jews played a leading role in western culture, in Europe and America. Their works and those of Europe's greatest writers (like Kafka and Proust) reflect the integration of Jews into non-Jewish culture in these societies, as well as the Jews' unique character and exclusion.

Judaism enjoyed extensive and varied development in all periods in which Judaism was open to the influences of other cultures – from biblical times to the twentieth century. During the short periods in Jewish history, when isolationism prevailed over openness, the development of Jewish culture came to a standstill, as in the case of Haredi Judaism.

The Bible, Monotheism, the Sabbath, the Synagogue – Jewish Contributions to World Culture

The beliefs and ideas of Jewish monotheism began to spread in Hellenistic and Roman times among many peoples, giving rise to circles of "God-fearers" – who did not join the Jewish religion, since they did not observe its many precepts, but professed exclusive belief in the God of Israel. Such God-fearers were among those addressed by wandering Christian Jews such as Paul of Tarsus, who proposed a religion similar to Judaism, without requiring that they observe the halakhic precepts.

When Christianity diverged from Judaism, going on to become the state religion of the Roman Empire, Judaism's fundamental principles and institutions exerted even greater influence – through Christianity, and later Islam.

Such influences can be found in specific products of Jewish culture adopted by many peoples on all continents: monotheistic beliefs, works of literature and philosophy from biblical to Hellenistic times, the New testament, some of the Jewish holidays – given new forms and content, the Sabbath and its impact on the organisation of human time, the synagogue and its influence on the organisation of society in cultural communities in western societies. The books of the Hebrew Bible would become part of the cultural heritage of many peoples, inspiring countless works of literature, art, theology and ethics.

The principles of ethical monotheism, a doctrine attributed to Moses, whereby God is one and incorporeal, justice-seeking, and one of the main protagonists in the liberation from slavery myth – spread rapidly. The prophets saw the Mosaic Law as the Law of justice and charity, demanding social justice above religious ritual. Hillel encapsulated "the entire Torah" in the supreme value of ethical humanism: that which is hateful to you, do not unto others. The unification of the divine world into a single creating and justice-seeking entity became a dominant concept in all of the cultures of the peoples that adopted the ideas of Jewish monotheism through Christianity and Islam. In each of these religions, and their respective streams, Jewish monotheism developed in its own unique form. All, however, adhere to the principle of the unity of God and the social justice he demands.

The Sabbath was an unprecedented invention in terms of the human concept of time and its division according to human needs, and in terms of its egalitarian nature – applying the laws of rest equally to men and women, parents and children, masters and slaves (including the humanitarian requirement that one afford rest to one's domestic animals as well).

The Sabbath, as a day of rest and leisure from labour and the burden of earning a livelihood, changed the human approach to time: no longer the province of the gods – measured in the seasons of the year, the movements of the celestial bodies and the cycle of life and death – but human time. The basic unit of time was henceforth the human week, ending in a day devoted to leisure and culture, pleasure and recreation; respite from toil, for all members of society.

The concept of Sabbath was distorted however by some Jewish streams, heaping countless restrictions upon their adherents, thereby imprisoning them within their towns and neighbourhoods, and precluding most leisure and cultural activities. These prohibitions do not affect the Sabbaths of most Jews today, or of the billions of people in the world who have adopted the principle of the Sabbath and made it part of their culture. In most cultures and societies throughout the world, the Sabbath is observed as a day of leisure – recently extended to two days in the West.

The synagogue, as an institution superseding the Temple, and representing the end of sacrificial worship, was also an unprecedented human invention. The concept of the Jewish synagogue, as an assembly-house serving a variety of communal purposes, spread to all peoples within the sphere of influence of the monotheistic faiths; replacing the various temples that had previously been at the centre of cultural life. Churches and mosques were instrumental in the proliferation of educational centres for children and adults among monotheistic peoples, and in the creation of communal and voluntary organisations, and social networks beyond family ties and tribal affiliations.

Through the various religious assembly-houses, classical Jewish literature spread throughout the world – alongside Christian and Muslim scriptures, based upon or referring to Jewish literature. The synagogues/assembly-houses became focal points for artistic expression in the fields of architecture, music, painting, sculpture, rhetoric and literature. Study of scripture, weekly sermons, and the hermeneutical literature that developed in all streams of the monotheistic faiths, infused new content into the cultural lives of members of these societies. Influenced by Judaism, the study of scripture – comprising the fundamental elements of cultural heritage – was open to all; no longer the exclusive province of the priestly classes. As a result, these societies also witnessed a corresponding proliferation of literacy skills; one of the primary motivating forces for cultural and communal development. The new education system was not designed to train professionals or prepare a ruling class, but to afford everyone the possibility of enriching their knowledge and range of experience, and the opportunity to become acquainted with their cultural heritage.

These Jewish contributions to cultures shaped by the monotheistic religions, inspired original works, increasingly removed from the Jewish works that influenced them, just as Jewish works had diverged from those of the cultures that had, in turn, exerted a profound influence upon them. Many of the works produced within monotheistic cultures relate to Jewish history and its protagonists as if they were their own (e.g. the Exodus, the Maccabean Revolt, the teachings of the prophets).

The Judaism that influenced Christian and Muslim societies also came to be influenced by them, as soon as the latter began to develop as distinct cultures. These influences are evident in lifestyles and modes of dress, synagogue rituals, relations between the sexes, language, mystical traditions and messianic ideas, and more recently – in the processes of secularisation and enlightenment developed in Christian societies, and adopted by ever-greater segments of Jewish society.

The Effects of Mystical Mythology on Jewish Pluralism

As noted above, "Judaism", as the culture of the Jewish People, is not – nor has it ever been – equivalent to the ethical monotheism conceived by Moses, entailing belief in a unique, abstract, and justice-seeking god.

Ethical monotheism exists within Jewish culture, alongside polytheistic religions and beliefs. This encounter between monotheism and polytheism in a single culture would seem improbable, but can be found in many Christian cultures as well (in Mexican Christian culture, for example), which preserve beliefs and rituals associated with divinities worshiped prior to their acceptance of the religion of the Christian god.

The religious history of the Jewish People describes an encounter between the ancient Jewish belief in a unique, abstract god (as in the Torah attributed to Moses), and a god represented by the image of a calf, like the gods of other peoples (as in the approach of Aaron). These two religions co-existed in biblical Judaism, alongside Canaanite religions, including those of Baal, Ashtoreth-Asherah, Moloch, Kemosh, and others.

With the disappearance of the Canaanite deities from Judaism (following the return from Babylonian exile), polytheism entered Judaism and its religion through mystical literature and movements, and through mythology inhabited by divine beings beyond Yahweh.

Such polytheistic mythology exerted a significant influence on leading Jewish streams in the Middle Ages, through kabbalistic writings and beliefs – especially through Hassidism, and other religious movements that accepted kabbalah as part of the Jewish religion while rejecting other elements of hassidic belief.

The multiplication of divine beings – angels and archangels, Satan and demons, as well as goddesses such as Shekhinah and Lilith – fundamentally changed the concept of a unique deity, incorporeal and wholly indescribable; replacing it with the figure of a denizen of a new Olympus, constructed in the words and stories of its human creators, like the pagan pantheons of any other culture.

Polytheism and Goddesses Enter the Jewish Religion

In the Jewish religion, as in Christianity, mythology has introduced divinities – male and female – in addition to God. God, who lacked a biography in early Judaism, is given a mother in Christianity, and a divine consort in Judaism. The goddesses that Jews worshiped within their culture, but external to that culture, are henceforth introduced by the new mythology, and become a part of the Jewish divine world.

The fertility goddesses worshiped throughout the ancient Near East were widely venerated in Jewish culture as well. Inasmuch as Yahweh was a unique and male god, according to Mosaic Law, many Jews adopted the female gods of neighbouring religions. The popularity of goddess cults such as that of Ashtoreth is evident, both from archaeological findings (figurines found in private homes), and from the literary works of the Bible, that reflect a spiritual and cultural reality with which their authors were familiar. In these stories, even Elijah does not dare challenge the religious establishment of Ashtoreth. According to repeated accounts in the Bible, the goddesses of femaleness and motherhood stood at the heart of the religious cultural life of most Jews. According to these accounts, Judaism was influenced by the cultures of other peoples, when the Jewish People ceased being a nomadic desert people, and settled in the Land of Canaan. The image of Asherah – the mother of all the Canaanite gods – was restored to the First Temple in Jerusalem every time it was removed by kings seeking to purify the temple of Yahweh of her presence. The image of Asherah stood in the Temple of Yahweh for two-thirds of its 370-year existence (according to the calculations of Raphael Patai in *Hebrew Goddesses*).

The cults of goddesses of fertility and motherhood addressed people's fears regarding the reproductive abilities of their families and farms. The presence of images representing these goddesses, and the rituals associated with them, would have appeared vital to anyone concerned with the future of her/his family and its livelihood.

All people, in their emotional and spiritual lives, have a primal bond to their parents – that lives on in their souls even after the parents' deaths. The mother figure continues, even after death, to fulfil roles that she fulfilled in life – in our dreams, visions, memories and subconscious. Woman and mother, as a loving and chastising figure, is a focal point for emotions and desires that play central roles in the conscious and subconscious, and in the artistic and religious creation of female deities – beautiful and good, or menacing and cruel; goddesses of love and war, generosity and malevolence. Such goddesses can be found in all religions and cultures within which Judaism developed – from India to Greece.

When the Jews ceased worshiping these goddesses in the context of other religious cults, creators of Jewish mystical mythology began to include them in the Jewish religion itself. The Shekhinah and Lilith appear as goddesses in the new Jewish mythology that developed in the Middle Ages, and the roots of which can be traced to the legends and mystical literature of the talmudic period.

The low status of women in society stood in sharp relief to the power of woman as mother, and as ruling, loving, chastising and concupiscent goddess. When women were raised to the status of goddesses, these two contrasting images were ostensibly reconcilable. All cultures that subjugate women manifest a need for a divine figure – female and maternal – a goddess of love and chastisement.

The inscription "To Yahweh and his Asherah" on a pottery shard dating from the period of the Judean kingdom, discovered in the Negev, strengthens the conjecture that there were already at that time, those who believed in Yahweh not as unique divinity, destined to a lonely and celibate existence, but as one who, like Baal, enjoyed the company of a goddess; his consort and Asherah. There is no evidence of this however, in the Bible or other ancient sources. Later – particularly following the publication and dissemination of the Zohar – this approach became an integral part of religious Judaism, as the Shekhinah was transformed from a concept to a distinct figure, and Lilith was made the protagonist of frightening tales that firmly established her presence in the consciousness of those who believed in her.

Belief in God as a Man
in Jewish Kabbalistic Mythology

The post-biblical book Shiur Komah, which describes God's cosmic proportions, detailing the precise measurements of his limbs – is one of the expressions of renewed anthropomorphisation of God in Judaism, the beginnings of which can be found in Genesis. In the cultural and spiritual lives of many religious Jews, the divine beings that inhabit the heavens are ascribed real existence. Others, such as Maimonides, view any attempt to anthropomorphise God as heresy. Stories regarding God's sex life with the Shekhinah and Lilith, and tales of the sexual exploits of the two goddesses with other male beings, make the denizens of the divine world all the more palpable to the inhabitants of this world.

Those who believe in the existence of such otherworldly beings also believe that they visit our world – which thus abounds in demons, whom we may not see, but whom we may encounter, as evidenced by the admonitions of prominent rabbis against encounters with the arch-demon Ketev Meriri, or other emissaries of Satan. The terrible Lilith – according to account-like stories – also wanders the world, appearing to powerful pietists as well as the vulnerable. Joseph Karo, on the other hand, reported regular visitations by a "Maggid" and the Shekhinah, who also dictated some of the content of his Shulhan Arukh.

Contrary to the biblical Yahweh, who lacked a personal and family life, the new Jewish mythology created detailed biographies for all of the divine beings. The angel Metatron for example, was not brought to heaven by God himself, according to the new mythology, but by the angel Anpiel.

Metatron rose in the angelic ranks until he became God's viceroy. When the heretic Elishah ben Abuyah (who also features in these mythological tales) reached the highest heavens and sees Metatron seated upon his throne, he wonders whether there are not "two domains in heaven" – for angels cannot sit, since they have no knees.

For this sin, Anpiel punishes Metatron with
pulsa denura – scourges of fire, painful even to angels.

Such tales can of course be understood merely as parables and allegories, expressing ideas, rather than a perception of reality. Many believers however, make no such distinction between reality and myth. To their minds, the world is filled with the characters that appear in these stories – further developed in the Middle Ages.

The story of Lilith's origins illustrates the use of legend for the homiletic interpretation of biblical texts, expressing an unequivocal ideological position regarding a woman's proper place in the family and human society in general. Lilith, according to one version, was the first woman created by God. Genesis 1 asserts the equality of man and woman, having been created simultaneously by God, in his image, and together called "Adam".

According to myth the first woman (Lilith) was insolent to her husband – demanding full equality in everything, including sexual positions. Adam sent her away, thus remaining alone. God then created a new woman for him (as in the story of the surgical procedure performed under general anaesthetic in Genesis 2, in which the woman is portrayed as a secondary creature, last-created, fashioned from a limb taken from the man's body, to serve as a helpmeet to him). This new woman, Eve, whose lot, according to this story, must be that of all women, was created for one purpose: to be a helper, a handmaiden to the man who rules over her, never insolent, always available for his sexual use, on all days of the month that she is not impure – the result, according to another myth, of having copulated with the snake, leading to the birth of Cain.

Lilith, Adam's "ex", went on to wander the worlds, copulating frequently, in the diabolical manner typical of a goddess and woman of her kind; a threat to all who cross her path.

As a result of the Shekhinah's exile, according to another

version, following the destruction of the Temple (also the chamber of her lovemaking with God, according to the evolving myth), Lilith copulates with God in her place, in order to relieve his loneliness.

One could claim that these too are merely allegorical allusions to the abstract ideas that form part of the kabbalistic vision of the universe. It is difficult to see the connection between these myths however, and Lurianic kabbalistic theory, based on tzimtzum (God's "contraction" of himself in order to leave room for the world), "the breaking of the vessels", and tikun (the restoration and integration of the vessels, that will be the Redemption; the end and ultimate goal of history). In the spiritual world of less sophisticated Jewish believers, the figures developed by writers and storytellers, based on, or influenced by the new mythology, are quite real; figures that became important elements of religious Judaism, through the Kabbalah disseminated by Hassidism and similar movements over the course of the eighteenth and ninteenth centuries. Other cultures and religions produced similar myths in the early stages of their development. In Judaism and Jewish religion however, mythology reached the height of its development some 2,000 years after the establishment of its unique status as a monotheistic religion, and toward the end of its hegemony within Jewish culture.

The new Jewish mythology has played a significant role in both religious and secular culture. It has enriched popular literature and provided secular Jewish literature with a wealth of materials. Popular stories and legends concerning these new divine beings – goddesses, Satan, demons, angels, ghosts – have been adopted and adapted in the works of Jewish authors such as: Y.L. Peretz, S.Y. Agnon, Bashevis Singer, Bernard Malamud and others.

The atheism that has spread throughout the West and Judaism has, in recent years, been accompanied by a revival of magical and mystical beliefs that adherents view as expressions of the "spirituality" lacking in their lives. These beliefs – influenced by the kabbalistic literature and the mythology it developed – have attracted renewed attention to this stream of Judaism.

The Bible as a Source of Inspiration for Contemporary Jewish Art and Literature

Judaism of the twentieth-twenty first century is represented by a wealth of Jewish and non-Jewish works – in the fields of philosophy, literature, theatre, film and art.

Our time is the richest, most prolific period in the history of Jewish creativity. Jewish works have been, and are being created in all languages, lands, artistic and communications media. The history of Judaism as the culture of the Jewish People in the twentieth-twenty first century is reflected in the Jewish works of writers, philosophers, artists, and creators of theatre, film and television – who have all played a part in the shaping of the culture of the Jewish People, expressing the changes it has undergone.

Most of these works have been created in a Judaism free from religion – the Judaism of most twentieth and twenty first century Jews. Even those works that deal with the subject of religious Jews, or with Jewish theology, are written from a non-religious or non-halakhic perspective. The range of works created by Jews, who have reflected, inter alia, trends in contemporary Judaism and its integration into western culture, stretches from Y.L. Peretz to Kafka and Bashevis Singer, from Heine to Amichai, from Goldfaden to Woody Allen, from Buber to Isaiah Berlin, from Mendelssohn to Bernstein, from Epstein to Danziger. The fact that many of these works are an integral part of the cultures of other peoples, in no way changes their status within Judaism – just as the works of the Bible continue to be a part of Jewish culture, although many of them have been adopted by other peoples.

Jewish artists and writers of the twentieth–twenty first century are free to make any judgements and express any opinions they may have, without fear of committing sacrilege or breaking any religious taboos; without fear of conflict between their views and their beliefs. In this sense, they reflect the process of secularisation, and humanistic beliefs in man as the sole source of authority in this world.

Jewish integration into western culture accelerated the process of change in the Jewish religion and its new streams, encouraging philosophical-religious development in all streams.

From Hermann Cohen and Rosenzweig to Kook, Heschel and Soloveitchik, Jewish religious thought flourished, although its influences were hardly felt by most Jewish artists and writers.

In Israel, centre of the rebirth of Hebrew as a spoken and creative language, and meeting-place of all ethnic and religious Judaisms, Israeli Judaism developed as a Judaism free from religion. Its ancient past, and the clashes that characterised it, quickly became one of the main subjects of Israeli Jewish literature, thought and scholarship. The creative world of Hebrew culture that first began to develop in early twentieth-century Palestine, grew rapidly over the course of the first fifty years of Jewish statehood. This sudden quantitative growth created a new cultural force: the thousands of Hebrew books published every year, along with dozens of stage, film and television productions, watched by hundreds of thousands every month, represent some of the many new faces of contemporary Judaism. Dozens of museums and art galleries exhibit Israeli art, and hundreds of thousands attend concerts performed by Israeli orchestras, including an ever-growing number of original compositions. One and a half million Jewish students are exposed to Judaism as culture and not as religion, at thousands of educational institutions and dozens of centres of higher learning. Eighty to ninety percent of Israel's Jewish population (numbering some five million) is exposed to Hebrew media and Israeli culture on a daily basis – in the printed and electronic news media, and in the dramatic and literary productions broadcast on state-run and private television and radio. At the same time, a few tens of thousands of yeshiva students devote their time exclusively to talmudic studies, with little effect on Israeli cultural life.

Such quantitative development is unprecedented in the history of Jewish art and literature. It is too early to determine the impact of this phenomenon on the quality of the works produced, but many Israeli Jewish works have already won recognition in Jewish and non-Jewish cultural communities throughout the world, Hebrew literature is widely translated, and Israeli scholars are invited to present Israeli culture in the cultural capitals of the world.

The sheer volume of works representing twentieth-twenty first century Judaism is daunting to anyone attempting conversance with the culture as a whole.

With the collapse of religion as a central, unifying force, magic and mysticism have spread, alongside atheism. It is a well-known phenomenon in all cultures, that magic and mysticism enjoy greater popularity specifically when national religion ceases to be a unifying force for most of society. Such was the case in Hellenistic society, as the pagan religious system broke down; and in Judaism, as the religious leadership and institutions lost their influence over most Jews.

Magic and popular atheism have a lot in common – most obviously the fact that believers in the powers and techniques of magic to cure illness or avert natural disaster, ignore God and trust in the magic practitioner: sorcerer, witch doctor, astrological prophet, herbalist or master of charms and spells. All of these methods are supposed to act directly upon nature, man and the universe. Like any medical or other technology employed in the secular world to fight illness or contend with the forces of nature, magic completely ignores God and his will.

The magical techniques employed in diverse cultures and religions thus tend to resemble one another. The magician does not openly declare his atheism, but acts as if her/his techniques are more efficacious than God or entreaties to him. People, whose belief in God has been undermined, need help from those whose technologies offer solutions to their problems. Since science and the technologies it has developed have failed to resolve all of man's ills, people seek alternative solutions. Magic offers just such an alternative, and even one who is not convinced of its efficacy, may believe that if it can't help, at least it can't hurt.

Such recourse to magic stems from a belief in the existence of unseen, supernatural forces – good and evil – all around us; in mysterious, inexplicable forces; and in man's inability to grasp them by means of reason and observation.

Belief in life after death; in ghosts that have the power to help or inflict harm in the course of their wanderings or at their gravesides; in the hereafter and the possibility of communicating with the dead – pervaded Jewish society, as its central religious institutions, the Temple and the High Priesthood collapsed. These institutions were integral parts of a Jewish political structure that painted a monolithic picture of Judaism.

The same phenomenon can be observed in Judaism today: alongside various atheistic beliefs, we find "spiritual" beliefs – beliefs in supernatural forces that can have no scientific or rational explanation – increasingly popular. There are a growing number of people who believe in the supernatural powers of sorcerers and enchanters, as well as sacred amulets, or tombs said to belong to saints, whose ghosts are able to offer those who visit their graves a great deal more help than they can offer themselves.

Magic is, as noted above, an ancient form of veiled atheism, asserting the supremacy of man and his ability to bend nature or divine forces to his will, as if there were no God.

131

The struggle against beliefs in astrology, sorcery, magic and necromancy, is as ancient as the beliefs and techniques themselves. Evidence of this can be found in the Bible, which tells of the efforts of religious and political leaders to wipe out necromancers and witches (Saul had recourse to a necromancer after having killed or banished all of her colleagues from his kingdom).

While some of the sages of the Talmud believed in astrology, religious philosophers such as Maimonides condemned all witchcraft and sorcery as heresy, or "atheism". When the kabbalists sought to establish the Jew's place in the restoration of the cosmos, the vessels of which having been broken at the time of creation, they raised their belief in magic to the level of a doctrine combining religion and magic, like the ancient Sumerians, who afforded man a crucial role in maintaining the cosmos, in partnership with the gods.

These trends in Lurianic Kabbalah – developed in Safed, following the expulsion from Spain – helped to establish the belief in Judaism that only Jews have a role to play in bringing redemption to the world. Observance of the halakhic precepts thus became, according to this belief, one of the crucial means of restoring the broken world. On the basis of this approach, Halakhah was redefined as a part of the magical technology capable of saving the world from the anarchy that had plagued it since the "breaking of the vessels".

Opposition within some streams of religious Judaism to the proliferation of mysticism, messianism and magic in their culture, is one element of the clashes between streams of thought and belief in contemporary Judaism, as in the past.

This multiplicity of streams, including those that deny any possibility of multiple views within Judaism, is characteristic of Jewish pluralism. The mystical and messianic beliefs espoused by a minority of the population, have become a significant factor in Israeli politics, affecting government decisions regarding peace and war, foreign and internal affairs, as well as education. Most Israeli Jews, as noted, are not swayed by religious, magical or mystical streams. Jews who call themselves "traditional" or "secular" however, share the belief that Judaism is a pluralistic culture, both in terms of the religious and secular streams it comprises, and in terms of the beliefs and views that exert an influence on its art, literature and society.

Atheism Joins Judaism's Many Beliefs

Atheism is one of the many beliefs within Judaism, and as such, is also a source of inspiration in Jewish art and literature. The clash between atheism and other Jewish beliefs enriches Judaism as a pluralistic culture – which develops through the addition of beliefs and customs, without cancelling previous ones. Monotheistic beliefs in Judaism did not remove earlier, polytheistic beliefs; and beliefs in a unique and omnipotent god did not eradicate beliefs in thousands of other supernatural forces that influence and are influenced by man. Atheistic beliefs have become a part of Judaism, without eliminating existing theistic beliefs.

Many religious Jews today, in Israel and abroad, continue to believe, as in the past, in God's power and ability to punish them, in the power of demons and evil spirits – and in the power of healers, sorcerers and amulets to protect them against these forces. Even the custom of expiatory sacrifice has survived to this day among those who believe that sacrificing a rooster or a chicken on Yom Kippur will atone for their sins, and spare them divine punishment.

The prevalence of these ancient beliefs among many population groups makes them a political factor, when used in electoral campaigns. The pluralistic culture of twenty first century Israeli Judaism includes both atheist and religious beliefs, as well as magical and mystical beliefs of every kind.

133

Like religion, atheism includes a variety of beliefs and customs. In every national or regional culture, people fashion their gods in a manner specific to that culture, ascribing unique form, character, and other attributes to various gods, or to a single god who assumes various roles. Such characteristics are shaped through literature, art and philosophy – in biographies and plastic images, unlike those found in other cultures. Even the one and only monotheistic God differs from culture to culture; his entourage, surroundings and appearance.

From the dawn of human culture, atheistic beliefs have developed alongside theistic (religious) beliefs, as shown by studies of tribes living in "prehistoric" conditions, isolated from known religious cultures (e.g. Australian aborigines and remote island peoples). Clear expressions of atheism appeared in India, in the second millennium BCE, enjoying a renaissance with the appearance of early Buddhism, in the mid first millennium BCE. Elsewhere, Buddhism became a religion, and atheism's strongholds in India all but disappeared. Today however, India once again boasts many centres and organisations for the dissemination of atheistic beliefs.

Most of the evidence regarding atheism in Judaism and pre-Hellenistic Greek culture comes from religious works that denounce it. Little of the work of early atheists has survived, apart from accounts of the humanistic and materialistic approaches of the pre-Socratic Greek philosophers.

Verses in Psalms denounce as scoundrels those who say there is no God; Elishah ben Abuyah was a Torah sage who left the religious fold, and believed he was not bound by the precepts of Halakhah; Plato (in *Laws*), suggested that atheists be committed to a house of correction for five years, during which time efforts should be made to convert them, but if these prove unsuccessful they should be put to death. The inventor of utopian totalitarianism viewed atheism as immoral, and a danger to the state and society. The atheism reflected in the theories of the Greek monistic and materialistic philosophers as early as the sixth century B.C.E., spread throughout Greece and the Hellenistic world beginning in the third century B.C.E., and many of its literary, poetic and philosophical expressions are extant, or are described by historians of the time.

Theogonic Theories in Atheistic Belief since Hellenism

Since Hellenistic times, when many kings were deified, it has been widely believed that people, at the dawn of religious development, also created their gods by deifying their ancestors and ancient leaders. The personification of inanimate objects and natural phenomenon joined belief in such ancestor-deities to create gods with unique personalities, life stories, and specific relationships with one another – shaped by mythology, art and literature. The fact that God is addressed as "our father" and "heavenly king" is a clear relic, according to this theory, of the process of God's creation by man.

The presence of deceased ancestors in the lives of human beings in every era is a phenomenon shared by theists and atheists alike. Parents, who were beloved and feared in their lifetimes, live on in dreams, visions and memories. They remain active in our conscious and subconscious minds, and in our memories – that both reconstruct and reinvent past. The capacity to include past and future in present spiritual life is uniquely human, and is what enables us to harbour religious beliefs, or the belief that the ghosts of the dead live on. Longing for the love and dreading the disapproval of those who were all-powerful in our childhoods, is both exciting and frightening, and analogous to belief in deities who live in an invisible and wholly other world like the "world to come", from which the spirits of the dead come, and to which the living go after their deaths. The next world and life after death are a part of most religious beliefs.

Atheistic belief in the sole existence of this world resembles the prevailing belief in the religious literature of the Bible, which also ignores the possibility of life after death. Judaism includes various atheistic beliefs – e.g. agnosticism, and belief in God as a literary figure, or as the wondrous order of the universe.

Emancipation – the liberation of Jews from the authority of their religious communities, opening the way for integration of Jews into non-Jewish society and culture – also triggered a process of Jewish spiritual auto-emancipation. Jews cast off the yoke of Halakhah and the taboo against criticising tradition hallowed by the religious establishment, and many shed belief in an omnipotent god who watches them and tells them what to do, seeing him rather, as a human creation, one of man's many cultural constructs.

In the eighteenth and especially the nineteenth century, such trends began to proliferate, and with them, agnostic, atheistic and humanistic views and beliefs.

These converged, in the minds of many Jews, with a belief in Judaism as the pluralistic culture of the Jewish People – including various and contrasting religious streams, as well as streams that are free from religion and from belief in God as fashioned in halakhic tradition. What all atheistic beliefs have in common is the belief in man as the ultimate authority in matters of ethics and faith; denying the existence of a personal god, capable of influencing human lives, and hence any obligation toward such a god.

Agnosticism for example, is atheistic in its view of man as moral authority, having the right to doubt and seek, unhindered by beliefs or religious taboos. Agnosticism does not espouse any belief or disbelief with regard to God's existence. It is the belief in our inability to know whether God exists or not. Agnosticism considers the very question "is there a god" to be meaningless and unanswerable – as did Protagoras and Socrates, who agreed that they knew nothing of the gods or their existence, and that the brevity of human life precluded the acquisition of any such knowledge.

Many agnostics believe that "God", as a concept, lies beyond the grasp of the tools with which man acquires knowledge – the senses and reason. God is therefore indefinable, and no attribute whatsoever can be ascribed to him – including existence or non-existence. Many readers of Maimonides' Guide for the Perplexed have come to this very conclusion, to the consternation of religious Jews who admire Maimonides as the greatest of Jewish philosophers. Consequently, the book has been banned in many circles, permitted only to mature readers; others have sought to destroy it by fire, lest it foster agnostic-atheistic beliefs among those who read it.

Agnosticism, like all other atheistic beliefs, maintains that man is free to choose the values by which to weigh, and adopt or reject modes of behaviour, religious precepts or laws. Accordingly, it repudiates the right of those who purport to speak in God's name to command, issue rulings, or otherwise impose halakhic precepts on others. It is the sole responsibility of the individual to determine her/his approach to any law – religious law included – on the basis of her/his moral convictions, personal judgement, and the information available to her/him.

Those who believe in God as a literary figure believe that he exerts an influence upon cultural and social life, inasmuch as he plays a decisive role in the artistic and cognitive experience evoked by the literature that shaped him and is central to the development of religious culture. A believer's artistic experiences thus combine with, or supplant, her/his religious faith.

Belief in God solely as a literary figure runs counter to religious belief, which recognises his existence beyond literature, and sees him as the author of the Bible, in which he is introduced to man as one of its protagonists.

Belief in God as a wholly literary figure is thus fundamentally atheistic. It sees man as the creator of God, morality and the biblical precepts; and fails to recognise God as an independent entity that can be exalted, prayed to, supplicated or feared. Even those who believe in man's need for the God created in these literary works, as a basis for moral authority, do not credit him with personal existence, independent will, or the capacity to command.

Pantheism is the belief in God's identity with nature – the divinity of nature. In this sense it is a belief in the existence of divinity, as a characteristic of nature and the universe. Jewish pantheism was first developed by mediaeval Jewish scholars in Arab lands, exposed – through Muslim philosophy – to Greek and Hellenistic influences.

Pantheism's first distinctly Jewish expression however, can be found in the seventeenth-century works of Spinoza – flowing directly from the twelve-century philosophy of Maimonides, flowing in turn from the works of the 1st-century philosopher Philo, based on the idea attributed to Moses, that God is existence embodying all potential existence; or in the words that the biblical author places in the mouth of his divine protagonist: "I will be that which I will be" (archaic pi'el, according to Albright; or in the third person: Yahweh).

Pantheistic belief eliminates the distinction between God and nature, thereby denying the possibility of defining God as a separate, creating, influencing, acting or supervising being. Like all of the beliefs mentioned above, pantheism also leads to atheistic conclusions: it is man who discovers the laws of nature, and creates laws and precepts in order to regulate his social and personal interaction. In the absence of a commanding personal divinity, man must contend with a freedom of choice, in matters of ethics and theology. Man does not have the right to renounce this freedom, and acquiesce to the dictates of clerics purporting to speak in God's name, since nature cannot speak in human terms. This belief charges man with responsibility for her/his actions and decisions, since these affect the world and nature – destroying it or saving it from destruction. Man's freedom is limited only by natural forces over which s/he has no control – genetics, mortality, and her/his physical and social environments.

Scientists such as Albert Einstein, who express awe at the natural order of the universe, on a micro- and macrocosmic level, throughout known and conjectured time, see religiosity in such awe. This belief in the wondrousness of the universe, its complexity and contrast-filled harmony, also, however, negates belief in a supernatural being.

Belief in the universal and eternal order of nature is atheistic, since it runs counter to belief in a creator, providence, life after death, or any other basic tenet of religious faith. (Einstein said: "I believe in Spinoza's God who reveals himself in the orderly harmony of what exists, not in a God who concerns himself with fates and actions of human beings".)

The Principles of Atheism

Atheism is the belief in man's sovereignty and freedom, responsibility for her/his actions, and ability to play a decisive role, under certain conditions, in determining her/his fate. As such, man is the source of authority, fashioning God and the humanistic or anti-humanistic values that serve as standards, by which all laws, precepts and customs are judged – to determine the extent to which they contribute to man's humanisation or dehumanisation.

Such atheistic beliefs are reflected in most twentieth-twenty first-century Jewish works. Within Judaism and western culture today, most people ignore God in their lives, although some may not reject the possibility of his existence. Few would term their beliefs "atheistic", due to atheism's bad reputation as heresy without belief, and attempts (since the days of Plato) to malign it as negating moral values and obligations to society.

Despite its etymology, atheism is a belief in its own right – opposed to religious belief, but not defined merely as "heretical" rejection of the latter. "Heresy" is what adherents of one belief call the beliefs of their opponents.

In Israel, the Bible is Once Again the Basis for Jewish Education

The development of Israel and Israeli culture has intensified Jewish cultural pluralism, both in Israel and in the diaspora. All of Judaism's ethnic, secular and religious cultures come together in Israel. Tension between them has grown, and the differences are greater than before – as are the differences between Israeli Judaism as a whole and the various diaspora Judaisms.

Throughout the diaspora, most Jews live in the language and culture of the lands they inhabit. In Israel, Jews live within a Jewish cultural environment, in which all streams of Judaism meet one another.

The influences of other cultures can be also observed in Israeli culture (lifestyle, dress, dance, media and its content), as in all national cultures developing in their own land and national language. These influences converge with each unique national cultural life and its creative efforts – in literature, theatre, film, secular and religious philosophy, art, journalism, national and personal holidays and celebrations.

In the new, secular Hebrew culture, the Bible enjoys greater prominence than in any other Jewish education system in the world. The language they speak, read and write creates a special bond between Israelis and the classical literature of the Bible. In the humanistic education offered by most Israeli schools, the Bible plays a central role at all levels – from pre-school to university. Familiarity with biblical themes is a basic element of the cultural lives of most educated Israelis and their children. Sightseeing – from school trips to family and individual outings – offers Israelis the opportunity to visit biblical locations. The Bible is perceived by most Israelis as a historical, literary and political document – disregarding scientific doubts concerning the veracity of the information it contains.

Biblical belief in the existence of a single world, coupled with the Bible's lack of angelic and mystical mythology, make it well-suited to the mentality of Israelis free from religion, as well as a source of inspiration and wellspring of references for many Israeli works – from literature and theatre to pop songs and political speeches.

Halakhic literature, and literature steeped in belief in the world to come, life after death, demons and angels that roam about unseen, have served as a source of inspiration for many Jewish works in the diaspora – including those of secular authors such as Bashevis Singer and Y.L. Peretz, who drew upon such myths in their ironic works (like "The Last Demon" or "If not Higher"). These authors, and others like them, were the products of Haredi education, based on the study of halakhic literature, religious exegesis and Midrash.

This body of literature is almost completely absent from the spiritual world of Israeli writers and their readers, just as it is absent from the spiritual world of most Jews; members of Judaism's religious and secular majority streams.

In light of these developments, the Bible has again become the common basis for Jewish culture in Israel – mainly among the secular majority and members of the religious-Zionist movements.

Only among the minority Haredi groups do the Talmud, Midrash and Kabbalah continue to be the focus of Jewish study.

In free Judaism, the Bible no longer serves as raw material for free midrashic interpretation, divorced from the plain meaning of the text. The Bible is again a literary anthology, understood by Hebrew-speakers, in its original language. In their lives, the Bible is no longer a religious book, nor are they familiar with its verses or half-verses merely as support for halakhic rulings or other assertions that have nothing to do with the original, literary context. They would find it strange and rather ridiculous to infer Esau's wickedness from the verse describing his return from the field. This is however, precisely what the Midrash does, reading numerous sins into the words "and Esau came in from the field, and he was faint"– including murder (since it is written in Jeremiah "for my soul fainteth before the murderers"), and rape of a betrothed woman (since the Bible distinguishes between rape in the field and rape in the city, where a woman might cry for help).

In Judaism free from religion, the works of the Bible have been restored to the status of independent works, unrelated to the midrashic interpretations that have been associated with them. We read them as literary works and historical documents, having religious significance only to the religious. Like all literature – both fiction and non-fiction – the works of the Bible are also historical records, providing information about life at the time they were written, and sometimes, even at the time they were written about.

Nationhood, Humanism and Tradition in Judaism Free from Religion

The distinction between nationhood and religion in Judaism began in response to anti-Semitic racism in the fifteenth century.

Atheism, in terms of its approach to lifestyle, religious precepts, rabbis and religious authorities, has been a significant part of Judaism, ever since this distinction was first made.

Proponents of the various atheistic beliefs do not recognise the existence of an independent, personal deity, who chose the Jewish People as its people. They do not recognise the existence of a watching, punishing and rewarding God, to which the Jewish People is bound by a special covenant. Such atheistic and humanistic beliefs are expressed in a broad range of contemporary Jewish works.

Agnostic pantheistic and other atheistic beliefs spread among Jews, in the wake of the shocks and changes that took place in European Jewish life from the fifteenth to the twentieth century. Jewish communities disintegrated as a result of pogroms and expulsions. Large numbers of Jews converted to Christianity, some of them secretly remaining Jews; while "New Christians" were persecuted as Jews in Spain and Portugal. All of this led to a new understanding of the term "Jew".

A new kind of anti-Semitism developed in Spain, following the mass conversion of Jews who had chosen to abjure their faith rather than leave the land of their birth, where their families had lived for generations. Consequently, "Old Christians" became increasingly hostile in their attitudes toward the New Christians, who had risen, upon conversion, to the highest echelons of Spanish society: the ruling classes and the Inquisition.

This change in the status of individuals still considered Jews by many Old Christians, even after conversion, transformed religious anti-Semitism into nationalist anti-Semitism, which considered Jews members of a specific people, regardless of the faith they professed. In response, many Jews began to develop a sense of national consciousness that was not equivalent to observance of the religious precepts, or acceptance of hallowed traditions and religious tenets.

Many New Christians, who had emigrated from the Iberian Peninsula to western and southern Europe, returned to Judaism when they were able to do so. Messianic movements – like that of David Reuveni and Shabbetai Zevi – aroused hopes for national liberation of a political nature, i.e. the establishment of a Jewish state. Disappointment with the failure of these movements led to the proliferation of mystical and kabbalistic beliefs, and to scepticism among the educated New Christians, some of whom had returned to Judaism after having become well- acquainted with European cultures, and had taken part in the Enlightenment movements of the sixteenth and seventeenth centuries.

New approaches to Judaism, as the culture of a people, began to gain credence among Jews, followed by the appearance of agnostic and pantheistic beliefs, closely resembling atheism in their conclusions. What these new approaches had in common was the distinction they made between the religion of Halakhah and Jewish nationhood – recognising the fact that one can still be a Jew, even if s/he is not religious by the standards of Halakhah-observers, even if s/he does not believe in God as an independent and providential force, and even if s/he does not believe in the duty to observe the precepts ascribed to God by those who purport to speak in his name.

Leaders of communities of New Christians who had returned to Judaism (like that of Amsterdam, for example) adopted religiously conservative positions, in order to ensure their re-acceptance as Jews. On the other hand there were intellectuals (such as Uriel da Costa and Spinoza) who expressed doubts regarding the sacred principles of religious tradition and its precepts. The community leadership resorted to the excommunication and public humiliation of anyone who – impelled by the passage from one religion to another, from one culture to another – dared to re-examine the principles of his faith and Jewish national identity.

Jewish communities adopted the same religious and intellectual intolerance that characterised the Christian authorities (both Catholic and Protestant). Uriel da Costa killed himself a short time after the establishment of the Portuguese Jewish community in Amsterdam (1640); having been excommunicated, humiliated and persecuted for his beliefs. The Jewish community excommunicated and banished from its midst, one of Europe's greatest philosophers – Baruch Spinoza – who had previously been a member of the community, and whose name appears on a list of contributors to the rescue of Jews expelled from Brazil by the Inquisition. At anchor in New Amsterdam (New York) harbour, they had not been allowed to disembark until their welfare had been guaranteed by the Jewish community of Amsterdam.

Spinoza was one of the first to adopt a critical approach to the Bible, and viewed the Torah as the constitution of the Jewish people at a given time in its history, rather than an eternal, religious constitution. He opened the way to approaching the Bible as the classical literature of the Jewish People, rather than the word of God. The biblical halakhic precepts appeared to him as the laws of an ancient national society, which would have to enact new laws were it to win renewed political independence.

The distinction between Jewish religion and nationhood was shaped by various factors that acted upon Jewish consciousness during the period of transition from the Middle Ages to the Modern Era. In addition to the racist-anti-Semitic factor that emerged in Spain in the wake of the New Christians' success; messianic movements – like those of David Reuveni and Shabbetai Zevi – encouraged Jews to think of redemption in national-political terms, and of Jewish nationhood as distinct from the Jewish religion of Halakhah. Another factor was the critical-philosophical approach advocated by figures such as Spinoza, who portrayed Judaism as the national-historical heritage of all Jews – religious and non-religious alike.

Non-Religious Humanistic Beliefs and Values Reflected in Most Contemporary Jewish Works

The number of Jewish works created outside the sphere of influence of Jewish religion and its prevailing beliefs, has increased steadily since the eighteenth century. The belief in man, not God, as the determinate factor governing individual behaviour and historical events, appears in a growing number of Jewish works. Beginning in the ninteenth century, but particularly the twentieth century, Jewish creative efforts, in Palestine/Israel and the diaspora, are directed primarily toward the fields of literature, philosophy, and the arts.

Most of the influential Jewish works of the ninteenth and twentieth-twenty first centuries are humanistic rather than religious: focusing on man and the ways in which s/he grapples with fate, rather than on God and the precepts attributed to him. Jewish works that have influenced contemporary culture – like those by Heine, Sholem Aleichem, Proust, Kafka, Saul Bellow, Bashevis Singer, Hess, Herzl, Buber and Isaiah Berlin – have been humanistic rather than religious, addressing moral dilemmas from the perspective of "what is good for man"; as opposed to most religious literature that addresses the question "what complies with the demands and precepts laid down by rabbis in God's name".

Most contemporary Jewish works – in the fields of literature, poetry, plastic and performance arts, theatre and film, philosophy and criticism – express belief in man and her/his freedom to act as s/he sees fit, within the limits of physical and social circumstances. In this sense, we see an affinity between Jewish works and various forms of atheism – based on the belief that the good of man takes precedence over all divine or other interests. Humanistic values as standards for evaluation and preference, striving for the good of man and her/his humanisation – are the measure of all things. In principle, these values are shared by religious and non-religious alike. Jewish religious humanists – like Yeshayahu Leibowitz – however, are aware of the contradiction between the universality of humanistic principles and the supremacy of the halakhic precepts.

True Jewish religious reformers, who follow in the footsteps of the Sages who created the Oral Law (found in all streams of Judaism, and not specifically those called "Reform", many of which tend toward halakhic conservatism), strive to resolve the contradictions between humanistic values and Halakhah. They work to change certain precepts, rewrite liturgy, reshape customs, in keeping with their humanistic convictions – granting equal rights to men and women in the selection of rabbis and religious court judges for example, or discarding offensive prayers, such as the blessing "blessed art thou who hast not made me a woman". Orthodox Jews, who believe they do not have the right to change any of the precepts or prayers, face an irresolvable dilemma, like that of Leibowitz.

Humanistic atheists believe it is their right and responsibility to evaluate and judge, choose or reject every law and precept, on the basis of values that strive for the good of all people – woman and men of all ages and races – since the good of man is the ultimate goal of all moral precepts. The essence of that good – the conditions and customs, values and laws capable of ensuring the greatest good for the greatest number – has stood at the heart of humanistic thought ever since the Socratic dialogues and formulated by Epicurus, Lucretius and Epictetus. Answers to this question have been the subject of art and literature throughout history. The "meta-values" of Hillel and Kant (that which is hateful to you, do not unto others; treat man always as an end and never as a means only; a law cannot be moral unless it is universally valid) have remained the measure of all humanistic values and actions. Even today, any human society committed to the good of its individual members must rely on these meta-values, although notions of "what is good for man" may change from generation to generation.

Atheists see nothing wrong with religious observance per se, as long as it does not conflict with these humanistic principles. Religious precepts that coincide with humanistic values – like the precepts of the Ten Commandments, or those based on the principles of justice and charity – are embraced by religious and atheistic humanists alike. They find precepts that conflict with such principles – like the halakhah that women may appear before a religious court, but may not sit on its bench – however, unacceptable and deserving of abrogation.

Religious traditions – Halakhah, prayer, piyutim, Midrash, stories, holidays and rituals – are all part of secular culture. The various atheistic beliefs view the halakhic literature of the Talmud as a unique body of literature, rooted in discussion and debate, as well as rulings that became binding precepts in the eyes of religious believers. The Talmud has aroused a great deal of interest, both as a historical record, and as a rhetorical and philosophical work. Its laws and precepts however, may be changed, abrogated or renewed, in accordance with changing needs and circumstances – as long as they serve the good of man. Atheists' beliefs allow them to choose religious precepts in keeping with their values, and reject or ignore those that are irrelevant or stand in contradiction to them. Atheists refrain from addressing benedictions, entreaties or prayers to God; considering such acts pointless or contrary to their beliefs, inasmuch as one cannot bless, entreat, or pray to something in the existence of which one does not believe.

Those who believe in God as a human creation – constantly changing, developing and being reshaped by human beings in different cultures and eras – do not bless or pray to him as if he had created them, or as if he somehow holds their fates in his hands.

Atheism does not deny its adherents the possibility of enjoying or employing artistic works in which God or his image appear, e.g. religious and secular piyutim, paintings or statues depicting God, stories and midrashim or mythological poetry. As long as they have independent poetic-experiential value, or afford pleasure in the roles they play in ritual and celebration, they are appreciated by Jewish atheists. Secular Jews may use religious poetry from Psalms alongside secular poetry from Song of Songs; religious poetry and prose from the Bible and the traditional Haggadah feature in the secular Passover Seder, alongside the secular poetry of Amichai or Naomi Shemer, Alterman or Ira Gershwin. Religious masterpieces like some of the Psalms, the philosophical drama of Job, or Michelangelo's Sistine Chapel, play a part in the spiritual lives of cultured people in general; secular and religious, Jews and non-Jews.

Poetry and other art forms play a fundamental role in the spiritual lives of all people; religious and non-religious. Every religion employs art and literature to fashion its gods and the rituals by means of which it celebrates its relationship with them, as well as its social and personal holidays.

Atheists, like all people, need ritual in their celebrations; whether national-traditional, or personal celebrations of life-cycle events. Such rituals were religious as long as society was religious. Secular Jews, however, seek ways of renewing ritual and adapting it to their beliefs and social needs. Non-religious Jewish culture has produced new Passover haggadot, as well as rituals for all of the holidays and celebrations, drawing upon both religious and secular literature and art. Among these new rituals we find for example: secular ceremonies for Kabbalat Shabbat and Havdalah (services marking the beginning and end of the Sabbath), Hannukah candle-lighting, and bat/bar-mitzvah celebrations for secular children. These ceremonies draw upon texts and poetical works from all periods and Jewish streams – religious and non-religious alike. Poems by Bialik, Tchernichowsky, Uri Zvi Greenberg, Heine, Manger and Alterman might appear alongside such patently religious poems as the Psalms, or mediaeval and kabbalistic piyutim.

One of the most important contributions of the first secular communities created by the Kibbutz Movement in Palestine was the systematic effort to recreate traditional Jewish rituals in a form consistent with the lifestyle and culture of their members. The creation and of these popular works and experience with them in dozens of secular communities in Palestine and the State of Israel, established new holiday traditions and ceremonies employing both ancient and new works.

Some of these traditions have served as a basis for the development of new rituals at secular synagogues and havurot in the United States. Some of these have been collected and are being researched at the extensive holiday and festival archives of Kibbutzim Beit Hashita and Ramat Yohanan. Today there are secular communities that do not use the name of God in their celebrations and rituals (e.g. the "Birmingham Temple" in Detroit), as well as many secular families and communities, that choose texts from both religious and secular traditions.

Chapter Four

Humanism and National Culture
Humanising and Dehumanising Education

Only man can become human, or inhuman – like Nazi murderers, Gulag jailers or Cambodian communists who slaughtered large numbers of their own people. All other animals fulfil the genetic potential of their species. Pico della Mirandola wrote in his "Oration on the Dignity of Man" (published in 1486):

> But upon man, at the moment of his creation, God bestowed seeds pregnant with all possibilities, the germs of every form of life. Whichever of these a man shall cultivate, the same will mature and bear fruit in him. If vegetative, he will become a plant; if sensual, he will become brutish; if rational, he will reveal himself a heavenly being; if intellectual, he will be an angel and the son of God. And if, dissatisfied with the lot of all creatures, he should recollect himself into the center of his own unity, he will there become one spirit with God, in the solitary darkness of the Father, Who is set above all things, himself transcend all creatures. (Translation by Robert Caponigri, Regnery Publishing, Chicago, 1956).

Humanism is the sum total of beliefs that view humanisation as a supreme value: the ultimate standard for the evaluation and preference of any value, mode of behaviour or form of government. Democracy is thus preferred over dictatorship; modes of behaviour that see others as an end in themselves are preferred over modes of behaviour that see them only as a means to something else; laws that ensure the human right to equality and freedom are preferred over those that subjugate some people to others. Subjugation and exploitation result in the dehumanisation of both subjugated and subjugator.

The processes that constitute humanisation – socialisation, acculturation and the development of critical and independent personality – flourish in the presence of democracy, and wither in its absence. They are guided by the humanistic belief that "human" man, one who has internalised humanistic values, believes – like Hillel and Kant – in the fundamental principles of morality: one may not do unto others that which is hateful to him; one may not treat man as only as an end; moral law cannot be applied to one group only.

Education – Socialisation, Culture and Personal Independence

Erasmus asserted that a man is not born a man, but becomes one – in a process that is dialectic inasmuch as it views socialisation as a precondition for individuation.

These two, seemingly opposed tendencies, in fact act in concert with one another in any process of humanisation; which is the ultimate goal of humanistic education:

1. Socialisation and acculturation – acclimatise the individual to society and its culture, acquainting her/him with its norms and characteristics, as well as with her/his own obligations and rights as a member of that society.

2. The development of critical ability and independence of personality fosters spiritual autonomy, the ability and habit of criticising and examining everything acquired through the process of socialisation and acculturation, as well as the creative ability to express one's individuality and realise one's potential.

These processes take place in the context of family, community and society that, in turn, exist within a national culture; but also include partial exposure to international communications media and other national cultures.

Today, we are witnessing the creation of an international communications and entertainment culture, common to many national cultures, within a single civilisation. It is precisely these developments that have also brought about the rise of movements promoting distinct national identity, striving to preserve and develop national language and culture, and to ensure the independence of their respective national groups, within federal or multi-ethnic states.

Virtually all of the wars fought since the Second World War have been the result of conflicts between national, ethnic or tribal groups – in Europe, Asia and Africa. The growing proliferation of international communications networks has raised awareness of national identity; while at the same time supporting the internationalisation of consumer goods, communications, culture and entertainment products – like pop music, information technology, or international suspense and horror films translated into national languages.

The humanisation process is the process of educating the individual in the society and national culture in which s/he is raised. There is no such thing as a cultural environment that is not national (ethnic or tribal). Every national culture is distinct from other national cultures in its language, concepts and associations, awareness of its historical and cultural heritage, customs and rituals, prevailing beliefs, group identity, and the otherness of societies that belong to other national cultures.

Various unique national cultures may develop within a single civilisation – such as twentieth-century European civilisation.

By the term "civilisation", we mean the sum total of the means and tools – technological and organisational – that supply man's physical and social needs. "Culture" refers to the phenomena and artefacts that constitute the spiritual environment in which man is educated.

In the masterpieces that represent a given culture we find expression of the isolation and uniqueness of their creators and of man in general.

Creativity and tradition are the two faces of culture. It is only together that they possess cultural value.

Recognising Israel's Jewish and Arab Identity

Diaspora Jews live and are educated in the national culture of their respective countries, and to an ever-lesser extent in the culture of their respective Jewish communities. The Jewish identity of American Jews differs from that of French Jews, just as their French or American identities differ from those of non-Jewish Frenchmen or Americans. Jewish identity continues, to a large extent, to preserve its unique character, despite increasing cultural assimilation among diaspora Jews, many of whom are breaking away from their Jewish communities, living in open, non-Jewish society, that encourages their integration into non-Jewish families and communities, and into the national cultural life of their country.

Israeli Jews live primarily in national Israeli-Jewish culture. Their Jewish identity and culture is unique – distinct from French or American Jewish identity – and develops within a largely Jewish cultural environment: in Hebrew, and in a Jewish education system that stresses conversance with Jewish historical and cultural heritage, the Bible, and a selection of other Jewish works.

Jewish culture in Israel develops alongside Palestinian-Arab culture – with Palestinians constituting a fifth of the population of the Jewish state. This culture is common to Arabs living in

Israel, Palestine and other Arab countries. Israeli-Arab culture also possess distinctive features that set it apart from other Arab cultures, including: bilingualism, exposure to Israeli media, expressions of the struggle of the Arab minority for equal rights in Israel, and its own unique accomplishments, in academia, literature and education.

These two cultures – Israeli-Jewish and Israeli-Palestinian – are influenced, like all cultures, by elements of international culture, while preserving and emphasising their own unique cultures: their respective languages, historical and cultural heritage, holidays, art and literature, customs, traditions, attitudes to religion and secularism, to the land, to those among their peoples who reside in other lands, and to members of other peoples.

At work within each of these two national cultures in Israel, are humanistic movements that promote humanisation, striving to improve quality of life, and struggling against the dehumanisation fostered by chauvinistic and racist-nationalist ideologies and movements.

Israeli humanistic education strives to develop awareness among Jews and Arabs, of their distinct cultures; to further education and artistic expression in each of these cultures; and to promote each group's ties with the culture of their respective peoples in other lands; while fostering mutual exchange, social interaction and co-operation in all areas of cultural and political life.

Humanistic education in both of these cultures shares many of the same goals, in terms of humanisation and the struggle against all forms of racism; just as both strive to further the unique character of their respective national cultures – through formal education and other social and communal institutions – while also seeking points of encounter between members of two cultures within a single state.

Such encounters between different national cultures occur in many countries, including: Switzerland, Belgium, Canada, Nigeria, China and Indonesia. Policies that recognise national-cultural differences can facilitate productive dialogue between members of different cultures within the same country.

In Israel, emphasis should be placed upon finding ways of bringing the two cultures together, and upon acquainting students and teachers in each culture with their own sources, classical works, historical heritage, national language and culture-specific concepts, cultural ties of each people with its diaspora, relations between religion and secularism, humanistic principles and movements for human rights and the struggle against their opponents, as well as the possibilities for co-operation between the humanistic movements of both peoples.

Internalising Equality and Safeguarding the Rights of Individuals and Society through Education

Humanistic education – in Judaism as in all national cultures – strives to instil democratic values, as the only system of government capable of safeguarding the rights of individuals and minorities in society. Democracy offers the best possible conditions for the humanisation of the individual, and the realisation of her/his unique potential, as well as ensuring the equal rights and obligations of all members of society.

Democracies allow minorities to educate their children in their own culture, as long as they fulfil their obligations to society – including the teaching of democracy, its laws, the obligations it imposes and rights it affords to all people. The ability of democratic society to safeguard individual and minority rights is contingent upon individuals fulfilling their obligations to the community. In order to ensure the rights of all individuals, the curricula employed at minority schools – religious or secular – must include language skills, particular and world history, as well as adequate preparation for further science and technology studies.

Recognising the legitimacy of debate entails recognising the illegitimacy of totalitarianism that silences all debate. Humanistic education highlights democracy's preferability to all other alternatives, inasmuch as it is the only system of government that ensures maximum realisation of the principles of equality in human society. Jewish humanistic education, beyond teaching democracy and equality, should also explore the ways in which these subjects are treated in Jewish sources.

Haim Cohn, in a series of lectures for the Israel Broadcast University (later published as *Zekhuyot Adam Bamikra Uvatalmud – Human Rights in the Bible and the Talmud*) discusses the issue of equality and difference in ancient Jewish sources:

"The first article of the United Nations Universal Declaration of Human Rights begins with the words 'All human beings are born free and equal in dignity and rights'. This notion was not invented by the authors of the Declaration, but – like most basic rights of man – can be traced back to Jewish sources.

The Bible teaches that God created man in his image: 'in the image of God created he him; male and female created he them'. Each and every person is created in God's image, and in this all men are equal. The one and only difference between them is mentioned in the very same verse, and that is the difference between male and female. Even the difference between the sexes however, is mentioned in the very same context, in order to stress the equality between them: just as the male was created in God's image, so the female was created in God's image. Not that God is of a specific gender (at least there is no reason why he must be of a determined sex), but the fact that there are physical and psychological differences between male and female, in no way affects the personal, moral and legal equality between them. Since every man was created in God's image, every man is equal to her/his fellow, and no man may say to another I am greater than you, my blood is redder than yours.

There is a debate [in the Talmud] between two sages as to what is the greatest principle in the Torah. Rabbi Akiva asserted that the greatest principle is 'love thy fellow as thyself', whereas Ben Azai, Akiva's cousin and disciple, claimed that the greatest principle in the Torah is 'this is the book of the generations of Adam. In the day that God created man, in the image of God created he him; male and female created he them'. What is the difference between Rabbi Akiva and Ben Azai? The former argues that man cannot be required to love all people equally; you cannot love a stranger, whom you do not know or understand. It is enough that you love those who are close to you, your family, your people. Ben Azai on the other hand, says that all were created in God's image, and just as you are required to love God, so the greatest principle in the Torah is that all men must be treated equally. What is important is the basic equality between human beings, and the obligation to treat each other as having been created in God's image is a great principle, upon which the entire Torah is founded."

The object of Jewish humanistic education should be the internalisation of individual and minority rights and obligations, and equality in their application, as well as the need of society to defend itself against those who would seek to subvert it by abolishing the democracy that guarantees these rights. Jewish humanistic education seeks to realise these beliefs, and strives to instil in its students the need to oppose any attempt to undermine equality between ethnicities, between men and women, or between the various streams of Judaism (Orthodox, Reform, Conservative and Secular) within Israeli Jewish society.

Nationalistic Education – a Threat to Humanisation

Religious and secular humanists reject relativism that shows tolerance and understanding toward nationalism, racism and chauvinism, "because they are a part of the culture of those who subscribe to them". Such relativism allows resources to be allocated for anti-Semitic education, or for propaganda advocating the abrogation of the rights of one people by another.

Nationalistic, racist and chauvinistic education results in dehumanisation, inasmuch as it causes people to perceive themselves as members of a chosen people, master race or superior sex. As such, they allow themselves to do to their fellows that which is hateful to them, to treat others as a means rather than an end, and to apply the principles of morality exclusively to members of their own sex or group.

Nationalistic and chauvinistic education is one of the causes of dehumanisation, since it undermines the three "meta-values" of humanism, as formulated by Hillel and Kant:

Humanistic education humanises its students, by bringing them to internalise the meta-values that ensure belief in equal rights for all, regardless of nationality, ethnicity or sex. Selfish education in all its forms – nationalistic, chauvinistic, racist – leads to the internalisation of belief in inequality.

In this fashion, selfish education entrenches false beliefs in the supremacy of man over woman, Aryan over Jew, Jew over "goy". By subverting humanistic values, such beliefs distort believers' perceptions of reality and diminish their own humanity.

Democratic, humanising society can only exist if we fulfil our obligations toward it, defending the rights of all people to equality, freedom and dignity. It is essential for the stability and continued development of such societies, that we defend them against racist and selfish ideologies.

Pluralistic humanistic education therefore rejects relativism that affords legitimacy, equal rights and public resources to nationalistic and racist education that subjugates its students to the dictatorship of leaders of any kind. There is no justification for education rooted in such beliefs, even if they are "authentic" expressions of traditional cultural environments.

Humanistic Values – Standards for the Evaluation and Criticism of Precepts and Laws

Values are, as remarked above, standards for the evaluation and preference of halakhic precepts or state laws. Humanistic education teaches a critical approach to all laws, based on the standards of humanistic values. The belief that it is man who creates values, and that their ultimate concern is the quality of human life, affords human beings the right to approve laws and precepts that improve their quality of life, and reject those that have an adverse effect on their lives.

Jewish humanistic education is based on these beliefs, as opposed to the belief that halakhic precepts come from God, and that the ultimate goal of human behaviour is to satisfy him by obeying those who purport to speak in his name. Ascribing divine origin to the precepts, denies man the right to judge them on moral or utilitarian grounds, adopting some and rejecting others.

Even religious rationalists, such as Saadiah Gaon or Maimonides, recognised the fact that some of the precepts are inexplicable and of no apparent benefit to man. Maimonides thus claimed that some of the precepts are temporary – to be abolished over time – like those pertaining to animal sacrifice, practised for many years merely because the Jews had been accustomed to bringing such offerings in their worship of other gods, and it is difficult to break longstanding habits overnight.

Jewish humanistic education approaches Judaism as an evolving culture, and therefore stresses this temporary aspect of its precepts. The halakhic precepts are not equivalent to Jewish values. Like the obligation to bring sacrifices, all of the precepts are temporary measures, valid at a particular time for a particular reason. When that reason ceases to exist in the eyes of believers, so does the need to observe the precepts associated with it – as in fact happened in the case of the Temple sacrifices.

Humanistic education encourages critical evaluation, and the rejection of laws or precepts that are inconsistent with moral values – whether explicitly stated in the Bible, or enacted by later authorities: the obligation to perpetrate genocide against the people of "Amalek" for example, or the commandment to kill one who violates the Sabbath laws, or the precepts that discriminate against women. Critical re-evaluation of all the precepts and laws, on the basis of the benefits they afford man, will lead many students of humanistic education to abandon observance of halakhic precepts they perceive to be unnecessary, anachronistic or incompatible with moral principles: the dietary laws, the prohibition against physical contact with a woman for a large part of every month, not watching television on the Sabbath or other days, etc. and the ability to enjoy the Sabbath as a day of rest and leisure.

These far-reaching changes will be judged not only as a

significant historical phenomenon, but also in terms of the benefits they have brought to religious Jews who wish to drive to the synagogue on the Sabbath and holidays, and to secular Jews who wish to spend the Sabbath engaged in other leisure activities, away from home.

Humanistic education does not believe in the sanctification of precepts and laws – whether due to their divine origin, or because they are a part of an age-old tradition.

Appreciation of customs and cultural traditions, including holiday and life-cycle rituals, stems from an appreciation for the contribution they make to the quality of human life, the way in which they enable an individual to identify with the cultural community to which s/he belongs, the ways in which they enrich our lives, through holiday traditions and the element of play involved in their annual repetition.

Humanistic education deepens this awareness, combining it with a critical approach, evaluating every custom, precept or law, in light of its potential benefit or harm to man.

Humanistic Education Depends upon Extensive Study and Social Involvement

Jewish humanistic education introduces students to Judaism as a specific and world culture, through extensive academic programmes that specifically address Judaism's openness to the influence of other cultures, and the influence it has, in turn, had upon them – focusing on elements common to contemporary western cultures in general, and the role that humanistic values have played in their development.

Such programmes afford students the opportunity to experience – on an emotional as well as an intellectual level – a range of works, representing Judaism's various ethnic cultures and religious streams. Curricula designed to familiarise students with the classical works of Jewish and other cultures, will help them internalise values of human solidarity and equality, and contribute to their understanding of the universal human dilemmas reflected in the classical works of all peoples.

Humanistic education must have the ability to introduce students to mankind's achievements, not only in terms of civilisation, but in terms of culture, as defined by Buber. Level of education and degree of exposure to the variety of works representing national and world culture, is one of the factors contributing to spiritual wealth or poverty, to the level and variety of conversation among family and friends, and to quality of life – which depends, among other things, on the type of spiritual activity in which one is able to engage. Such education is essential to social adjustment, and to the students' ability to participate in the national and international culture in which they live. The success of humanistic education depends upon its ability to combine an extensive academic programme with social involvement, fostering critical evaluation and personal creativity.

Social Involvement

In humanistic education, children and adults are encouraged to take on certain tasks and obligations within the family and community, creating a sense of responsibility and purpose. Social involvement also serves to raise awareness of the moral issues that affect the lives of people in the society in which they live. Children and teenagers for example, might participate in campaigns for children's rights, or equality for minority groups; join community activities or educational programmes to help younger children; take part in protest movements, against nuclear war, threats to the environment, nationalism, chauvinism, etc.

In Mandatory Palestine for example, the fact that many young people took part in the activities of the youth movements and the Haganah, preparing the ground for the establishment of the Jewish state, and providing direct and indirect assistance for the illegal immigration of Jews from post-Holocaust Europe, had a decisive educational impact on generations of Israelis, in terms of their internalisation of values of national and universal human solidarity. The lack of appropriate frameworks and the failure of the existing education system to provide volunteer programmes for children and adolescents – on behalf of children's rights and equality for women and minorities – have had an adverse effect on the internalisation of humanistic values among Israeli youth.

Many Israelis have extended the sense of solidarity one feels toward members of one's own family and community to include all Jews – wherever they may be in distress as a result of their Jewishness, such as Soviet Russia or Ethiopia.

Jewish humanistic education, like all humanistic education that is national but not nationalistic, requires the constant expansion of circles of solidarity and responsibility. Such expansion deepens one's awareness of the need to act in ways that allow individuals to influence the fate of national and human society. Internalising the importance of national solidarity converges with a sense of universal human solidarity – reinforced by involvement in social and political activities, like the struggle by young American Jews and other "whites" for equal rights for African Americans in the 1960s and 70s. Humanistic education is also committed to political activism, for the rights of people of every age, sex and nationality. Humanistic curricula must therefore teach social issues, philosophical approaches to them, declarations that have sought to guarantee human rights, their origins in classical Greek and Jewish sources, and in European humanistic thought and literature; the declarations of rights produced by the American and French revolutions, and the United Nations' declarations of human rights and children's rights.

An education that combines social involvement with a broad cultural background, critical ability and personal creativity, will heighten value-consciousness, on the basis of which one may evaluate existing laws, precepts and traditions, and aspire to social change for the improvement and enrichment of human lives.

The Role of Classical Literature

Classical works (also called "masterpieces") are referred to as such, because they fulfil a function in public and personal cultural life, and they retain that designation only as long as they continue to do so.

All humanistic education is based upon providing students with a thorough introduction to the classical works of their culture, the elements common to all of its streams, and the influence exerted by these works on other cultural works throughout its history.

"Classical literature" comprises works that represent the culture of a people or group of peoples; "timeless" works that are products of the period in which they were written, but continue to provoke thought, evoke emotion and influence the culture of readers in subsequent eras; works that address universal human dilemmas from a unique perspective, and through the personal experiences of their protagonists (such as: Jacob, Joseph, Job, Medea, King Lear, Don Quixote, Faust, etc.).

Intellectuals and critics in different eras value classical works as masterpieces of the genres in which they were written, exerting a profound influence on education and artistic development in their own cultures. Familiarity with a culture's masterpieces is the key to understanding that culture – like the works of Homer in ancient Greece, or the works of the Bible in Jewish culture; both of which were to become classical works in western culture as a whole. Other works attain the status of classical works only later in cultural history, like the Greek tragedies – recognised as masterpieces of western culture only in the Renaissance; or the works of Philo and Josephus – recognition of which, as classical works of ancient Jewish culture, is only just beginning.

"Classical works" of art, literature or philosophy, evoke an intellectual and emotional response in those who experience them. Such is the case with many works of the Bible, that continue to function as classical works in contemporary Jewish culture, representing and influencing spiritual and creative life in all of Judaism's Judaisms – secular and religious.

Works become and cease to be classical works, in accordance with the cultural and social functions they fulfil. Greek classics for example, ceased to function as classical works in Europe at the close of the Hellenistic era, and remained so for centuries, returning to fulfil this function upon their rediscovery and introduction into western humanistic education.

Many works of the Talmud and Midrash functioned as classical works in mediaeval Jewish culture, alongside the works of the Bible, but ceased fulfilling this function in most twentieth-century Judaisms. This was the result of enlightenment and secularisation processes, the split of religious Judaism into Reform and Orthodox streams, and the far-reaching changes effected in most Jewish education – from Talmud to Bible-based curricula that combined Jewish and general culture.

Works of the Talmud and Midrash, like those of the Kabbalah, Halakhah and religious exegesis, continue to function as classical works in Orthodox Judaisms, but no longer do so in most religious and secular Judaisms. The literature of the Talmud, Kabbalah and Halakhah continue to function as "Jewish sources", representing certain periods and religious streams in Jewish history, but no longer play a significant role in the creative and cultural lives of most secular Jews.

Students in all of Judaism's Judaisms are introduced to the classical works of their respective cultures, at various levels. In secular Judaism, the works of the Bible continue to function as classical works, alongside western classics. In western cultures as well, the works of the Bible continue to function as classical works, as part of their common heritage – alongside the classical works of individual national cultures.

What do Classical Literature's Sinful Characters Contribute to Humanistic Education?

Ever since Plato, educators and philosophers have pondered the educational value of classical works in which the protagonists commit sins, break the law or violate moral principles – from Abraham to David, Agamemnon to Medea, Macbeth to Faust.

In classical works, the protagonists are not held up as paragons of virtue. No one would want her/his child or student to behave as Abraham did toward his sons, or as Isaac did toward his elderly and blind father, or as Yahweh behaved in withholding knowledge and morality from man. The main characters in most of these classical works behave in morally reprehensible ways.

In what way do these works contribute to humanistic education that strives to instil moral and critical values?

The educational value of classical literature lies not in the role models it provides, but in the human truths it reveals (as Tolstoy claimed), through the poetic truths it evokes in those who experience it (as claimed by Aristotle); in the human face it holds up before us, indefinable except in truly great art and literature (like the works of Shakespeare).

Such human and poetic truths reveal the potential within man, and are far more enduring than historical truths that change as historical and archaeological scholarship advances and unravels their meanings. Poetic truths which, according to Aristotle, report things that might happen, as opposed to things that have happened, bring to light man's ability to cope with universal dilemmas. Classical literature, in all its genres, portrays universal human reality, confronting every person with her/his failure. Coping with irresolvable problems is part of the human condition, and a pre-condition for man's humanity. The more sensitive and revealing the work, the greater the confrontations it creates between protagonist (and reader) and irresolvable problems – like those of Hamlet, Oedipus, Jacob and Joseph; or the dilemma faced by Eve, who broke a clearly immoral law, that sought to proscribe the distinction between good and evil.

Great works of literature portray human dilemmas through the transgressions – legal and moral – of their protagonists. In this fashion, literary masterpieces, reveal the human capacity for evil (like David who arranges the murder of Uriah), for resisting evil (like Jeremiah who risks his life for the sake of peace), for despair at the futility of everything (like Koheleth), and for love (like the Shulamite in Song of Songs).

This type of revelation of human truths through poetic truths can be found in all classical literature – in which protagonists do not act like pathetic victims, but like valiant heroes grappling with fate and with themselves. In classical literature there are no absolute saints or happy endings, and no unequivocal moral; merely a unique portrayal of the human capacity for emotional greatness, depth of thought and sublime expression, and the ability to plunge into the depths of failure and human suffering and confront them (as in the works of Euripides, Shakespeare, Dostoevsky, and Primo Levi).

Poetic truth discovered through the experience of reading

classical works is accompanied by a rare sense of certainty that what has been revealed is indeed true, and requires no factual proof. The style and form of a work of literature afford emotional and spiritual pleasure, despite any shock we may feel at the sin and evil we discover therein. The feelings evoked by a great work of art or literature, include the excitement and pleasure we derive from form and content, from our encounter with the work's characters and their creator, from the unique forms of expression they employ, and from the ability of the whole to convey poetic and human truths.

One of humanistic education's greatest contributions to spiritual wealth and quality of life lies in the ability it imparts to its students, to derive such poetic experiences from classical works of art and literature.

Value-oriented education also conveys sensitivity to the human condition. Humanistic education strives to impart not only a sense of justice, but also compassion and generosity of spirit; the ability to look beyond the rules that derive from the moral meta-principles, or in the words of one of the sages of the Talmud: Jerusalem was destroyed because judgement was exacted there in accordance with the [strict letter of the] Law – and not with compassion.

Great literature exposes and condemns sinful actions, but does not judge its protagonists according to the strict letter of the law. Readers are led to re-examine the values by which we define actions as sins or transgressions, and wonder at their own capacity to sympathise and identify with sinful characters.

The feelings we experience toward literary figures are not of pity, but of kinship and identification, based on the human capacities we share. The depth of kinship between reader and protagonist does not depend upon the character's righteousness, but upon her/his human greatness, as conveyed by the author or artist. We identify more with King Lear than with his saintly daughter, and Raskolnikov is closer to us than the good Sonia. We feel a greater affinity with Joseph than with Judah, who was prepared to sacrifice himself in order to spare their father further pain. David inspires greater sympathy than Absalom, who sought revenge for his father's indifference to the rape of his sister Tamar.

Eve and Prometheus

Eve in Jewish mythology and Prometheus in Greek mythology, are literary figures that have become symbols of humanism in western culture. They symbolise man's liberation from ignorant submission to nature; rebellion against tyrannical laws designed to enslave her/him and deny creative freedom. Such freedom requires the type of thriving civilisation made possible by Prometheus' fire, and the knowledge bequeathed by Eve – the ability to distinguish and choose between good and evil, without which there could be no human nor creative development. Man's humanity would have been impossible, had s/he remained in rain forests like those of the garden in Eden, in a state of servility to nature or God, ignorant and unable to distinguish between good and evil, lacking shame that is a product of knowledge and conscience.

Today, with the threat of relativism and post-modernism looming over humanistic education, and with education in many places offering only professional training – cultivating narrow expertise and failing to develop students' humanity – we are in danger of a return to an Eden of cultural ignorance and inability to distinguish between good and evil.

It is incumbent upon humanistic education to reawaken interest, and engage students in these fundamental dilemmas of our humanity, employing – among other means – such classical works as the story of Eve in Genesis and Aeschylus' *Prometheus Bound*.

Developing Poetic Sensibility in Humanistic Education

Classical literature and art are essential to humanistic education, inasmuch as they are essential to the development of one's ability to discern the beautiful and the good in human works. Most of the entertainment products to which we are exposed – plays, films, television and radio programmes – are works of entertainment designed to elicit instinctive responses (car-chases, pornography, war and crime). In many ways, such spectacles of violence and murderous conflict are the modern equivalents of the ancient world's gladiatorial contests.

Rarely do plays and books designed primarily to arouse feelings of desire, horror or suspense – without emotion or thought – also evoke a poetic response to the work's unique style and meaning. Poetic experience comprises both instinctive thrill and emotion, aroused by the form and content of a work of art or literature. Thought and feeling are aroused by the human dilemmas they portray, while we marvel at their unique form.

Human beings need the excitement of suspense, laughter, pity and fear – afforded by dreams and daydreams, film and theatre, games, masks and costumes, competitions, etc. These sources of excitement appear to be realistic, but those who experience them are aware of the fact that they are figments of the imagination that cannot physically harm them.

Such games are common among children and adults alike. The function they fulfil differs from that of the poetic experience elicited by works of singular form and meaning – called "poetic" precisely because of their ability to evoke such a response.

We describe experiences by the things that evoke them, when we find ourselves unable to describe the experiences themselves. We thus refer, for example, to "sexual experience", "gastronomical experience", "experience of natural beauty", or "poetic experience".

Jewish Education and the Development of Artistic Sensibility

Exposing students to works of Jewish literature and art evoking a poetic response will open a world of pleasure to them, enriching their souls and spiritual lives. Works that evoke such a response will live on their memories, creating a bond with the collective memory of the culture in which they live. Such experiences broaden and deepen one's conscious and emotional ties to the cultures represented in the works that elicit them.

The poetic experiences evoked by masterpieces such as Ecclesiastes, Song of Songs, the novel of the Patriarchs and Matriarchs, songs from the Psalms, and works of religious and secular Jewish prose and poetry that have developed over the millennia that have passed since the completion of the Bible – will introduce students of Jewish humanistic education to the unique poetic works of their culture.

Developing poetic sensibility while exposing students to classical Jewish and other works from all periods also enhances their awareness of the historical and cultural heritage of the Jewish People and surrounding cultures. The pleasure they learn to derive from literary and artistic forms of expression and structure, combined with the excitement, emotions and thoughts that accompany such exposure, will strengthen their affinity with the works that represent the various periods and streams in Jewish culture.

Most people today do not receive a humanistic education. They are therefore accustomed to making due with works of entertainment, titillation and excitement that are forgotten once they are seen, and make no lasting impression on man's cultural consciousness. In most cases, the education system makes no attempt to contend with the spiritual poverty of those whose cultural diet consists entirely of works that elicit instinctive responses, without challenges, thought or emotion, without appreciation for uniqueness of form, or interest in the thoughts or lives of the people who made them.

A cultural life consisting entirely of entertainment and thrills, results in a dangerous sense of emptiness; an ailment of one's neglected spiritual and emotional organs. The emotional lives of those who consume only thrill-oriented entertainment are like the emotional lives of people who are sexually satisfied, but have never experienced love.

In humanistic education, the internalisation of moral values and development of emotional intelligence converges with the cultivation of artistic sensibility. This kind of education expands knowledge and hones students' ability to discern and appreciate works of art that evoke spiritual experiences; and through these – introduces them to the culture of their own and surrounding peoples. Systematic exposure to works of art and literature capable of evoking a poetic response in adolescents creates spiritual needs that a person continues to fulfil throughout her/his life. These needs can be satisfied through frequent encounters between the individual and the works that represent her/his culture. A person is not born with a thirst for unique or sublime poetic works, but only in man can the thirst for and pleasure derived from masterpieces of literature, art, music, painting, sculpture and the performing arts be cultivated.

Critical ability and spiritual independence are developed through exposure to masterpieces of literature and art, and through the cultivation of the ability to discern the unique elements of such works, the characteristics they have in common with other works, and the things that evoke a poetic experience, or feelings of repulsion.

Works that are judged "masterpieces" by the intellectual elite in a given cultural community for generations are re-evaluated by each and every generation. Works that are accepted as masterpieces by the new intellectual generation, become part of the system of aesthetic values that help foster critical ability and the capacity to enjoy literature and art.

"I-It" and "I-Thou" Relations in Humanistic Education

Buber distinguished between I-It and I-Thou relations. We perceive the "It" as a means to satisfying our needs, due to her/his role as a provider of services – as in the relationship between teacher and student, doctor and patient, vendor and buyer, ruler and subject, etc. The "Thou" or "You" is revealed in all others when we recognise them as unique personalities, above and beyond the functions they serve.

In love, art and faith, we develop an affinity with the "Thou" in others. We develop a sense of kinship with the unique personalities we discover in love and friendship; in great works of art and literature; and in the faith we have in man or God. By virtue of these things, the world we live in is enriched with beings who live in our souls, beyond the tangible and the present, like loved ones who live on after their deaths, and like God in the hearts and minds of those who believe in him.

Humanistic education that strives to develop sensitivity toward the other as an independent personality, cultivates familiarity with the great works of art and literature that centre on man as artist and artistic subject; and distinguishes between such works and works that present the other as "It", as a means, as a being whose entire essence lies in its narrative function, in the role it plays in the composition of a painting – a meaningless shape.

Developing artistic sensibility helps to develop sensitivity toward others, complementing the process of internalising moral values, while cultivating the capacity for enjoyment and poetic experience, and the ability to discern between artistic failures and achievements.

The sense of identification we experience with a literary protagonist both conflicts and converges with our critical approach to her/his character and actions. These feelings are part of the complexity of the poetic experience, and one of the sources of the kinship we feel with literary figures and their creators.

The encounter with an author or artist through her/his work and the characters s/he has created is a spiritual event that casts convention in a new light and brings us face to face with ourselves.

Rarely do we find the courage or opportunity to face ourselves and consciously experience the contrasts in our souls.

The protagonists of poetic works often embody these contrasts. Their literary features reflect the conflicts within our own souls – like Hamlet or Don Quixote, Faust, Job or Koheleth. And in these reflections, we encounter ourselves.

Our awareness of the singularity of the subjects of art and literature and their creators, contributes to the development of our awareness of individuality as one of man's defining traits. Awareness of deviations from the norm and of the unique nature of each and every individual develops our ability to accept others and ourselves.

Humanistic education includes systematic, interpretive and critical exposure to the classical works of the culture in which we live, contributing to our awareness of ourselves and our independence as thinking personalities, capable of experiences that enrich our spiritual world and our affinity with others.

Education as a Means to Humanisation

Classical humanistic education included exposure to music and the arts, literature and philosophy, rhetoric and dialogue, the culture of the body and aesthetics, mathematics and the sciences. As consciousness of universal human culture (in Hellenism and the Roman Empire) grew, so education in the cultures of surrounding peoples became a part of education in national culture.

In the Hellenistic period, many Jews were educated in the history of their people and its classical literature, as well as in the culture and classical works of Greece – including philosophy, literature and art. From that time to the present, in Judaism, as in other national cultures, there has been a tendency toward openness to world culture and its inclusion in national cultural education – as for example in the Middle Ages, in areas under Islamic and Christian influence; during the Renaissance and Age of Enlightenment, in central and western Europe; and today, in Israel and in all countries of the diaspora.

The poor in spirit, who perpetuate poverty of spirit through insular education enclosed in a single stream of Judaism, ignoring the creative wealth and variety of contemporary Judaism, also ignore world culture.

Education systems today, which offer only professional or scientific training, teach ignorance and disregard the cultural heritage embodied in the classical works of national and world culture. Their students are, however, exposed to whatever entertainment is in fashion – and only as long as it is in fashion; thrill-oriented productions that have lost all distinction as products of a particular national culture or expressions of a unique personality.

Without humanistic education, professional and specialist educational institutions produce effective professionals – "creatures with the head of a computer and the body of an animal", to quote one late-twentieth-century criminologist. Humanistic education is essential to the existence of human society. Erasmus asserted that "a man is not born human, but becomes human" (in a dialectic process: individuation is a product of socialisation); and Pico della Mirandola wrote, in his "Oration on the Dignity of Man" that only man possesses the ability to choose between brutish sensuality, angelic intelligence, vegetative indifference, and divine contemplation and understanding.

Man is the only creature that requires systematic education in order to realise its defining characteristic – being human. All other animals are what they are by virtue of the genetic and instinctive mechanisms with which they are endowed at birth. These mechanisms do not compel man to be human – they enable her/ him to become human. The genetic and instinctive mechanisms that propel man's development as a biological creature can just as easily enable her/him to become inhuman. Man's humanity is contingent upon the processes of humanisation or dehumanisation effected by education. Education that disregards the goal of humanisation, and fails to cultivate the spirituality and personality of the individual – becomes a destructive force in human society. The identity crisis suffered by many students in today's educational systems, undermines their ability to distinguish between good and evil, their commitment toward others and toward society, and their awareness of the rights that society owes to them.

Those who commit murder or other crimes, and are not motivated by economic or class disadvantage, act as psychopaths, lacking the ability to distinguish between good and evil, lacking sensitivity toward others as unique personalities entitled to certain rights. For society, this is one of the most dangerous effects of the lack of humanistic education.

Humanistic education that brings students to internalise man's obligations to others and to the society in which s/he lives, also brings them to internalise awareness of the rights to which every individual in society is entitled. Without such awareness, individuals cannot coexist within a human society capable of defending itself against the destructive forces from within.

Teaching Democracy and its Jewish Sources

Humanistic education also instructs students in democracy – not only as the most efficient form of government (in economic and defence terms), but as the only system that defends the rights of minorities and individuals, and affords cultural, educational and creative freedom.

Humanistic education offers students practical experience of the democratic process at every age, introducing them to the beliefs and opinions that fostered democracy among certain peoples at certain points in history. Such study and discussion equips students to deal with the problems inherent to democracy and the democratic process. One such problem concerns the principle of decision by majority, adopted by the sages of the Talmud – influenced by elements of Greek democracy, and rooted in the biblical verse "incline after a multitude". The very same verse however, cautions "thou shalt not follow a multitude to do evil", thereby revealing the difficulties involved in accepting the principles of democracy as fast rules. The commandment to accept and obey the decision of the majority is accompanied by a warning against being led astray by the evil decisions of an unjust majority (as in the case of German National Socialism, that rose to power through the democratic system).

Many of the talmudic sages concluded that the majority should be obeyed, but the opinion of the minority must be preserved, because it could prove right at some future date (Rabbi Judah). Under no circumstances however, should the right of decision be afforded to a single individual, even if that individual is God himself (as implied by the story of Akhnai's oven).

It is on the basis of these approaches in Jewish tradition that democracy developed in many Jewish communities, in which leaders were elected and rabbis appointed and replaced by community decision – as is the practice to this day in religious Jewish communities throughout the world.

It is also on the basis of these principles that the State of Israel was established as a democracy, in which both secular and religious leaders and movements were able to take part. It was only at a later stage that the demands of some of the religious movements came into conflict with democratic principles.

Education in democracy is based on the experience of the large democracies of the West – accumulated since the foundation and decline of Greek democracy – referring also to its manifestations in Judaism, and to Jewish philosophical and critical works on the subject.

Since the days of the Talmud, most Jewish thinkers have rejected the notion that any person can speak in God's name, or that one's status in a community of rabbis, or tradition, can confer infallibility (like the Pope). Jews have never hesitated to criticise or dissent from the opinions of halakhic or philosophical authorities widely acclaimed the greatest of their generation. Even Maimonides' *Mishneh Torah* was criticised by many, and failed to win acceptance as a binding constitution in most Jewish circles. Maimonides himself did not hesitate to condemn the words of talmudic sages, when he judged them liars and preachers of superstition – as in his letter to the community of Montpelier, in which he denounces astrology as a lie, yet cites talmudic sages who believed that a man's fate could be discovered by calculating the positions of the stars at the time of his birth.

There are of course, other, blatantly anti-democratic approaches within Judaism, whereby certain individuals and "Torah Giants" are afforded the right to rule on every matter, personal or political, halakhic or legal. Many Jewish religious groups continue to live in anti-democratic societies, both in terms of decision by majority and in terms of respect for human rights. Such anti-democratic approaches have become the province of a small and shrinking minority in Judaism.

The Jewish state was founded upon the democratic principles cited in Israel's Declaration of Independence, which coincide with the principles set forth in the American Declaration of Independence, and the United Nations' Declaration of Human Rights.

Humanistic education will familiarise students with democratic principles, universal humanistic values, related topics in Judaism, Jewish and non-Jewish works that express the fundamental ideas of democracy and the struggle against those who seek to destroy it.

Developing Linguistic Ability

Humanistic education cultivates that which distinguishes man from all other living things: language – the ability to communicate by means of verbal symbols that change their meaning according to context and the conventions of those who use them.

The first stage in the development of linguistic ability is the acquisition of a mother tongue, within the national culture in which one lives. In diaspora Judaism in the past, language skills developed at a very early age, due to the exposure of children to a number of languages in addition to their mother tongue – including Jewish languages (e.g. Hebrew, Yiddish, Ladino, Maghrebian, Tat and Jewish dialects of other languages), and the languages of the peoples among whom they lived.

Linguistic ability is enhanced by exposure to works of literature, drama, and television, radio and cinema that employ rich and varied language, to the extent that such exposure is accompanied by the cultivation of speech, dialogue, rhetoric, organisation and clarity of thought and expression. Humanistic education must therefore include the study of practical rhetoric – oratory, discussion and debate – from an early age, drawing upon all genres of literature.

The importance of developing language skills lies not only in the facilitation of communication between people for purposes of work or trade. The development of linguistic ability is essential to democracy, providing the means with which to exercise one's rights and fulfil one's duties; to listen, criticise, express opinions, or influence voters and elected officials alike.

Developed language skills and vocabulary allow one to experience a broad range of ancient and modern literature, to understand them and discuss them with friends and family, thereby enriching one's spiritual world and improving one's quality of life, by providing an additional field of interest, beyond one's daily needs or the pursuit of a career.

Human language – contrary to the communication systems of other animals – includes a world of concepts that transcend the tangible. These concepts become and represent "objects" that exist beyond the boundaries of existence and becoming – past and future. They express such things as aspirations, principles of evaluation and preference (values), ideals, and sources of anxiety.

All linguistic constructs – concepts, thought, conversation, morality, knowledge and literature of all kinds – are created within a national cultural environment, as it interacts with other cultures.

The development of linguistic ability – in one's own national language and in other languages – is one of the most important ways in which humanistic education strives to introduce its students to the culture in which they live, and enables them to realise their full human potential.

The study of the Hebrew Bible as the basis of Jewish national culture and of its national language is essential to humanistic Jewish education.

Part II

Bible as Literature

Biblical Literature and
its Role in Secular Jewish Culture

Chapter One

Approaching the Bible from the Perspective of Cultural Criticism

Although biblical criticism and Bible research do not engage in cultural criticism the study of cultural artefacts and phenomena throughout Jewish history they do address characteristic features of biblical literature, the roles the Bible has played in Judaism as a culture, and the roles it plays in the spiritual and cultural lives of contemporary secular Jews.

Jewish cultural criticism reveals the unique role the Bible has played, as the only fundamental element common to all forms of Judaism. All other bodies of Jewish literature, thought and art have functioned as an impetus and driving force within the boundaries of a particular form of Judaism, past or present, such as: Hellenistic Jewish literature in the Greek-speaking Jewish diaspora; the Zohar in Kabbalistic Judaism; the Talmud in rabbinic Judaism; the *Tanya* in Habad (Lubavitch) Judaism; Ahad Ha'am, Bialik and Buber in secular Judaism; modern Hebrew literature in Israeli Judaism.

Each of these Judaisms is wholly or partially ignorant of the fundamental texts of the other Judaisms. The Bible, to which all Jewish literature relates, is the only basis they have in common.

All Judaisms are familiar with the Bible or parts of it, and in all Judaisms biblical literature shapes national consciousness, the historical legacy upon which it is based, and messianic hopes (religious and secular) of return to a Jewish land and the re-establishment of political and cultural independence. In all Judaisms, the Bible has inspired a broad range of creative works: in painting, sculpture, writing, theatre and cinema, music and poetry.

The perspective from which cultural criticism approaches the

Bible differs from that of other disciplines, such as biblical criticism, biblical philology, comparative study of the Bible and other ancient near-eastern literature, traditional commentary sanctified by Orthodox Judaism, or Bible study in the context of Jewish history and archaeology.

Perceiving the Bible as the only fundamental element common to all Judaisms (cultures of the Jews), presumes that knowledge of the Bible does not afford knowledge of Judaism as it has developed over the two millennia that have elapsed since the Bible's completion. Clearly, Jews who view rabbinical literature as essential to their Judaism, will study – in addition to the Bible – Talmud, Midrash, commentary and philosophy ascribed to the Rabbis. It is equally clear that Jews for whom rabbinical literature does not sufficiently represent Judaism of the Hellenistic-Byzantine period, will select works they perceive as being more representative of that period, including: rabbinical works, Philo and Josephus, the New Testament, the frescoes of Dura Europos, *Exodus* by the playwright Ezekiel of Cyrenaica, poetry, parables and stories from the Apocrypha and the Pseudepigrapha, *Sefer Hayetzirah*, *Shiur Komah*, the virtual journeys of the Merkabah and *Hekhaloth* literature, the Dead Sea Scrolls of the Qumran sect, etc.

All of these different bodies of literature relate to the works of the Bible. Only a sample in which all are represented can accurately reflect the broad range of Judaisms that existed alongside, within and often against one another, during the Second Temple period and throughout a large part of the first millennium CE.

When I say that the Bible is the only fundamental element common to all Judaisms, I am not implying that it is the sole foundation of Jewish culture. The study of Judaism as culture shows how each Judaism has created it own distinctive elements, in addition to the Bible.

Questions for Discussion Regarding the Roles Played by the Bible in Judaism as Culture

– What roles does the Bible play or has it played in the past, in Judaism as the culture of the Jewish People?

– How have the literary works of the Bible influenced historical and cultural consciousness among Jews?

– In what sense does the Bible constitute a historical record of the prevailing cultural, spiritual and social reality in Judaism of the first millennium B.C.E?

– What unique characteristics does this literary anthology possess that enable it to play its various roles in the culture of the Jewish People?

– What roles does the Bible – both religious and secular works play in secular Jewish culture and education?

– How do the beliefs of secular Jews affect their approach to the Bible and other Jewish sources?

– Why is the prevailing approach among secular Jews that of Buber, whereby one's first encounter with the Biblical works should be "naked", without consulting traditional commentaries, midrash or scientific research?

The above questions are all addressed in the following chapters.

Secular Jewish Beliefs Shape Secular Jewish Approaches to the Bible

Secular approaches to the Bible – i.e. not bound by halakhic precepts, the authority of traditional religious commentary or the sanctity of the Bible – are a function of prevailing secular beliefs. These beliefs are not always clearly articulated in formal statements or even in the minds of secular Jews. They are expressed in their lives, in the education they give their children, in the selection of Jewish works they view as their "Jewish sources",

187

and the ways in which they read the works of the Bible – the only basis common to the cultures of all Judaisms.

With the proliferation of secular Judaism in the 18th and 19th centuries – becoming the predominant Jewish culture in the 20th century – the Bible began to resume a central role in Jewish education. It was once again viewed as the basis of Jewish nationhood – consciousness of a cultural and historical heritage common to all Jews in all times. In this sense, the Bible replaced the talmudic studies that continue to play a central role in Orthodox religious education. In secular and Reform religious Judaisms, the Bible is studied in a variety of ways: as the classical literature of Jewish culture, as the source of the monotheistic Jewish faith that has spread to so many other cultures in its Christian and Muslim forms, as a collection of historical records documenting the social and cultural life of the Jewish People during its formative period.

In order to acquaint ourselves with secular Jewish approaches to the Bible, we must first take a look at prevailing beliefs among secular Jews, and the influence these beliefs exert upon their adherents.

Among the secular Jewish beliefs that guide the ways in which biblical literature, its content and its messages, are approached:

– The Bible, God, moral values, and the precepts and laws derived from them, are all human creations.

– A "value" is a criterion for evaluation and preference of conduct, civil law, religious precepts, customs and traditions.

– Each human culture creates a different God. In all literature created by believers in God's existence beyond the realm of literature and art, laws and precepts are attributed to the created God – laws which adherents are bound to uphold even when they are not in keeping with universal moral values.

– The evaluation and acceptance of a given law or custom

is guided by belief in specific values, the goals of morality, knowledge of the reasons behind the laws and customs and possible consequences of adherence to them.

– The goals of morality and values are the improvement of mankind and the quality of human life. The attainment of these goals is contingent upon moral conduct, i.e. conduct guided by values in keeping with the principles articulated by Hillel and Immanuel Kant:

What is hateful to you, do not unto your neighbour.

Treat humanity always as an end and never as a means only.

There is no moral law that is not universally valid.

– Man's "natural" inclination toward morality and humanity is the result of education as a process of humanisation, practised within a moral society.

– Education and humanisation always occur within a national culture, because there are no a-national cultures.

Secular humanistic Jewish education must therefore develop knowledge/affinity for and understanding of Judaism as the culture of the Jewish People, and of the cultures within which Jews live and have lived in the past.

The educational process includes instruction in the culture of the national society within which one lives, and in the cultures of the peoples among which the nation resides, introducing students to the artefacts and phenomena of the cultural and historical heritage of the people and its foundations, such as knowledge of the Bible in Judaism.

The development of knowledge strengthens belief in the principles of morality. Historical knowledge provides examples of the possible consequences of one's actions, thereby strengthening belief in the advantages of all open, democratic societies that safeguard human rights – as opposed to the disadvantages of all closed, undemocratic societies in which tradition takes precedence over human rights. The inferiority of such societies is reflected in the quality of life enjoyed by the individual and by society, the level of economic development and standard of living, the state of personal and national security, the level of humanising education, and the development of human resources.

Separating the Plain Meaning
from Midrashic Interpretation

Biblical works should first be approached as complete works of literature, free of all deconstructive midrashic interpretation or academic analysis.

Presenting the literary works of the Bible in this fashion will enable us to write about the works themselves, and not about some other literary or academic work: midrash or "biblical criticism" for example. Associating each and every part of the Bible with these other literary works results in a distortion of the original work, both in terms of literature, and in terms of the influence it has exerted upon the historical and cultural heritage by virtue of which the Bible has played such an essential role in our cultural lives.

The character of Abraham for example, is distorted in the minds of those who associate it with the midrashic story of the boy Abraham who broke all of the idols in his father's shop, while the Abraham of the Bible in fact showed respect even toward El Elyon – the chief of all Canaanite deities – to whom he made a sacrificial offering, when a guest of the Jebusite priest Melchizedek, king of Jerusalem.

Readers of the Song of Songs cannot experience the grandeur of this masterpiece of erotic poetry, if they first understand it in keeping with its homiletic interpretation – in terms of love between Yahweh and the Catholic Church or the People of Israel.

The book of Job cannot be experienced as a poetic and philosophical work, among the most important and influential in Jewish culture, if we engage in a discussion of the various theories regarding its apparent composite parts, rather than simply reading the work itself.

The book of Genesis and the patriarch and matriarch narrative it includes, combine to form a contiguous unit, unique in world literature, which cannot be fully appreciated unless a clear distinction is made between reading it as a unit and engaging in the scholarly study of the Yahwist, Elohist and Priestly sources upon which the editors drew to create the text.

Historical Evidence in Biblical Fiction

All fiction, biblical fiction included, is a source of historical evidence. Fiction-writers, using their imaginations, create new situations out of familiar reality. The reality that is the raw material of their work reflects in the social, cultural and spiritual world of the fictional characters they create based on their own experiences.

Following Carlisle, we find literary characters – like King Arthur or Jesus of Nazareth – that have become historical figures, as a result of the roles they have played in national and world history, regardless of the historicity of the accounts of their lives, as presented in the stories that have shaped their characters.

That is how Ahad Ha'am viewed Moses – shaped by biblical narratives, retroactively becoming a historical figure when he began to play a part in Jewish history, religion and culture, social and political thought and its application in Jewish life. Although we lack proof of the "archaeological truth" of the events recounted in the Life of Moses, Ahad Ha'am asserts that the literary works that shaped Moses should be treated as if they had established a historical figure.

Fiction may therefore play two distinct roles:

1. Establishing literary characters – divine as well as human – capable of becoming historical figures.

2. Representing the social, cultural and spiritual reality within which the author lives or which he describes, as he weaves stories from authentic historical materials that he observes rather than invents.

Although the accuracy of the events recounted in the literary narrative cannot be determined, they offer a glimpse of the social and cultural reality they reflect, evidence that may be corroborated by historical research and archaeological findings. Knowledge acquired in this fashion builds a sense of heritage and develops the collective memory of a people represented in such founding literature.

The Bible functions in this capacity, developing the collective memory of the Jewish People. The Bible reveals, through such historical evidence, the social and cultural circumstances of the Jewish People during the period of its development as a distinct people. This historical evidence has played a role in fostering messianic hopes and beliefs – religious and secular – including belief in the eventual return of the people to the land of the Bible in order to establish an independent state within its confines – like the three states founded during the course of the first millennium BCE.

Scholarly theories regarding the lack of authenticity of the biblical account of events, do not change the role this historical evidence has played in the culture and history of the Jewish People. The fact that no archaeological evidence of the exodus from Egypt has been discovered to date – other than the 2,500-year-old writings we possess – does not change the importance Judaism has ascribed to the exodus as a fact, and the role the exodus narrative has played in world culture (see Michael Walzer, *Exodus and Revolution*).

Familiarity with historical and archaeological scholarship expands knowledge regarding the possible historical background of events recounted in biblical literature. Such studies are used in the field of biblical criticism, and help reveal anachronisms – references to things that cannot be assumed to have existed in a given period – such as the camels included in the gift Pharaoh bestowed upon Abram in return for the three days Sarai spent in his palace. (Other studies claim it is not an anachronism, since the remains of domesticated camels dating from the fourth millennium BCE have been found in Iran, and deposits of camel bones from the third and second millennia BCE have been found mixed with sheep bones in the Negev – apparently attesting to the existence of domesticated camels in the period to which the events in the story of Abram are attributed.)

In most cases, Biblical criticism – which employs historical and archaeological research – strengthens the historical evidence provided by the Bible in its description of social and cultural circumstances: in comparisons between the Hammurabi code and biblical family and inheritance laws for example, or in the picture that emerges (based on documents from the Amarna and Mari archives) with regard to literary works discovered in the twentieth century that predate those of the Israelites. According to the Bible, the Israelites worshiped Canaanite gods, similar in status and function to the gods described in Mesopotamian mythology; Mesopotamian royal documents refer to wars described in the Bible between invaders from Mesopotamia and the Israelite kingdoms; and the word "Israel" appears on an Egyptian stele dating from 1207 BCE. – as the name of an ethnic group that Pharaoh Merneptah (in the thirteenth century BCE) believes he has annihilated to the point of having no progeny or future.

The literature created by the Jewish People during the first millennium BCE reflects a multiplicity of opposing streams of thought, religion and belief. These can be observed in the testimonies of the prophets of Yahweh, who believed in God's exclusive divinity. The wanderings of the "Hapiru" or "A'piru" and their relations with the ancient cities of Canaan along the route of their migration throughout the Fertile Crescent – resemble those of the families of Abraham and Jacob (which names or similar ones appear in the aforementioned archives).

The Bible provides numerous examples of the affinity between the cultures of the peoples of the Fertile Crescent and that of the ancient "Hebrews", later called "Children of Israel" or "Jews". According to the Bible, the ancient Israelites spoke Hebrew ("Judean" in Jerusalem) – a language closely resembling Phoenician, and the Children of Israel were frequently upbraided for worshiping many of the Canaanite divinities, alongside or instead of Yahweh.

Based on the evidence provided by biblical literature, belief in life after death was not widespread among the Israelites, and none of the biblical authors profess such beliefs (with the exception of the author of the book of Daniel). The Bible does however attest to the existence of deviant beliefs, and to the practise of necromancy – as in the story of Saul's encounter with the deceased Samuel.

Much of biblical literature reflects the development and singularity of the moral monotheism of the Prophets, which even if shared only by a minority of Jews at the time, exerted a decisive influence over the development of Judaism and of western culture as a whole. The Prophets' most original and revolutionary innovation was their commitment to social justice – above religious and ritual requirements, i.e. animal sacrifice and prayer.

The Prophets thus laid the foundations of western social justice, and inspired those who many centuries later would see the values of social justice as the standard by which all laws – religious and civil alike – must be judged.

The biblical texts are archaeological records – some of them written over two thousand years ago – copies that are at least in part remarkably accurate: witness the comparison between the book of Isaiah discovered at Qumran and the Isaiah that appears in the thousands of printed editions of the Bible.

The antiquity of the biblical texts reinforces their status as historical documents reflecting prevailing circumstances during periods close to the times in which they were written. The proliferation of printed editions of the Bible has caused many to forget the extreme antiquity of biblical literature, some of which was translated as early as the third century BCE.

In all of these senses, the Bible should be considered a collection of historical records reflecting observed rather than invented reality, although fiction writers do not provide legally admissible factual accounts of events, but reality reflected in the plot, the characters, and the words the author feels they should utter.

Just as the Iliad and the Odyssey should be viewed as reflecting the social and cultural milieu of certain tribes that lived prior to the eighth century BCE and were later called "Greeks", so the stories of the Bible should be seen as attesting to and reflecting the social and cultural reality of the Hebrew and Israelite tribes later called "Jews", who lived in the Middle East and the Canaanite lands in the first millennium BCE and perhaps even in the second half of the previous millennium.

Those who have obsessively and vocally sought to deny the existence of the ancient Israelites based on the lack of unequivocal archaeological evidence, have ignored the first rule of any historical or legal investigation that "the absence of evidence is not evidence of absence".

The wild theories of the Israel-deniers – whereby rebellious Canaanite slaves fled the Canaanite cities and settled in the hills of Samaria and Judea, creating an Israelite history for themselves, beginning with the Exodus from Egypt – are invented reality, reflecting only the imaginations of their authors.

When faced with the Merneptah Stele – dating from 1207 BCE and containing a direct reference to "Israel" – the deniers of ancient Israel's existence merely acknowledge bewilderment, although admittedly, the only document attesting to Israel's existence is in fact a declaration of its destruction and thus non-existence.

The Bible in Secular Education - Humanisation in Judaism as National Culture

The aim of all education is the humanisation of the being called man – capable of attaining humanity and acquiring social and cultural behaviour, possessing moral inclinations, as well as the critical ability to distinguish between good and evil. This aim can be achieved through education in national culture, since there is no such thing as non-national culture.

This type of education involves two opposing tendencies:

1. Adapting man to society and its conventions, while conveying its historical and cultural legacy, effecting the internalisation of universal moral values, and the acquisition of skills essential to the individual's ability to study and work within that society.

2. Promoting individuality, creativity and a critical approach to the conventions of society and to the products of its historical and cultural heritage, striving to realise the unique potential of each individual, and fostering knowledge of the rights and obligations that stem from membership in national, communal and familial society.

These two tendencies are served by education and introduction to the classical works that lie at the core of national
and surrounding cultures.

Developing a familiarity with these works as well as an
emotional bond to them, facilitates both the adaptation of the
individual to society and the individuality that places her/him at
odds with that society and culture.

Fostering Poetic Sensibility and Critical Ability

Prevailing secular Jewish beliefs advocate furthering
knowledge, and fostering the ability to derive pleasure and spiritual
enrichment from biblical works, alongside a general critical
approach, unencumbered by religious or other constraints.

Developing an aesthetic and ethical critical approach to the
works of the Bible, the divine and human characters, lessons and
precepts they present, renders the Bible a source of emotional
and poetical gratification, enriching the reader's affinity toward
the foundation of Jewish culture and its relation to other cultures.

Furthering these goals requires familiarity with the literary units
of the Bible, noting their form and content as if they were complete
literary works, alongside and beyond the discussion of their various
sources and components.

Reading and contemplating works of art and literature are a
part of the aesthetic and ethical pursuits and education of every
cultured person, requiring – in the words of Coleridge – the
"willing suspension of disbelief".

We must experience the poetry, while exercising our ethical
critical abilities, and suspending scientific criticism that seeks to
reduce the works of Shakespeare to their respective sources, or in
terms of biblical scholarship: determine what is of "Yahwist",
"Elohist" or "Priestly" origin.

Approaching biblical works as integral units, even if scholarship has shown the book of Job for example, to be a "blemished perfection" (as it is termed by Yair Hoffman in his excellent book on Job), ensures an encounter with the philosophical drama Job, before scholars have broken it down into its component parts.

Discussion of biblical literature must first revolve around its poetic value, the human and ethical messages that stem from the manner in which the narrative and its protagonists are presented, the moral dilemmas that arise in the lives of the story's protagonists and in our own, as with the short account of the conflict between the literary figures God and Eve, resulting from God's original sin: denying man knowledge and morality by forbidding Adam and Eve to eat from the tree of knowledge of good and evil. Knowledge is both "conscience", and "consciousness" of the distinction between good and evil.

Fiction Reflects and Embodies Human Experience

A great literary work has the ability to introduce characters and circumstances on a plane that lies beyond historical and scientific discoveries. Science, like everyday language, speaks in generalities, assigning concepts and names to them. Human experience consists of individuals, to which only language and scholarship refer in general terms, abstractions and laws. People long to encounter the unique – in literature and art, which reflect and relate to the singular and the ephemeral.

The power of literature lies in its ability to penetrate the barriers of generalisation that stand between us and human reality. The desire to reach out and touch the individual, whose unique personality is lovingly revealed to us in a work of art, is an emotional need we all share. Art and literature create a new and autonomous reality that challenges as well as reflects our lives.

The surprise that accompanies our encounters with the human experience in art entails the sudden realisation that the figures represented - despite their foreignness, and the differences between us – have the ability to represent us.

The reality lived by members of every culture includes the reality portrayed in the classical literature to which they have been exposed. From kindergarten to high school, most Israelis become acquainted with the reality and protagonists portrayed in biblical literature. This awareness exists on many different levels of experience and knowledge, just like awareness of present social and cultural circumstances.

The reality depicted in great works of literature forms part of the spiritual reality common to members of all national cultures. Art and literature – in their form and content, figures and stories – help us escape the sense of transience, the flow of events, the changes and immediate responses to change, we experience in our everyday lives.

Literature reveals the universal – the moral dilemmas we all share, but the full meaning of which only writers and artists have the ability to bring to light – through the particular. By describing the lives of unique individuals (as we are all unique), literature affords us the opportunity to encounter life on a symbolic level – like the life of Jacob, who overcame his destiny and his god, and became Israel, like that of Don Quixote, who became disenchanted with reality and lived his own nobility and battle for justice in his imagination.

While everyday life represents only itself, life as portrayed in literature at its best, represents the human dilemmas and potential we all share. Such works, like many of the books of the Bible for example, depict what Aristotle called "poetic truth" – not an account judged by the extent to which it corresponds to "what really happened", but a story that reveals potential: "what could have happened", to the story's readers as well as its protagonists. The power of the story of Isaac's binding is, inter alia, its ability to focus our minds and hearts on the idea of sacrificing that which we love most in the world for the sake of our beliefs.

Therein lies the universality of classics, their ability to transcend national culture, to become classics in other national cultures as well: the *Iliad, Hamlet, War and Peace, The Trial, Job, Jonah,* or the two versions of creation at the very beginning of the Bible, which are an allegory for the human condition – man's capacity to create and resemble God (knowledge of good and evil being prerequisites for man's humanity) or to repress knowledge and freedom; in the words of Pico della Mirandola, man's ability to be "as base as a devil and as sublime as an angel".

Chapter Two

Literary Genres in the Bible

Biblical literature comprises all of the main literary genres present in the European literature it has influenced, including:

Lyrical Poetry – Hymns, as in the book of Psalms, complete with instructions for performance and musical accompaniment; secular poetry, such as the poems that make up the Song of Songs, the song of Lemech, or the satirical poem attributed to Yotam on the subject of elections in Shekhem and the trees who sought a king.

Epic Poetry – Songs like those of Deborah and Moses, recounting tales of war and bravery, heroes and divine succour in battle.

Sagas – Like that of the patriarchs and matriarchs in the book of Genesis, recounting the stories of the members of a family that would later become a nation; with the twists of plot, dialog and streams of consciousness that shape unique literary characters. The saga, which tells the stories of four generations, begins with Abram and Sarai, who set out for a new land, leave it and return – as do their descendants of the third and fourth generations, at which time the family splits into separate tribes inhabiting different regions.

Rhetoric – Such as the sermons collected by the redactors in separate books, each attributed to one of the prophets of Yahweh; or other works of rhetoric that stand as independent literary units within larger works, like Judah's monologue, Nathan's sermon on the "poor man's lamb", Samuel's sermon against monarchy, Micaiah's sermon to Ahab, etc.

The Philosophical Drama of Job, and the poetic monologues in Ecclesiastes, rare works that reflect currents perceived by Dubnow as anti-religious, clearly challenging God's ability to influence life and nature, and the justification of a god capable of entering a pact with Satan to bring a holocaust upon the family of a righteous man such as Job.

Historiography in the books of Exodus, Judges, Samuel, Kings, Ezra, Nehemiah and Chronicles – Providing methodical accounts of the linear history of the Jewish People, from its birth at the time of the Egyptian Exodus to the return of a fraction of its members from Babylonian exile. These works are written in ancient historiographical style, based upon source materials rather than research. Such sources include oral traditions and variant accounts of the same events, representing different approaches to Jewish history – as demonstrated by Yaira Amit in her book on biblical historiography.

Proverbs – A large collection of proverbs, reflecting a variety of beliefs and ideas, philosophical and religious approaches, traces of which can be found in other biblical works.

Mystical literature – Represented by the book of Daniel, an unusual work that also relates to the world beyond, to the quickening of the dead and other supernatural events; as if the redactors wished to include a sample of this rare genre as well, in the anthology representing the culture of the entire people.

Short Stories – Classical works in this genre, that focus on plot rather than character development, and whose narrative structure guides readers to a specific point the author wishes to make, affording special meaning to the entire story. Such works include: Jephthah and the sacrifice of his daughter – The story of Jephtah – son of a harlot, shunned by his brothers, but chosen by them as their leader in wartime – who promises to sacrifice to God whatever shall come to meet him when he returns home victorious. He is thus compelled to sacrifice his beloved daughter on the altar of Yahweh after she has returned from the mountains, where she goes with her friends to mourn her lost youth.

The story of Deborah – The first woman to be judge, poet, and victorious commander with the help of another woman, Jael the Kenite, who lured Sisera into her tent, and murdered him as lay at her feet.

Jonah – A surrealistic story included in the book of Prophets, although not a work of rhetoric, but rather an event-filled narrative, leading up to the final dialogue between Jonah and God, on the subject of an eternal moral and political dilemma.

Esther – A short political romance, written in realistic style as a historiographical account of the thwarting of history's first "final solution". Based on life at the Persian imperial court, the story leads the reader from amusement to horror at the revenge exacted by the scheme's spared victims.

Biographies of the Prophets – Presented alongside their rhetorical works. The greatest of these is the book of Jeremiah, the prophet and poet credited with authorship of Lamentations – a landowner from Anathoth who left his estate (which he continued to run from afar) to wander the streets of Jerusalem denouncing the social injustice caused by the city's rich and the corruption at the royal court, as well as the Jewish People's betrayal of its covenant with Yahweh in violating the principles of justice and charity and in taking part in the cults of other peoples' gods – including the sacrifice of sons and daughters by their parents on the altar of Molech in the Hinnom Valley.

When Zedekiah forges an alliance with Egypt, thereby betraying the Babylonian king who had appointed him, and Nebuchadnezzar subsequently lays siege to Jerusalem, Jeremiah dares to demand that the Judean king save the city and its temple by surrendering to the Babylonian forces. As a one-man opposition, Jeremiah is hounded by the civil and religious authorities, who condemn him to a slow death by sinking into the mire that filled the dungeon in which the king's officers had imprisoned him. He is rescued and brought to the palace by the Ethiopian eunuch Ebed-melech, but adamantly continues to advocate surrender, which he believes to be both essential and right. From his new prison, he shouts tirades against the royal court and the people to his secretary.

At the end of the story, after Jerusalem is laid waste by the Babylonian armies and the exiled Zedekiah's eyes are put out, Jeremiah chooses to remain at the court of Gedaliah, Nebuchadnezzar's Jewish governor, who tries to reconstruct Judea, but is murdered by Jewish terrorists, guests in his home. This political assassination continues to resound in Jewish history through the only annual fast day dedicated to the memory of an individual – the governor of the Babylonian occupation of Judea, whom Jeremiah supported until his own exile to Egypt at the hands of Gedaliah's murderers.

This story exemplifies the unique character of the institution of prophecy in ancient cultures: an active, critical and menacing moral opposition, conducted for centuries by lone individuals, who lacked party, family or tribal backing, but whose words have been preserved within Jewish cultural and historical heritage, and have served as one of the foundations of western humanism.

Historical Novels – Developing complex and multi-faceted literary characters that have become, thanks to the works that have moulded them – historical figures that have shaped the course of Jewish history. These works include:

The Life of Moses – Stretching over four of the five books of the Pentateuch, and including the first autobiographical monologue in our literature, in which Moses, in the book of Deuteronomy, tells his version of his life story. Moses (an Egyptian name) was adopted by an Egyptian princess and lived as a prince in Pharaoh's court until compelled to flee to the desert, after having murdered an Egyptian who had been beating a Hebrew. He then married the daughter of the head of a desert tribe, whose flocks he tended, until he heard the voice of God, emanating from a burning bush that was not consumed.

The God Moses encountered was unique among the known gods of the ancient world: invisible, without shape or form, constituting all that will be, and whose name was "I will be what I will be". Moses returns to Egypt to guide his people, against the will of its leaders, and convinces Pharaoh that the disasters that have plagued Egypt and killed its children will come to an end only if he allows Moses' people to go forth into the desert.

Moses leads a people of slaves – including slaves of other nationalities as well – into the desert, where he is accused by the masses of having brought them to the brink of annihilation as a result of their liberation – the hunger, thirst and suffering freedom entails. Were there indeed not enough graves in Egypt that Moses had to bring them to die in the desert?

The story underscores Moses' loneliness, vis-à-vis his people and his God. When he is accused of nepotism by his political opposition, he buries its leaders alive in the desert. He barely manages to convince God not to destroy his ungrateful people, for fear of what the Egyptians might say when they found out. Moses is the man who gave his people the commandments of morality as a covenant with God. He is also the one who broke the tablets upon which the commandments had been written by the finger of God's hand. The man who declared "thou shalt not murder", orders his army to kill three thousand of the revellers of the golden calf – a representation of the God who had taken them out of Egypt, in the eyes of the People and the high priest.

Moses appears as a moral, cruel and lonely figure, residing outside the camp, in a tent he erected for himself and as a place in which to meet with his God, without altar, sacrifice or image;

only a pillar of smoke and cloud – substances that are both created and consumed at the same time. His first wife calls him a "bridegroom of blood". He afflicts his sister Miriam, the dancer and poet, with leprosy, for having opposed his later marriage to an Ethiopian woman – although it is Miriam who saved his life as an infant, when she placed him in a basket upon the Nile and brought her mother to the Egyptian princess, to serve as the child's nursemaid.

After forty years, when the People finally stands on the frontier of the promised land, on the eastern side of the Jordan, Moses – the elderly leader who refuses to relinquish his position – still stands at their head. His younger lieutenant, Joshua, goes with him alone to the mountains, from which they can observe the land that was the goal of their long journey of liberation. From atop Mount Nebo, Moses sees the land he will not enter. Joshua returns alone from his journey with Moses, replacing him as leader of the tribes, and to this day, the story concludes, no one knows the place in which Moses is buried.

Kafka said that the story of Moses represents the fate of all men: at the end of their days, they stand on the verge of achieving their goals, see the promised land from afar and die on its frontier.

The plots of the Bible's other historical novels are no less complex, developing the multi-faceted characters that have served as a paradigm for European prose and drama – from Shakespeare to Tolstoy, from Dostoevsky to Proust. Works such as:

The Life of Saul – Israel's first king, one of the saddest figures in the Bible. He was crowned by Samuel, who opposed the very institution of the monarchy, but conceded to the people's desire to be like all the nations, that they might stand up to the Philistine incursions. Samuel expressed his opposition to monarchy when he selected Saul, a driver of she-asses, the tallest man in the land, to be king.

Saul became mentally unbalanced when he was suddenly

crowned king over all the tribes of Israel, to lead them against the triumphant Philistine armies. When his people emerged victorious, thanks to a shepherd boy named David who split the skull of the swaggering Philistine champion, he began to suffer fits of depression and rage. In order to soothe his troubled mind, the shepherd boy, who was also skilled musician, was brought before him – the same David who was admired by all the women in the land, for his success in battle and for having consequently won the hand of the king's daughter.

In a sudden fit of rage, Saul tried to kill the haughty young musician. Saul's paranoia caused him to suspect, rightly, that David wished to rule in his stead. It was only due to Saul's daughter Michal, whom David had wed, that he succeeded in escaping when Saul's soldiers came to arrest him at home. Despite Saul's victories against the Philistines and the Amalekites, Samuel accused him of having failed to fulfil his duty to the God of Israel, since he had not slain the entire foreign population he had conquered – women, children and livestock included. Samuel further subverted Saul's rule by anointing the young David as future king of Israel. Even Jonathan, Saul's son, helped David, whom he loved, to escape his father's wrath. David provoked the king, demonstrating his superiority by carrying out nocturnal raids upon Saul's camp, that the king might know that he lives only by David's grace.

The death of Samuel – Saul's primary adversary, who made his life a misery by crowning him king – breaks the heart of this disturbed and insecure man. Although Saul had driven out all of the necromancers – those who conducted mystical séances in which they summoned spirits from the world of the dead to converse with the living – he now sought out one who had survived, because he could not stand the absence of Samuel from his life. His encounter with the dead Samuel however, was no better than his encounters with the prophet while he was still alive.

Saul knew that his end was near. David had established a private army, aided by the Philistines, who stepped up their attacks. By the time Saul and his army were defeated in the decisive battle at Mount Gilboa, all that remained to Saul was to ask his armour bearer to thrust him through with his sword; and when he refused, to fall on the sword himself.

The Life of David – Like a sequel and counterpoint to the historical novel recounting the life of Saul. Although it was Saul who founded the united kingdom, David reaped all the glory – even though he collaborated with the Philistines, divided the kingdom before reuniting it following his victory in the civil war, eliminated the descendants of the previous king, retained a court prophet who reprimanded him but bowed to his authority, and behaved like a ruthless despot. He is sane, sober and successful even when his succes s is tragic, like his victory over his son Absalom's rebel army.

The novel has contributed to David's historical image as a young, charming, triumphant, poet, warrior and king of all Israel, from whose descendants the messiah will be born. The authors endowed him with heroism and success from early youth – as a shepherd fighting beasts of prey, daring to challenge the Philistine giant and killing him with the first shot, the king's son-in-law, a skilled musician, who loved the kings son and was beloved of women.

The novel also portrays David however, as the leader of a band of desperate thieves, who flock to him and obey his every command, live off plunder and the extortion of landowners, and gladly join the Philistines – Israel's enemies – seeking even to join the Philistine army in the decisive battle in which Saul and Jonathan were to find their deaths. When David hears of the deaths of Saul and Jonathan, he kills the messenger who brought him what should have been good news, and utters one of the most beautiful laments in the Bible – a song of David's love for Jonathan, which was more wonderful to him than the love of women.

In emphasising these apparent contradictions in David's actions and personality, the story shapes a living, breathing figure, who sins and loves, is ambitious, cruel and overbearing: the essence of human potential, often unfulfilled but present in all of us.

David appears in this historical novel as flesh and blood, a man who is certainly real, even if he never actually existed. Its authors do not portray him in an idealised fashion. It is history and culture art, legend, tradition, song and commentary – that have reinvented David as a model king, forebear of the messiah. The Biblical literature describing David, like all of the realistic works in the Bible, reveals the humanity of the living man within the literary figure, not the desired traits of an imaginary hero.

David did not fight on the side of the enemy at Mount Gilboa, because he was cast out of the Philistine army as it went to battle against Saul. With both Saul and Jonathan dead in battle, David founded his own kingdom at Hebron, splitting the kingdom of Israel, initiating a civil war, and bringing about the systematic assassination of nearly all members of Saul's family. Following the murders, David's tiny kingdom assumed control over the tribes of Israel, and he established a site for Yahweh there. Instead, he built himself a house of cedar in the City of David, from which he could look out upon the roofs of the city's inhabitants, until one day, he spied Bathsheba bathing on her rooftop. He immediately had her brought to the palace, lay with her and sent her home. When he discovered that she was carrying his child, he summoned her husband Uriah, who served in David's army, encamped at Rabbah, and tried to get him to sleep at home with his wife, that the pregnancy might be attributed to him. When Uriah refuses, he seals his own death. David sends him back to his commander with a letter detailing the method of execution: set Bathsheba's husband in the forefront of the battle and retreat suddenly, leaving him to face enemy alone. Now David can bring the widow of a soldier in his army to the palace to join his harem.

David's court prophet, Nathan, reproves him with the parable of the poor man's lamb, but being a court prophet, does nothing further. He does not go out to the city squares to decry the adultery and murder committed by the king, like prophets not bound to the royal house. The parable of the lamb that the rich man stole from the poor man who loved it and even slept with it, takes an unequivocal stand regarding the primacy of justice over royal prerogative. This position however, changed nothing in David's life or court.new capital in a city belonging to neither kingdom – the ancient Jebusite city of Jerusalem, which David cunningly took by surprise. Jerusalem henceforth became the capital of the united kingdom. Already in the days of David's grandson Rehoboam however, ten of the tribes of Israel seceded to form their own kingdom, building two temples to Yahweh the golden calf, and saying "what portion have we in David?"

David's personality is given greater depth through the stories that highlight his cruelty and ingratitude toward Michal, to whom he owes his life. After having neglected her for so long, he wrests her from her new husband and cloisters her in a house in Jerusalem, where she remains, childless, until the end of her days, ashamed of David when she sees him dancing and uncovering his nakedness at the head of a riotous procession escorting the ark of the covenant with Yahweh to Jerusalem.

The king's interest in running the kingdom (extended on both banks of the Jordan by his generals) wanes, as his children multiply and grow up. David does not even intervene in court life when his son Amnon brutally rapes his daughter Tamar, sister of Absalom – who takes revenge upon his father for his indifference. Absalom takes his father by surprise, leading a military revolt against him, forcing him to leave Jerusalem, laying with the king's wives before the whole city, and pursuing the exiled David, who had established an alternative capital on the other side of the Jordan. When the war is over, and David's forces have defeated the rebels, the king's heart is broken by the death of his son Absalom – his enemy, most beloved of all his sons.

The authors of the David narratives, like those of all of the historical novels in the Bible, do not judge their protagonist. They create, develop and shape him, like the great prose writers who followed in their footsteps, while discovering their character's unique humanity, which is in fact the embodiment of life, of the potential traits and weaknesses present in all people.

In the epilogue, David appears as a man who is no longer interested in anything other than his young love, who lies with him and warms the elderly king, disappointed with his life. He has no interest in the future of his kingdom or the court intrigues surrounding his future heirs' struggles for the throne. Finally, David yields to the alliance forged between the court prophet Nathan and Bathsheba, by whose initiative her son Solomon is crowned "with the crown wherewith his mother crowned him", as the author of Song of Songs wrote. Solomon quickly gains fame, but after a short period, according to the authors of this novel, David's kingdom crumbles, his son chastises the people with whips and his grandson promises to chastise them with scorpions. The people abandon him, bringing about the demise of the great kingdom of Jerusalem, reduced to the tiny kingdom of Judah – the only part of David's realm to return to life after many centuries of destruction and exile.

In all of the historical novels in the Bible – from the patriarch and matriarch narratives in Genesis to the Life of David – the authors present their realistic accounts as historiography, describing reality, rather than fiction. Their power of persuasion rests entirely upon their literary merits. They provide no evidence that the events portrayed, in fact represent reality, but rather create their own unquestionable reality, the existence of which – like all reality created by great novelists – does not depend upon the physical evidence archaeologists have unearthed or failed to unearth to date. Andrei Bolkonsky, Pierre Bezuhov and Natasha Rostova undoubtedly exist, like the Karamazovs, Proust's Marcel or Joyce's Bloom – like biblical literature's Abraham, Moses, Saul and David. They exist in our cultural reality, and require no proof of their existence.

The uniqueness of the Bible's historical novels stems from the role they have played in the culture of the Jewish people and other peoples it has influenced. While the protagonists of modern novels form part of our experiences and moral consciousness, the protagonists of the biblical novels influence the historical consciousness that has marked the course of Jewish history.

Belief in the historicity of Moses, Saul and David has played a central role in the development of the consciousness and belief in the three-thousand-year existence of the Jewish People, whose present-day members follow in the footsteps of a people born at the time of the Exodus from Egypt, under the leadership of Moses. The actions of the characters in this body of literature have the power to effect change in our own lives, to bring the Jewish national movement to strive for and achieve the return of the Jewish People to the Land of Israel in the twentieth century, to cause Jewish political parties to struggle with one another over the integrity of Jerusalem as if it had always been the eternal capital of the Jewish People, to wrangle over what may be sacrificed for the sake of sovereignty over the tombs of Abraham and his family at the Cave of Machpelah, to hold rulers and prime ministers to the same standards by which Nathan judged David or Jeremiah Zedekiah.

In this sense, corroboration or refutation of theories regarding the "historicity" of the stories of Moses and David, or whether this historicity differs from that of the stories of Ahab and Herod, are of no importance. It is the quality of the literature that affords its protagonists their quality of reality, and culture that determines the roles they will play – regardless of what archaeologists have or have not yet discovered.

Religious, Cultural and Ideological Pluralism Reflected in Various Works of the Bible
Two Versions of Creation: The Poem of Creation of the Universe and the Story of God's Original Sin.

The poem of creation with which the biblical anthology opens, and which Longinus admired in late antiquity (in his book *On the Sublime*), begins to fashion the literary figure God – in man's image. God, both male and female in the creation poem, creates man in her/his image. The divinity's humanity is underscored by her/his exultation and pride upon completing each day of creation and admiring her/his handiwork, deeming it "good" and even "very good". At the end of a hard work-week however, even God needs to rest, and s/he desists from all labours of creation, thereby inventing the Sabbath and its laws – the first egalitarian laws in history.

The author of the creation poem perceives the creation of the universe and life on Earth as an evolutionary process: from the burst of light energy within the void, the creation of celestial bodies and their orbits that create time and divide it into day and night, the division of the void into heaven and earth, the gathering of the waters, the creation of life in the waters and their incursion into air and land as multiplying creeping things, to the appearance of mammals, which at the height of their development – man, male and female, both first and equal at the time of their creation – come to dominate the Earth and everything in it.

The second version of creation differs from the first in most of its narrative and ideological elements. God exists within the world rather than beyond it, he creates life through deeds rather than words, provides his garden with an irrigation system, sculpts with his hands that which he plants in the garden of Eden, one of the Earth's regions, fashions the statue of man and breathes life into him. When it becomes apparent that "it is not good that the man should be alone", he sculpts small and large statues in the forms of all the animals, and breathes life into them. God is disappointed when man gives them all names indicative of their inability to assuage his loneliness. The author describes how his farmer-sculptor protagonist becomes a gifted surgeon, anaesthetises the man he had created, removes a rib from his body, and using an ancient cloning method, creates a helper for man – not first-created like Adam, but the last creature placed upon the Earth, a creature with a distinct vocation: to be watchman and gardener's assistant in God's garden.

God's last creation rose up against him. All of the animals, including the human male, were willing to accept the only law in the world – that which forbade knowledge and morality, or as it is termed by the author, "knowledge of good and evil". Only the woman, created from man, refuses to come to terms with this draconian law, is intrigued by the fruit of the tree of knowledge "to be desired to make one wise", eats of the forbidden fruit of distinction between good and evil, thereby crossing the threshold from "animality" to humanity, and also gives the man with her to eat, thus saving all of humanity from psychopathy (the lack of distinction between good and evil), and from eternal life within an unchanging natural state.

In light of the first woman's success in her insurrection against God's original sin – trying to keep knowledge and morality from man – the author develops the theme of confrontation between human and divine figures, a central motif in many of the biblical works.

Since Eve, like Prometheus in Greek mythology, rebelled against the draconian laws of the ruling divinity, Yahweh punishes her and all members of her sex, with pain and sadness during childbirth, with subjugation by men who do not suffer such travails, and worst of all, with desire and love for the men who will dominate them in every patriarchal society from that time to the present.

This primordial curse that defines the socio-biological tragedy of women, could only have been written by a woman, claims the great literary critic Harold Bloom (in The Book of J). The story and its manifold meanings – according to the literalist and midrashic commentaries that have accompanied the text for tens of generations – reverberate to this day, in art and philosophy throughout the world. Misogynists like Augustine tried to make it the story of woman's original sin. Those who followed in his footsteps made "original sin" an article of their faith, establishing the universal guilt of all human beings born of woman – who is inherently sinful by virtue of being a descendent of the first defiant woman, who succeeded in defeating God.

The ability of a great work of literature to transcend the culture within which it was created, is demonstrated by the history of the Garden of Eden story, in the second chapter of Genesis. Like every classical work of literature, this story continues to play a role in Hebrew language and culture, while translations fail to convey its full literary intensity. It is difficult to find a translation for the meaning-laden expression used to describe Eve's moment of indecision and truth, when she sees that the fruit of the tree of knowledge is "desired to make one wise" (*nehmad lehaskil*) – an amalgam of playful sensuality and irrepressible intellectual curiosity.

In order to emphasise the importance and greatness of Eve's rebellion against God, the author gives voice to the fears of Elohim (the plural form of the divine) that man was actually becoming like them, no longer merely a reflection of their image. Having acquired knowledge, what was to prevent man from eating of the tree of eternal life? What pre-eminence would God then have over man?

Due to divine fear, man was released from the Garden of Eden and, equipped with the knowledge given to them by Eve, her descendents began to create and produce, to develop civilisation and economy, culture and art – as described in the story of the sons of man who left the Garden in the region of Eden and began to conquer the Earth and all its lands.

Human creation begins to rival divine creation, thenceforth the literary figure God will clash with human literary figures in the great works of biblical literature – from the tales of Abraham, Jacob and Moses, to the stories of Jonah and Job.

How Perceiving God as a Literary Figure Affects Approaches to the Bible and its Place in the Moral Education of its Readers

In secular Jewish culture, the prevailing belief is that God – a character in biblical literature – was created by man. In Genesis, God was made in the image of man (male and female), in other works he is depicted as an incorporeal figure, omnipotent like

216

nature and human in character, speech and temperament. Yahweh, god of Israel, created in the Israelite literature of the Bible, differs from the gods of other peoples, also created by man in the ancient myths of the Fertile Crescent and Greece. Contrary to the many gods created in the myths and literature of polytheistic peoples, Yahweh is alone in the world, without family and without a specific abode (like Olympus). Yahweh is portrayed in the Bible as a god who preceded the universe and nature, which he created out of the void and with which he continues to struggle.

In their belief that God created the world and man, the authors of the Bible ascribe to God all of the laws that govern individual and social human behaviour, thereby eliminating the difference between religious precepts (man's duties to God – e.g. cult and ritual) and civil laws (man's duty to his fellow man and to the society within which he lives). This kind of theistic belief makes it incumbent upon the individual to obey religious leaders, their laws and precepts, since they are perceived as representatives of God, creator of the universe and human society, king and overseer of all they do, who metes out rewards and punishments as he sees fit.

The belief of secular Jews that God and moral values are human constructs frees man from the authority of religious establishment leaders, the Halakhah they have created, the commandments they have spoken in God's name, and the system of rules called religion, which they impose upon those who believe in them and in the ability of human beings to speak on God's behalf. Such belief is essentially a-theistic, since it rejects the authority of religion and religious leaders to impose a specific set of beliefs or rules of conduct.

A-theism takes many different forms, e.g. various pantheistic approaches, which identify nature with the divinity, inasmuch as

217

they (like Spinoza) view nature as divine; or conversely, identify the divinity with nature (God has no specific abode, because he is all-encompassing).

Agnostics reject the authority of religion, because they believe that it is impossible to know whether God exists independently of the literature that shaped him; and that consequently, religious leaders claiming to speak in God's name should not be believed, since he cannot be known, encountered or heard.

Deists (like Voltaire) have postulated that a supreme force one might call God could exist, but that such a force is far-removed from humanity and from individual human beings, so that those who purport to speak in its name should not be believed or obeyed.

An analogous approach is that of the religious philosophers (such as the author of the Guide for the Perplexed), who assert that the human mind is incapable of grasping God, to whom no characteristic – including existence – should be ascribed. Advocates of this approach believe God to be the supreme wisdom manifest in creation, accessible only to a select few scholars and scientists; or (as Einstein believed), "God" is what we call the enigma of the orderly harmony of all existence – microcosm and macrocosm – order that can be studied, but the source of which can never be known.

What all adherents of the aforementioned beliefs, pantheists, deists, agnostics and declared atheists, have in common are the following:

a. A perception of the biblical God as a literary figure created by the authors of the various biblical works; given human form (mouth, arms, etc.) and human characteristics (speaking, commanding, striking) in order to provide unsophisticated readers with an allegory (as Maimonides claimed in *Guide of the Perplexed*), to which they could relate and in which they could believe. The literary figure God, fashioned by the works of the Bible, is anthropomorphic, and can therefore be said to speak words with a mouth, perform actions with an outstretched arm, express rage or disappointment when the Israelites are ungrateful and complain about the conditions of their liberation from slavery, etc.

b. An "a-theistic" approach to established religion, in the sense of a belief that one who is free of theism, religion, religious leaders and their precepts, is committed to the man-made moral values upon which life in human society – the only structure within which one can be fully human – depends. When religious precepts and customs violate human moral values (like the binding and sacrificing of a child upon an altar, or any precept/custom that discriminates against the female half of society), they must not be obeyed and should be outlawed. Rather than integrating Halakhah and civil constitutional law, a clear distinction must be made between the two. Both are man-made, and both should be judged in accordance with the principles of human justice. When Halakhah and religious precepts clash with the constitution and democratic law, democratic civil law must take precedence, as long as the latter complies with the principles of justice, safeguarded by the supreme courts.

The distinction between God as creator of man, and God as literary figure created by man, is thus a decisive factor in determining one's approach to life within society, and to society's creations – the Bible included. Those who believe that man is sovereign, free to create laws, abolish or change them in keeping with moral values, adopt a critical approach to the biblical laws and precepts, as well as to the actions and statements of all the characters depicted in the Bible. Such a critical approach – whereby one may accept or reject any biblical precept, statement or action of God, Abraham or Moses – is part of the moral education served by acquaintance with the works of the Bible.

Even the biblical authors who truly believed in God as creator of the universe and supreme judicial authority, were extremely critical of Yahweh's morality. Abram asks whether it is right for the judge of all the earth to mete out collective punishment; readers of Job know that God and not Job was responsible for the latter's woes; the authors of Ecclesiastes and Jeremiah know that there is no justice in Yahweh's world, in which the wicked prosper and the righteous suffer. Like all literary figures in classical literature the world over, God sins in terms of the readers' moral values. That is also how the characters behave in the Iliad, the Odyssey, the dramas of Aeschylus, Sophocles and Euripides, Shakespeare, Molière and Goethe. Plato was wrong about authors who depict sinful protagonists, when he suggested that they be garlanded with praise and expelled from the city. Characters in literary masterpieces – Yahweh included – are not paragons of virtue. They represent human, emotional, social, religious and moral reality.

Relating to sinful protagonists in a lenient fashion because of their "sacredness" in religious tradition is detrimental to moral education and the development of critical ability. In terms of the values of a humanist reader, there is no moral justification for Abraham's blind obedience, deceiving his son, leading him to the place of the sacrifice, laying upon Isaac the wood with which he intends to immolate him, binding him on the altar, bringing the knife to his throat in order to slaughter him, because that is what he believed his god had commanded him to do. God's commandment to Abraham that he sacrifice his son is blatantly immoral, as is Abraham's obedience, and the intrigues he employs in order to carry out the order.

Perceiving the God of the Bible as a literary figure allows one to read the works of the Bible and develop an affinity for the characters they present, including Yahweh. Such an affinity is part of the poetic and intellectual experience afforded by literature.

The Philosophy of the Prophets of Yahweh: Recognising ours as the Sole Existing World and the Supremacy of Justice and Charity

Biblical literature reflects the prevailing thoughts and beliefs of the period, in stories, poems, and orations delivered by its protagonists – the prophets for example. Belief that the ability to distinguish between good and evil is conditional upon knowledge is first expressed in the Garden of Eden story, and is reiterated with every denunciation of evil as proceeding from foolishness, lack of foresight, and unwillingness to recognise the death and destruction to which it leads.

Knowledge, including the knowledge of good from evil, is essential to man's humanity, since only knowledge affords man the freedom to choose between existing alternatives or to create new ones (the fundamental difference between man and beast, according to Bergson).

It is clear to the author of the Garden of Eden story that the snake was right and that God acted selfishly, as one who had not eaten from the tree of knowledge of good and evil. Lacking foresight, Yahweh failed to understand that he would lose the faithful keeper of his garden, and that knowledge cannot be withheld forever. Human beings will rebel against any who would deny them the freedom to choose between good and evil. According to the author, not only does knowledge significantly reduce the difference between man and God, but it also releases man from dependence upon the natural environment provided by God. Man could henceforth create a new natural environment, far from Eden – considered by all of the biblical authors to be the beginning rather than the end of human history.

Placing the Eden story at the beginning of the biblical anthology, is one of the many ways in which the Bible reflects the belief in this world as the sole existing world, and in death as the dissolution of the human body, which thus returns to the earthy matter from which it was created. The one-way road from Eden is one of the greatest innovations in Jewish thought of the biblical era. For the most part, neighbouring cultures of the time believed in the existence of an afterlife, a world beyond the boundary between life and death, in which the dead continue to live, alongside the gods, for all eternity. Biblical Judaism rejected, or disregarded the world to come and life after death – a radical turning point in the history of western thought.

Belief in eternal life and the hereafter (mentioned in the Bible only in the book of Daniel) were widespread in post-biblical times, particularly in the Hellenistic era and the Middle Ages; contrary to the views of philosophers such as Maimonides in his Guide for the Perplexed, who perceived eternal life of the soul only in terms of coalescence of the human mind with the divine.

Rejection of the existence of an afterlife – a radically innovative departure from prevailing beliefs in the ancient world – became, in western culture of the Enlightenment period, the shibboleth that distinguished between believers in the monotheistic religions, and the growing number of sceptics, agnostics and atheists. The belief that there is no world beyond the one in which we live was the basis of the prophets' preference of ethical behaviour and social justice over religious ritual. Belief that reward and punishment can come only in this world and this life, produced the demand, reiterated much later by Bialik, in his poem On the Slaughter ("*Al Hashehitah*"): "If there is justice – let it appear at once". In Bialik's view, this was a sine qua non for belief in divine authority and justice in the world, leading him to declare in the same poem: "If after my death justice should appear – let its throne be cast to the ground".

In the Prophets as well, knowledge that ours is the sole existing world is accompanied by a demand for justice here and now, not only because "the dead praise not the Lord", but primarily because there is no other world in which those who have been wronged in this world can be compensated. The prophets understood that wickedness and disregard for justice are foolishness, being the opposite of wisdom that is foresight, i.e. recognising the consequences of one's actions, beyond their immediate benefits.

Leaders of the monotheistic religions based their demands for absolute compliance with the precepts and customs pertaining to ritual upon the Bible, threatening terrible physical punishment in the next world, where the fires of hell burn for all eternity. It is in the works of the Bible however that rejection of the world to come developed, providing a basis, during the Enlightenment period, for the movement for liberation from religion and the control of religious leaders. The Enlightenment witnessed the re-emergence of the belief that there is no world beyond this world and no life beyond this life, belief in human rights – the source of ethical values, and belief in the duty to apply these values here and now, since there is no other life in which they can be applied. Thus agnostics and atheists were also able to appreciate the contribution of the biblical authors and the prophets of Yahweh they portrayed, who were the first to declare social justice preferable to prayer and sacrifice to God.

The prophets' belief in the validity of ethical values was based upon the knowledge they possessed, and upon extreme dissatisfaction with the social, economic, political and religious leaderships of their times. Compelled by the ability to distinguish between good and evil, the prophets condemned wicked and foolish priests, wealthy landowners and kings who failed to foresee the consequences of violating the covenant with God – the essence of which is acting justly – accusing them of leading Israelite society to destruction.

Belief in values is meaningless without the power of inference – the ability to foresee the consequences of one's actions or failure to act. The belief that ethical values provide an absolute standard for good and evil – as expressed by Hillel and Kant – entails belief in the essential role such values play in any society capable of humanising its members. Societies in a process of degeneration, such as those governed by the totalitarian regimes of the Nazis and the Taleban, witness the deterioration of man's humanity, with dehumanisation replacing humanisation, and education – rather than striving to better the lives of all – promoting subordination to the dictator, religious and cultural coercion, human sacrifice and suicide.

Just as belief in values, and the ability to choose between good and evil are conditional upon the knowledge that enables us to discern between the two, the ability to prefer the better action or reject the worse depends upon knowledge of the consequences of our actions. Without belief in values, there would be no standards by which to judge and choose between good and evil. Without knowledge, it would be impossible to apply moral values to that choice.

The Conflict between Man and God in Biblical Literature in Light of Secular beliefs in God as a Human Creation

One of the common themes in many biblical works is the conflict between the literary figure God and human literary figures. It appears in realistic stories such as the patriarch and matriarch narrative in the book of Genesis: beginning with the debate between Abram and God regarding the morality of collective punishment, when the latter sends his messengers to destroy Sodom and Gomorrah. Abram accuses God, "the judge of all the earth", of acting unjustly, since the holocaust of these two cities and their inhabitants, righteous and wicked alike, cannot be considered just.

One of the of the climaxes in the struggle between the human and the divine appears in the story of Jacob, who constantly struggles with and overcomes his destiny, finally defeating God himself at "Peniel" (face of God) – so designated by Jacob to commemorate his encounter with God, "face-to-face".

The conflict between God and man re-appears in surrealistic works such as Jonah and Job. Jonah accuses God of being too forgiving and merciful toward wicked kingdoms, while Job opposes the theodicy of righteous fools who believe the deaths of Job's sons and daughters to be the result of his sins. The biblical author of Job denounces those who – like Job's friends and their present-day counterparts, members of the hassidic sects of Lubavitch and Satmar – blame the victims of a holocaust in order to exonerate an omnipotent God. In the prologue the author explains that Yahweh conspired with Satan to visit a holocaust upon the pious Job, in order to test his piety.

Each of the stories of conflict between man and God sheds light on the unique personalities of both human and divine protagonists, thereby affording insight into man's universal struggle against his destiny – i.e. the natural and historical processes that lie beyond his control or moral judgement, and which religious believers ascribe to God.

The Conflict between Man and God in Biblical Literature Reflects Man's Struggle against the Forces that Shape his Destiny

The forces that shape the destiny of each and every individual are addressed by both religious and secular beliefs, and are represented in biblical literature by man's struggles with God.

In secular belief, destiny is seen as a force in our lives that is independent of will, yet may be influenced both by will and character – similar to the balance of forces or vector sum in physics, whereby many different forces, although acting in various directions, may influence the resultant force. Leaders and others are among the forces that exert an influence upon our lives, independently of our will. Individual will may however also be one of these forces – in many cases the dominant one.

In religious belief, destiny is perceived as being divinely ordained, since everything that happens is the result of the gods' omnipotent will. In Greek tragedy (Oedipus Rex for example), destiny prevails over man's will despite all of the efforts he may exert, since that which has been decreed by the gods cannot be changed.

In biblical literature (the stories of Abraham, Jacob, Joseph and David for example), the protagonists struggle against genetic and environmental factors to overcome their destiny – like Jacob who strove with God and with men, and prevailed. In these biblical narratives, man's will and character number among the many forces that determine his destiny. The life of an individual does not correspond exactly to his will, yet individual character and force of personality exert an influence over the process, sometimes altering the course and outcome that would otherwise have resulted.

Jacob overcame his destiny as the younger and therefore unentitled son according to the custom of the society into which he was born. After having successfully overcome even his god however, he was unable to prevent the course of events that forced him to flee Shekhem: the slaughter visited upon the city's inhabitants by his sons, in revenge for their sister's rape. Despite his preference for the son of his beloved Rachel, Jacob was not spared years of loneliness and bereavement, when he believed

Joseph to be dead. His favourite son had in fact risen to greatness in a neighbouring land, yet failed to send word not only to the brothers who had sold him into slavery, but also to the father who had doted upon him.

Man's destiny, in these stories, is influenced by his personal initiative and ability to apply his talents to the challenges that present themselves. Individual liberty is reflected in the capacity to face the forces that lie beyond one's control – one's own passions, the limitations imposed by society and its conventions – and in the ability to follow one's own path, seizing opportunities and overcoming adversity.

Most of the characters in biblical literature strive to change their destinies, by force of will and initiative. Abram finds an unconventional way of abiding the famine and poverty that pose a threat to his family and jeopardise his plans to be the father of many nations. He asks his beautiful wife Sarai to say that she is his sister rather than his wife. The servants of the Egyptian king thus take her to the royal palace, where she remains for three days. In return, Pharaoh makes Abram rich, giving him sheep, oxen, asses slaves and camels. Abram was just another destitute nomad, like the "A'biru" or Hebrew clans that crossed the Great River, wandering the length and breadth of the Fertile Crescent – from Ur via Haran to Egypt. In this story however, thanks to his ingenuity and the cooperation of Sarai in the great act of deception and seduction, Abram came to head a great clan, with a private army numbering hundreds of slaves, capable of defeating the armies of the four Syrian kings who attacked his Canaanite neighbours. As a result of his success in the Egyptian royal court and on the battlefield on the outskirts of Damascus, Abram won the respect and admiration of the kings of Canaan. Melchizedek, the Jebusite king of Jerusalem, priest of the most high god father of all the Canaanite gods, invited Abram to sacrifice at his altar, and Abram struck roots in Canaan by buying a family tomb from the Hittites in Hebron.

This reversal of fortunes was the direct result of the protagonist's initiative, will and ability to flout the social conventions of family and marriage, thereby drastically changing the course of his life and that of his family.

Jacob Struggles and Overcomes his Destiny and the God who Stood in his Way

Jacob, more than any other character in the Bible, personifies the ability to contend with one's destiny and one's God. Jacob's story, the greatest of the tales of struggle, stretches from the time before the hero's birth to his death, and employs the unique constructive prose of the patriarch and matriarch narrative – a style unparalleled in all of ancient literature, according to Robert Alter.

The story of Jacob's life begins with his unsuccessful struggle in the womb to be born first. Even during birth, Jacob attempted to delay his twin, grabbing him by the heel. The amused parents thus named the child "Ya'akov" (from the Hebrew word *akev*, heel – tr.).

Jacob's failure in his attempt to be firstborn sealed his fate in the family and society into which he was born. He would always be the second son, denied all the rights afforded to his elder sibling, although Jacob would turn out to be brighter, more cunning and generally more capable than Isaac's favourite – the hunter Esau, so-named for his precocious hairiness. The blind old man was in fact, mainly fond of the venison provided by his elder son and the savoury meat prepared by his wife.

Esau is depicted by the story's author as unintelligent, lacking foresight, moody and impulsive; the type of person who is never hungry, always "famished". Returning from a failed hunting trip, he is tired and hungry, when his brother the tent-dweller entices him with a lentil stew he is cooking for himself. The author stresses Esau's crude nature. Longing only to eat "of that red red stuff", he does not even bother to ask Jacob what it is. His desire is so great that he accepts Jacob's indecent proposal, and sells him his birthright in exchange for the lentil stew.

The biblical authors are omniscient, and recount not only things that are done or said aloud, but also things that the characters say to themselves. In this case, the author reveals Esau's inner thoughts. He reasons that he is about to die of hunger, so what good is a birthright to him anyway – thereby convincing himself to do as Jacob has suggested and sell his birthright for some lentil stew.

The story of the encounter between the two brothers is one of the literary gems included in this surrealistic narrative in four parts, each of which features a different generation of father and mother figures: 1. Abraham, Sarah and Hagar; 2. Isaac and Rebecca; 3. Jacob, Rachel and Leah 4. Joseph and Osnat – forebears of the tribes of the northern kingdom of Israel; and Judah and Tamar – progenitors of the kings of Judea. The editors set the patriarch and matriarch narrative at the beginning of Israelite history, when the Jewish people was a single family, splitting up as early as the fourth generation into a group of tribes – alternately coming together and breaking apart, in a kind of pluralism later to become a characteristic element of Jewish culture.

In the third part of the narrative, the author focuses on the personality of Jacob who, like the story's readers, is aware of his initial failure to obtain the birthright, and awaits his chance to acquire the blessing as well.

The sale of the birthright for some lentil stew was to become a cultural icon. In the biblical story however, it is merely Jacob's first step toward "striving with God and with men", toward overcoming the forces beyond his control that constitute the greater part of destiny. In order to gain sanction for his purchase of the birthright, Jacob must also obtain the blessing bestowed by father upon firstborn – a formal will, transmitted orally in the age before writing.

The tale of deceit, disguise and theft of the blind, senile father's blessing is told in the author's characteristic laconic style. In this case however, one can sense timbres of mockery and sadness between the lines: the farce of an old man enticed to pretend he cannot tell his sons apart, and the tragedy of an honest, simple man cheated out of his birthright by his brother and father.

From the time of the terrible trauma of Isaac's binding on the altar at Mount Moriah, when his father tied him to a bundle of kindling and held a knife to his throat, Isaac lives as if in a state of shock. He is a sedentary nomad, a man without initiative who failed to marry because he never got over his mother's death – precipitated by news of her son's binding. Only at the age of forty, his father's aged slave returns from a distant land with a cousin willing to marry him, who falls off her camel at the sight of him, brings him into the tent, comforts him and lies with him, thus becoming his first and only wife.

The author underscores Isaac's passivity and stunted spirituality, compared to his elder brother Ishmael whose "hand is against every man and every man's hand against him", his energetic and enterprising son Jacob, or his father Abraham who left his native land to seek and find his fortune and future in distant lands. Lacking initiative or originality, Isaac imitates his father, including an attempt to lend his wife to the king of the Philistines in order to make his fortune, but fails even at this. Unable to restrain himself, he makes love to his wife who is supposed to be his sister, and the king discovers the deception.

The characterisation of Isaac as a weak and broken man sets the stage for the grotesque scene in which the father gives the firstborn blessing to his younger son, disguised in goat skins the elderly shepherd should easily have distinguished from the hairy limbs of his son Esau. In this scene however, he too falls in Jacob's snare, like Esau before him, since he cannot resist the tempting aroma of the delicacies his wife has prepared, which he will clearly be able to enjoy once he has bestowed the blessing. In this final tableau, blindness and old-age combine with Isaac's other characteristics. When Jacob appears dressed in bristly goatskins, Isaac concedes that the arms are indeed those of Esau. He knows however, although he cannot see his son, that the voice belongs to Jacob.

The old man probably guesses that he is once again being tricked (as he was by his father on the way to Mount Moriah), but since he is Isaac, he cooperates this time as well. Knowing that he will soon be able to eat the savoury meat Rebecca has prepared, he gives Jacob a blessing worthy of Abraham's grandson: the entire promised land, with all of the rights and privileges that might accompany such a promise and such a land. Isaac's blessing to Jacob is so exhaustive, that there is nothing left with which to bless Esau. By the time the latter arrives to fight one last time for his birthright, it is too late. The father is as helpless as the son, and the atmosphere changes from mockery and farce to sadness and tragedy.

Esau is a victim of his destiny: his character, personality, lack of cunning, and an unhelpful father. He seeks to kill his brother – the only way to get back that which is rightfully his – but fails at that as well. Jacob has already fled, having guessed at and heard of his brother's plans for murder and revenge.

The Genesis author does not judge his characters, sticking merely to the "facts". Other biblical characters however, freely criticise the actions of their peers. The prophet Hosea, like Esau, has harsh words for Jacob. Jacob on the other hand – destitute and fleeing for his life, but in lawful possession of the blessing and the birthright – thinks only of his future. He carries nothing but his staff, but immediately begins to dream of greatness. The place in which he spends his first night appears to him to be God's house and he names it Beth-el (House of God). The stones upon which he lies in the middle of nowhere appear to the sleeping Jacob to be the base of a ladder leading to heaven and to the God he believes in when he is awake. At this point however, he begins to impose conditions for relations between them: if God will make him successful and abide by all of the conditions he has set forth – above all ensuring his return to the promised land – Jacob will agree to do things for God, including the establishment of a place of worship, like the one later built and restored by Jeroboam at Beth-el, with which all readers or listeners in biblical times would have been familiar.

The author's sympathy for his protagonist who has been promised everything but has nothing is evident at the beginning of the second part of the narrative devoted to Jacob. The author uses this contradiction between Jacob's seemingly hopeless present and the bright future he has been promised, to create a sense of tension and expectation.

Jacob, who is initially portrayed as a grave sinner – like all protagonists in the masterpieces of ancient literature – undergoes a surprising transformation in his later struggles with destiny, leading up to his ultimate struggle with God. The surprising change in Jacob's character, selfish and thus far wholly engrossed in his ambition to obtain the birthright, is revealed in his great love for his cousin Rachel. His love is so great, that he vows to toil for seven years without payment in order to win her hand. On Jacob's wedding night, the author again surprises us, when the protagonist falls into a trap set for him by the sisters and their father, preying on his male weakness. In the dark, he lies with Leah, thereby becoming her husband. In the heat of sexual desire, he fails to notice that she has switched places with her sister, his beloved Rachel.

This incident however, claims the author, has no effect on Jacob's love for Rachel. He continues to love her deeply, vowing to work another seven years without pay in order to win her hand as well. The change Jacob has undergone is also reflected in the manner in which he now goes about attaining his goals. He is deceived rather than deceiver, works faithfully for more than twenty years, and steals nothing. He increases his employer's and his own wealth honestly, thanks to a rare knowledge of the planned breeding of sheep and goats. From a destitute exile, Jacob becomes head of a family and tribe endowed with herds, women, children and slaves, finally able to depart for the promised land, after having fulfilled all of the other promises on his own.

Scientists have calculated and discovered (see *Olam Hatanakh*, "Jacob in Aram") Jacob's experiments and successes in the breeding of sheep and goats to be highly feasible, as if the author wished to lend further credibility to the story, most of which is recounted in realistic fashion, i.e. describing what might have happened rather than actual fact.

At this stage, Jacob's struggle against his destiny reaches its climax. The man who has become a father and a wealthy Aramean leader, now seeks to fulfil the divine promise given to his grandfather and his father, and which he himself inherited when he bought and stole the birthright. Once Laban is satisfied that Jacob has not stolen his household gods (neither he nor Jacob entertain the possibility that Rachel might have taken them), the two men make a covenant, swearing to go their separate ways. Jacob now stands alone on the frontier of the promised land, having sent his family across the Jabbok.

After all of these adventures, Jacob discovers that his way to the promised land is in fact barred by a nameless individual who, like all men, is the living image of God. (Perhaps God's resemblance to all men makes it difficult even for those who believe in him to recognise him. According to the Midrash, human monarchs strike their portraits upon coins and all the coins are alike, whereas the King of Kings imprints his image on all who are made in his likeness, yet each is different.)

The author heightens the sense of realism, by naming a well-known place as the venue of that fateful encounter between Jacob and his god. At first, Jacob did not know with whom he was struggling at the Jabbok ford – a place everyone called "Peniel" even in the author's day.

In Peniel near the Jabbok ford, the author tells us, a great struggle went on through the night. The contest is a physical one and Jacob is injured in the thigh. By virtue of his strength and determination however, he prevails over his adversary, who remains locked in his grip. At daybreak, the stranger seeks to depart, but Jacob refuses, demanding to know his opponent's name. Left with no choice, God reveals his identity when he tells Jacob that he must change his name from Jacob – so named for having held his brother's heel at birth – to Israel – one who has striven with God and prevailed. Jacob, now known as Israel, releases the god he claims to have seen "face-to-face", naming the place in which the struggle has taken place "Peniel" (face of God), and is finally able to cross into the promise land. The experience however, has left its mark upon Jacob-Israel, whom the author tells us "limped upon his thigh".

This unusual story, in which man prevails over God, reflects the belief of the biblical authors and redactors in man's ability to strive with God and destiny, and prevail. Many readers have viewed this story as the source of the name "Israel" – a people for whom, like its mythological forebear, constant, seemingly hopeless struggle has become a way of life. Other readers have been so frightened by the obvious significance of the original text, that they have interpreted it beyond recognition. Catholic painters and other religious commentators pounced on the story in their interpretations, removing God from it – contrary to the firsthand testimony provided by Jacob, the event's only eyewitness, according to the very same commentators. Instead of the god with whom Jacob claimed to have struggled, they invented a winged angel, of the kind created by Judaism and Christianity in post-biblical literature. The influence of the religious commentators upon readers of the Bible has been so strong, that many remember the biblical story as that of "Jacob and the angel", despite the fact that no angel appears in the Hebrew text.

The face-to-face struggle between Jacob and God is not only the climax of the story of man's struggle with destiny. It also sheds light on the concept "God", suspended as it is between the abstract and the concrete. "God", according to the Genesis authors, is an entity unto itself, distinct from all others. The stories about God and his relations with man however, lend new meaning to man's struggle with destiny, a battle one must sometimes fight with oneself. In Kafka's first story, "Description of a Struggle" – inspired by the biblical account of Jacob's struggle – a man goes out into the night, and struggles with someone standing in his path, until dawn, when it becomes clear that there was no one there but himself. French director and writer Chris Marker called his documentary film about the State of Israel, "Description of a Struggle", after Kafka's story or its original inspiration.

The biblical author is aware that within the world he has created with his words, these are indisputable facts, not just ideas. As if to bring us back to reality, following the amazing story about God and man, he adds, almost incidentally, that Jacob crossed the Jordan and entered the Promised Land limping. Only he and we know the reason for this limp, which in our imaginations imparts flesh and blood to this literary character.

Opposing Views on Collective Punishment of Wicked Kingdoms in the Book of Jonah

Even the Bible's surrealistic works, like Jonah and Job, shed light on the conflict between man and God whose actions, according to the protagonists of these works, lack moral justification. Man, in these works, discovers his own helplessness against the forces of the universe, nature and the course of history, all of which he ascribes to God.

As in Jonah and Job, the authors carefully mould the characters and their personalities through their behaviour and the dialogue in which they present their views on morality.

Initially, it is unclear to the reader why Jonah tried to flee God's command that he go to Nineveh and cry against it. The reader knows that Nineveh is the capital of a wicked empire that subjugated, killed and forced many peoples into exile. There is no doubt in the reader's mind, as emerges later in the story, that Nineveh is worthy of destruction – just like the wicked capitals the destruction of which was foretold by Amos, for example.

Jonah however, is not a book of prophecy. It is the story of a prophet who did not believe that his prophecy would come true, and consequently that his soft-hearted, merciful and gracious God could not be trusted. Written in the short story genre, Jonah numbers among the Bible's rhetorical works, casting aspersions – in an ironic gesture by the editors – on the ability of prophecy to actually foretell the future. A masterpiece of the genre, Jonah offers an exciting reversal-filled plot, leading to an ideologically surprising climax in which God's humanistic outlook is juxtaposed with the fanatical position of those who believe in relentless justice.

The story begins with an almost realistic account of the mission with God has charged Jonah, like the tasks set before the fourteen other prophets in the section of the Bible devoted to their oratory. Jonah's reaction is unlike that of any of the other prophets. He attempts to escape both the task and God, hastening to the great port of Joppa to find a ship that will take him to the other side of the world. The author weaves descriptions of minor events into the fabric of the story, lending credibility to the reality he has created. Jonah hastens to pay his passage, and once the voyage is underway, sinks into a deep sleep, as one who is fleeing consciousness itself.

Only at the end of the story does Jonah admit that he tried to flee from God because he has no faith in him or in the prophecies he utters in his name. At this early stage, no explanation is offered for Jonah's strange behaviour, which also surprises the mariners fighting the terrible storm sent by God. Each prays to his god in hope of saving the ship, which was "like to be broken" while Jonah continues to sleep below deck, until the shipmaster wakes him with the bewildered cry "What meanest thou, O sleeper? Arise call upon thy god".

When Jonah awakes and the mariners cast lots, they discover

that Jonah is the cause of their plight. They ask him his occupation and his origins, and Jonah admits that the storm is indeed on his account: he is a Hebrew fleeing the god who created both sea and dry land, and their only hope for deliverance therefore, is to cast him into the sea.

This is Jonah's first encounter with simple folk "that cannot discern between their right hand and their left hand". Even after he has confessed his culpability to them and informed them that only drowning him will save them from death, they continue to row, in the hope of overcoming the storm. When all hope is lost, they pray to God to forgive them for what they are about to do, and throw Jonah overboard.

Only at this point does the plot cease to be plausible, taking on the surrealistic features that may be the reason the story became engraved so deeply upon the cultural memory of western peoples. God who is interested in Jonah's compliance rather than his death, dispatches a "great fish" and commands it to swallow Jonah, but the obdurate Jonah keeps silent for three whole days trapped inside the fish, until he can stand it no longer and prays to God for deliverance. His plea makes no reference to his dispute with God, resembling instead a lyrical prayer of the type found in the book of Psalms.

The fish disgorges Jonah upon dry land, God reiterates his command to Jonah that he go to Nineveh and inveigh against it, and Jonah, knowing that he has no choice, goes to Nineveh as instructed. The author once again remarks on the city's vastness – a city of three day's journey. After a single day's journey into the city, Jonah delivers his message, as if performing a duty with which he has been charged against his will. Rather than a poetic, imagery-filled oration, like the prophecies of other prophets, the author has Jonah utter a telegraphic parody of fire and brimstone: "Yet forty days, and Nineveh shall be overthrown". Anyone familiar with the story of Sodom and Gomorrah would have understood what that meant, regardless of the extreme terseness of the message.

The king decrees that every man and beast in the city abstain from food and drink, wear sackcloth, and turn from violence and evil, in the hope that they might be spared. God responds immediately: he changes his mind and calls off the disaster he had intended to visit upon Nineveh. And the capital of evil – like those before and since, up to the present day – returns to its daily life, as if remorse and prayer can erase one's crimes.

Only one man, according to the author, could not forgive God's forgiveness. When it becomes clear that he had been right, and that his prophecy had been a false one, he grows very angry. He accuses God of being "gracious, merciful, slow to anger, of great kindness, and repenting of evil" – and that is why he tried to flee to Tarshish. Jonah confesses that he would rather be dead than alive, but God continues to provoke him, asking him "art thou greatly angry?" He then leaves the city, repairing to the east, to patiently and incredulously await the disaster that would never come.

Jonah is the only biblical work to address the morality of forgiveness and mercy. Are all wicked people worthy of forgiveness – even if they have shown remorse for the evil they have done? Is there really justification, asks the book of Jonah, for a reprieve granted by a gracious and merciful god, who is slow to anger and repents of evil – even when the subject at hand is Nineveh and its ilk? Was Jonah right that prophecies of just chastisement and destruction, like the one that he was commanded to utter, stand no chance of being fulfilled, because God is not the god of justice, but the god of kindness and mercy?

The author strives to answer all of these questions in the last part of the story, returning to the realistic style employed in the opening verses, this time with the tale of a gourd in the desert, where Jonah has gone to await the outcome of his prophecy, under the scorching Iraqi sun. The gourd, despite its poor foliage shades and delivers Jonah from the heat of the day, but God sends a worm that causes the gourd to wither and die, exposing Jonah to the sun once again.

Ostensibly, there is no connection between the main story and this botanical interlude recounted in such detail by an otherwise economical author. It is however swiftly incorporated into the broader narrative, as it becomes the basis for the author's main philosophical argument.

When Jonah faints from the heat, the gourd in which he so rejoiced having withered and died, God provokes him again, asking him whether he is greatly angered for the withered gourd, and Jonah replies vehemently "I am greatly angry, even unto death". The author expresses his viewpoint in the following words, attributed to God in the book's closing verses: "Thou hast had pity on the gourd, for the which thou hast not laboured, neither madest it grow; which came up in a night and perished in a night. And should not I spare Nineveh, that great city, wherein are more than sixscore thousand persons that cannot discern between their right hand and their left hand; and also much cattle?"

This position, defended by the author of the Abraham narrative in the debate between Abram and Yahweh regarding the morality of collective punishment, is taken up by the author of Jonah, who places it in the mouth of his divine protagonist – in the form of a question that redirects the reader's sympathy from Jonah to God. Up to this point, author and reader would appear to identify with the story's main character – Jonah the frustrated prophet, who seeks only fulfilment of a just prophecy demanding that the wicked be punished. At the story's end however, the tables are

240

turned, and the moral position – presented by God this time – argues that ordinary people, most of whom cannot discern between right and left, must not be punished, even when its leaders are as wicked as those of Nineveh.

Jonah is part of the body of philosophical and ethical literature that represents the mosaic of Jewish thought in the biblical era. Many of the ideas expressed in these works run counter to one another. The position taken by the author of Jonah for example, is antithetical to that of most of the biblical prophets, who did not hesitate to promise wicked cities – Israelite and other – destruction, exile and annihilation.

Like the choice of Berlin as a metaphorical capital of evil in modern works, the choice of Nineveh in Jonah is not incidental. Nineveh's crimes against humanity are well known. To this day, they are documented and exhibited in ancient Assyrian clay tablets that depict victory processions in which soldiers of Nineveh bore the heads of their vanquished enemies on the ends of their spears.

The author uses historical events as a backdrop for his story of the personal and spiritual tragedy experienced by people like Jonah, tormented by the knowledge that there is no God who punishes those who are guilty of crimes against humanity.

The message conveyed in the book of Jonah closes one of the many philosophical circles presented by pluralistic biblical thought: from accusing God of being "the judge of all the earth who does not act justly" to accusing him of being of being "gracious, merciful, slow to anger, of great kindness, and repenting of evil".

In Job: Who is to Blame for the Holocaust?
Its Innocent Victim or an Omnipotent God?

One of the most poetic works in all of biblical literature is the drama of Job, which questions the principles of faith in a God of justice and his involvement in the lives of human beings. The authors of Job set the victim at variance not only with God, but also with all who believe that a holocaust is necessarily retribution for sin – known or unknown to the sinner.

Job is the collective work of a number of writers, and an editor who combined and reworked the various source materials to produce the final text as it has stood for some two thousand years. It may be possible to study the individual sources that make up the integral whole, but it would be, as Robert Alter suggested (citing Edmund Leach), "unscrambling the omelette".

The integrity of Job, as it appears in the Bible today, is reflected in the roles played by all of its component parts in creating the import of the work as a whole. The epic prologue, the dramatic dialogue between Job and his friends, the epilogue comprising Yahweh's two monologues, and the short epic ending intended to provide this tragic work with a happy end – combine to achieve the overall significance and unique character of the book. Although Job appears to be a "blemished perfection" – the title of Yair Hoffman's excellent book on the literary, aesthetic, philosophical and ethical aspects of Job – it still deserves to be read as a single work, one of the great classics of world literature that has withstood the test of time and inspired countless other works of poetry and philosophy throughout the ages.

The "author" of Job makes it clear from the outset that Job is right, and his friends are wrong in claiming that only sin can explain the great tragedy visited upon Job and his family. The sincerity and commitment of Job's friends to their groundless beliefs turns the intellectual clash between them into an expression of dramatic personal conflict.

Holocausts are caused by human beings attacking other human beings, or by forces of nature, like the earthquake that destroyed Sodom and Gomorrah. In Job, the author cites two causes of the holocaust visited upon his protagonist: Sabean and Chaldean marauders, and the great wind that brought his eldest son's house down, killing all of his children. Believers ascribe such events to God, whom they must then justify by laying ultimate blame upon man's sins; or conversely, charge with satanic wickedness, as the author does in his prologue.

In the prologue we discover that the tragedy Job and his family will experience is the result of a pact between God and Satan. God allows Satan to torment Job and his family, because of Job's great righteousness, not his sin. They meet at a periodic gathering of the sons of God, and Satan wagers that Job's faithfulness will not endure a satanic holocaust.

In the eyes of righteous fools like Job's friends, God can do no wrong. Blame therefore must always rest with man – even when he is a sinless victim or an innocent child.

When disaster strikes Job's family and fortune, and the boils with which he is inflicted force him to wallow in ashes, his wife advises him to curse God and die. But Job does not curse God. He believes in his god, and seeks to know why he has been the victim of such injustice. Unwilling to accept the arguments of his religious friends who justify God without knowing the truth, he seeks to come together in judgement with God himself. He seeks justice from a patently unjust god.

The poetic part of the book opens with a shocking imprecation against the dawning day and the shining light; Job curses the day he was born and life itself, preferring the inexistence of the never-born. He does not however, curse or blame God as the cause of all his misfortunes, since he is unaware of the circumstances known to the reader.

When Job's friends come to visit him during his illness, they try to convince him that only sin can explain the holocaust that has been visited upon him. They too are unaware that God is in fact to blame for having been drawn in by Satan and allowed the murder, pain and affliction. Job knows that they are wrong, and that he is not at fault, but he does not know where to lay the blame.

Job's tragedy and song of longing for inexistence that is better than such a life, stand in contrast to his friends' absurd claim, which runs counter to the experience of anyone who has ever observed life in an unprejudiced fashion. The opening words of Eliphaz the Temanite, the first among Job's friends to speak, present their main argument – later repeated in various forms – in support of the conventional religious position: no innocent man has ever perished and all affliction is caused by human rather than divine sin, because mortal man simply cannot be more just than God.

Job, like the reader, knows that this is not true. The author condemns the baseless claims of the religious holocaust justifiers and explainers, both in the way Job's friends views are presented, and in God's rejection of their claims in the epilogue.

Job, the book's main character, is depicted as a religious man in terms of faith (as opposed to those who are religious in the observance of halakhic precepts). He believes with all his heart in his god – that god's existence, and until now, in his righteousness as well. It is precisely for this reason that he cannot agree with his friends, and insists upon understanding the reasons for the holocaust he has experienced. He cannot accept the belief that God is incapable of wrongdoing. As a religious man, Job also attributes to God all of the disasters experienced by man at the hand of nature or his fellow man. He therefore demands that God appear and justify these actions, for which he bears sole responsibility. It is clear to Job that should God agree to stand trial before him, the claim of Eliphaz and his friends that man cannot be more just than God would be proven false.

The story's clever structure allows the reader to know that there is no convincing reason behind God's actions, because God – or the forces of nature and history ascribed to him – often causes bad things to happen. Other biblical authors, such as the creators of Jeremiah and Ecclesiates – committed like the author of Job to truth rather than faith in God's absolute righteousness – knew that the righteous often suffer, while the wicked obtain their hearts' every desire.

The author turns the philosophical debate between Job and his friends into a dramatic personal conflict between individuals, both convinced of God's immanent presence, who espouse irreconcilable opinions. Job continues to believe in God even when he is the victim of an unjustifiable disaster, refusing to curse him, yet – unlike his friends, or the rabbis of Lubavitch and Satmar – also refusing to justify him.

Through the dialogue between Job and his friends, the author raises the question that has shaken the faith of many in our time: how can there be a just God in a world of oppression and mass murder on the basis of ethnicity, class, race, opinion, religion or health? The God character who appears in the prologue, enters into this discussion only at the very end of the book. His words, like the entire background story, refute the claims Job's "friends" who in their blind faith in God's righteousness and the system of reward and punishment with which he runs the world, place all who doubt this righteousness on trial. In the epilogue, Yahweh condemns Job's friends for not having spoken "the thing that is right" and for having levelled false accusations, for which they must atone and beg Job's forgiveness. Through Yahweh's monologues, the author explains that God is not responsible for man's suffering, which must not be seen as punishment for sin, since God can only be perceived in terms of the creation of the universe and its mysteries, which man cannot explain (a view reminiscent of Einstein's belief in the mystery of what lies beyond science – the mystery of order in the universe).

Yahweh, appears in the epilogue as acquiescing to Job's request that he explain his actions. His two monologues, composed entirely of rhetorical questions, fail to explain the holocaust he has caused, according to the background story, in agreeing to Satan's plan. The author's unique use of rhetorical questions enables his divine character to present the debate between Job and his friends as irrelevant to the nature of divinity and its role in the world. Rather than belief in a personal, punishing and rewarding God, the author of Job proposes a belief system similar to Voltaire's deism: God is creator of the universe and everything therein, but exerts no influence upon human beings, their actions, or the pain and suffering they endure in their lives. The questions that Yahweh poses to Job in his first monologue show that man cannot comprehend God's actions – which pertain entirely to the process of creation and the establishment of physical and biological systems wholly unrelated to sin and punishment, pain or happiness.

In the second monologue, the author further describes his belief in God as a symbolic mythological figure, pitted against monsters of chaos, such as the behemoth and the leviathan – reminiscent of similar creatures in Mesopotamian creation mythology. In this monologue too, God is portrayed as transcending the human world – making any assertion of divine responsibility for human suffering absurd.

These conclusions proceed from Yahweh's monologues, written as unique nature poems, consisting of a barrage of questions directed at Job – by means of which the poet attempts to illustrate the infinite chasm he perceives between God and man, the insignificance of man when compared to the universe and God, which he tries in vain to understand and judge according to human values such as morality and justice. Almost none of Yahweh's words relate directly to the debate between Job and his friends, apart from the assertion that they are wrong. Yahweh thus tells Job that it is pointless to blame God for having violated the principles of justice, or to accuse him of evil: "Wilt thou even make void my judgment? Wilt thou condemn me, that thou mayest be righteous?" (Job 40:8).

The book's allusion to Abram's ancient claim against the judge of all the earth who does not act justly, reminds us that the present debate is merely a link in the long chain of confrontations between human literary figures and the literary figure God in the Bible – from Genesis to Job.

Since Yahweh's arguments depart from the subject of their dispute, Job has no fitting answer to them. Precisely because the basic premise of all of Yahweh's questions is his own omnipotence however, Job continues to claim that he cannot understand why this terrible injustice has been visited upon him and upon his family. "I know that thou canst do everything and that no thought can be witholden from thee," Job says in his short reply to Yahweh, "therefore have I uttered that I understood not; things too wonderful for me, which I knew not" (ibid. 42:2-3).

Finally, the author provides his divine character with an answer to Eliphaz the Temanite – the first of the friends to speak, and the one who presented the essence of their arguments: "My wrath is kindled against thee, and against thy two friends, for ye have not spoken of me the thing that is right, as my servant Job hath" (ibid. 7).

In the epic conclusion, the author proposes a happy outcome to this tale of misery and woe. God, he tells us, blessed Job with renewed wealth and offspring, with daughters who were the fairest and richest in the land (for Job allowed them to inherit alongside their brothers), and what is more, Job lived to see four generations of his descendants. None of this can erase the horrors, raise from the dead those who died in vain, or cancel the terrible conspiracy between God and Satan. Our life experience has taught us that holocaust victims cannot be compensated for their suffering. Their pain and grief persists and can never be justified – as asserted by this rare religious work in its criticism of God.

As if to stress the universal nature of the problem, the author never mentions Job's nationality. Job's righteousness is unrelated to observance of the religious precepts of the Jewish or any other religion. Job was righteous because he was perfect and upright and eschewed evil. Job "feared God" – but not necessarily the one the Jews called Yahweh.

In giving Job no specific national identity, the author emphasises his role as the protagonist of a metaphorical work, which presents two opposing views: the one whereby everything that happens to man is an act of God, and the other that perceives the universe and nature as being morally neutral and indifferent to man's fate – like God in the book of Job.

God in the book Job is wholly unlike God the father or king, God of the High Holidays who keeps individual accounts in the Book of Life and Death, which he updates at the end of every year. God at the end of Job also differs from the God who appears at the beginning of the book. The epilogue portrays the god Yahweh as an entity manifest in the act of creation and the endless struggle against the monsters of chaos that threaten all existence (i.e. cosmic order), whom man will never know or understand.

Historical Evidence of the Existence of a Multiplicity of Religions in Biblical Judaism: Separating National and Religious Identity

Biblical literature, as noted above, is a valuable source of historical evidence inasmuch as it reflects the social, cultural and religious reality in which its individual works were created and which they depict.

In addition to the variety of beliefs presented by the various biblical authors, the Bible also contains numerous descriptions of religious customs and rituals common among Israelites at the time. Historiographical works such as the books of Judges, Samuel I and II, Kings I and II, and the orations of the prophets of Yahweh, depict an Israelite culture of many religions – prevalent among the common people, in the royal courts, and among the hundreds of Israelite prophets of Baal and Ashtoreth. Polytheism was typical of most of the People of Israel, in both Israelite kingdoms.

The critical stance of the historians and prophets who denounced this phenomenon, strengthens the credibility of their testimony to its existence. According to the evidence provided by these works, most of the Israelite population – townspeople and villagers alike – worshiped the Canaanite divinities, alongside or in place of the worship of the Israelite god Yahweh. A statue of Asherah, mother of all the Canaanite gods, stood in the temple of Yahweh in Jerusalem, according to biblical historians, for two thirds of its three hundred and seventy-year existence (Raphael Patai). Statues of Ashtoreth and Baal were erected by Israelite believers "on every hill and under every green tree" (according to the biblical prophets and historiographers). Israelites made sacrifices to gods such as Molech and Chemosh, and kept household gods, apparently as gods of medicine and healing.

This multiplicity of cults and statues attests to a widespread multiplicity of religions and beliefs in biblical Israel, as well as to the split that occurred within the Israelite religion itself when the cult of Yahweh the golden calf was established in the kingdom of ten of the twelve tribes. In the temples of Beth-El and Dan, at which the majority of the Israelites worshiped, sacrifices were offered to Yahweh the golden calf, the god who had taken them out of Egypt (according to Jeroboam, following the tradition of Aaron, the first high priest). In the temple of Jerusalem, the minority of the Jewish People practised the cult of Yahweh represented by the cherubim – figures with human faces, and wings that spanned the breadth of the Holy of Holies.

The prophets continued in the tradition of belief in Yahweh as a being without shape or form – a belief ascribed to Moses, and expressed so beautifully in the story of the prophet Elijah, who knew that God was not in the earthquake or in the great wind, but in the voice of thin silence.

From Genesis to Ecclesiastes and Job, biblical literature presents a broad range of beliefs concerning God, his morality, essence and appearance. Through narrative, poetry, philosophical treatises, rhetoric and drama, the Bible paints a pluralistic picture of Jewish thought and culture of the period. From the time of early settlement to the destruction of the first two Jewish kingdoms, a national consciousness developed – a sense of belonging to a single people – despite vestiges of membership in the different tribes, and unrelated to the national religious identity of the believers and worshipers of Yahweh as sole and universal God.

The "Israelite religion" – the ethical monotheism of the believers in Yahweh as a sole, formless deity – was already a national religion at the time, inasmuch as it was the religion of a single people. The People of Israel and the Israelite religion however, were separate from one another.

At the height of the Northern Kingdom's political and economic prosperity, during the reign of King Ahab, the religion of Baal and Ashtoreth was declared the official religion of the kingdom. The prophets of Yahweh were banished, and hid for fear of execution by the Israelite king.

During the construction of the first temple to Yahweh, Solomon built temples to all of the gods of the neighbouring peoples in Jerusalem, thus creating a polytheistic metropolis, in which monotheism was also practised. Before his idealisation in Jewish tradition, Solomon was condemned by the prophets of Yahweh for having promoted and established the multiplicity of religions that prevailed in the Jewish kingdom prior to its division.

Centuries later, on the eve of the destruction of the Jewish kingdom and the first temple in Jerusalem, the custom of sacrificing children on the altar of Molech was still practised in the Hinnom Valley (located today between Mount Zion and the Jerusalem Cinematheque), according to Jeremiah.

There were Israelites who made human and animal sacrifices, and Israelites who took part in erotic rituals in Canaanite temples, at which they served as sacred prostitutes (also found at the Jerusalem temple). According to the prophets, religious Israelites did not refrain from oppressing anyone they could exploit or subjugate: the poor, widows, orphans, slaves and day-labourers. The prophets asserted that Yahweh would forgo religious sacrifice and prayer if only the Israelites would follow the rules of justice and charity, which they believed to be the essence of the covenant between Yahweh and his people. In the eyes of the prophets of Yahweh, the struggle against "idolatry" – i.e. the worship of foreign gods – was an integral part of the struggle against social injustice, which they believed would bring about the destruction of the Jewish state.

Biblical Jewish Pluralism Continues to Develop in Jewish Culture throughout the Ages

Following the destruction of the first temple, and particularly during and after the Second Temple period, Jewish culture and society continued to be marked by a multiplicity of beliefs and outlooks.

In every generation, Judaism has been characterised by the disputes that have divided it and contributed to its development, to the contact between its parts and factions – and thereby, to the continued existence of a distinct Jewish culture. It is precisely the friction and clashes between the various Jewish factions – despite vast geographical and cultural differences separating Jewish communities around the globe – that have drawn Jews closer every time a new dispute has shaken the Jewish world. Such was the case of Sabbatean messianism and the controversy it sparked, and such has been the case of Zionism and the debate regarding its justification and chances of success.

Religious and ideological disputes have brought secular and religious Judaism together, deepened each Judaism's familiarity with all of the others, and consequently heightened national consciousness, which – as in biblical times – is not the same as religious identity.

Judaism, which comprises many different "Judaisms", is not an ideology, but rather the culture of a people – multifaceted, of variegated religious and secular beliefs that differ from one another and clash with one another, causing individuals to respond, to be aware of their Jewishness.

The assertion "Judaism says" is therefore incorrect, as is the statement "the Bible says". The most one can say is "in Judaism it is said" or "it is said in the Bible". "Normative Judaism" is a misleading designation, since it reflects the belief of one of the various Judaisms that it alone represents the true "norm". That is how the Orthodox who continue to believe their Judaism to be normative perceive themselves, although most of the Jewish People and even a majority of religious Jews, reject the ways of Orthodox Judaism, its lifestyle, education, and many of its sacrosanct beliefs and precepts.

Monotheism – belief in the existence of a single, incorporeal and moral God – as described by the authors of the Moses narratives and the books of the Prophets, is one of Judaism's most profound contributions to world culture. Even in biblical times however, monotheism characterised only one of the Judaisms of the day. From the Hellenistic period until the Haskalah, Jewish religious identity converged with Jewish national identity. Jews were, in their own eyes and in the eyes of others, those who professed the Jewish faith and observed its precepts. The Jewish religion was a national religion, the religion of a single people – as opposed to Christianity and Islam, which are international.

The split came about this time within the Jewish religion. Different streams held divergent beliefs and viewpoints, and practised different rituals. Contrary to the belief of biblical times in a single life and a single world, there developed within the Jewish religion a belief in life after death, a world to come, and the postponement of punishment and reward to the hereafter. In place of the exclusive belief in Yahweh, the Jewish religion witnessed the influx of a large and growing population of divine beings: angels, Satan and demons, goddesses (divine consorts) such as the Shekhinah and Lilith. Divine beings appeared in works such as the Merkabah and Hekhaloth literature as early as the Hellenistic-Byzantine period. In these works, the palace of Yahweh resembles that of a Persian monarch (as suggested by Yosef Dan). Presiding over the royal court is a viceroy, the angel Metatron – formerly a man called Enoch, whom the angel Anpiel brought to heaven, and whom he flogs occasionally with scourges of fire, like the time when the heretic Elisha ben Abuyah, who also appears in these celestial tales, asked whether there were not two domains in heaven – that of Yahweh and that of Metatron. Such tales express beliefs entirely unlike those of

Moses and the prophets, in the solitary God of heaven and earth, whose place cannot be defined, for he is "place" (makom).

Contrary to the belief professed in the Moses narratives in God's complete incorporeality, God's human form is restored to him in the Jewish religion, and particularly in mystical works such as Shiur Komah, in which God appears as a human figure many times the size of the universe – or, in more moderate versions (like that of the Zohar), as a king who regularly engages in sexual intercourse with his consort.

The belief that Justice and charity are the heart and soul of the Jewish religion is superseded by the belief that its essence is observance of the halakhic precepts ad verbum – that is according to the words of those who codify them in books such as the *Shulhan Arukh* or its derivations.

Religious philosophers, like Maimonides in *Guide of the Perplexed*, perceive God not only as beyond all substance, but also beyond all human conception. Wisdom and philosophy are the only means by which that the human mind may approach the supreme mind that is the godhead. According to this belief, there are temporary precepts, such as those pertaining to animal sacrifice, which is merely the legacy of the cults of other gods.

Contrary to the beliefs espoused by the rationalistic philosophers, mystical beliefs also arose within the Jewish religion – beliefs like those of Lurianic Kabbalah, which asserts that observance of the halakhic precepts will bring redemption not only to the Jewish People, but to the entire world – since the primordial light of creation shattered the vessel as it burst forth, its fragments intermingling with the "husks" of matter – and only the Jewish People can redeem the world, the Shekhinah and God from exile.

Hillel's moral principle whereby one should not do to another that which is hateful to oneself, has been superseded in Orthodox halakhic Judaism by the male-chauvinist belief that women can be treated in any way that would be hateful to men, who have appointed themselves legislators, interpreters and guardians of a law that considers women unclean for half of every month, and treats them as inferior beings who may be isolated and discriminated against in the synagogue, the courts, education, politics and leadership, marriage and divorce.

Contrary to the biblical belief that sorcery and necromancy must be eradicated, along with all who practise witchcraft by incantation or amulet, and pretend to supernatural powers, the Jewish religion has seen the proliferation of belief in the power, prestige and leadership of magicians and other thaumaturges, living and deceased, who employ tombs for example, as a means of remedying spouselessness, infertility or malignant diseases. The spread of magic in religious Judaism continues to this day, despite the inherent similarity between magic and atheism – both depend upon human initiative and action, bypassing or ignoring God, his divine will and power.

Spiritual Affinity for Biblical Literature in Secular Judaism and Particularly in Secular Judaism in Israel

Many of the prevailing beliefs in secular humanistic Judaism closely resemble those of the ethical monotheists of biblical Judaism and the books of the prophets – apart of course from the secular belief in man as the creator of God, contrary to the biblical authors who fashioned God in their writings, but believed that God created man. Like the prophets, secular Jews prefer acts of justice and charity to prayer and sacrifice. Like the biblical authors, secular Jews do not believe in life after death or the world to come, and therefore also believe that justice must be done here and now, since reward and punishment cannot be postponed to a hereafter that does not exist. Like Moses and the prophets, secular humanistic Jews believe in universal values, like those that appear in the Ten Commandments, by which all peoples, including the People of Israel, are judged. God has no special preference for Israel, which is but one of the many peoples cared for by a universal God, or in the words of the prophet Amos: as the Ethiopians, Philistines or Aram. In secular Judaism, as in biblical monotheism, it is believed that sorcerers and witches, wizards and magicians who pretend to supernatural powers and defraud the public for political gain, should be cast out.

Since the halakhic literature and discussions of the religious precepts and their observance serve no function in the daily lives of secular Jews, their role in secular Jewish culture and education is limited. Biblical literature on the other hand, due to the spiritual affinity secular Jews feel toward it, plays a central role in moulding secular Jewish national consciousness – as their historical and cultural heritage.

Secular belief in the sole existence of this life and this world creates a bond with biblical literature in which such beliefs are common, exerting an influence over the themes of its works, the ethical views of the prophets, and its approach to humanity and human life. This approach is reflected in most of the biblical narratives, which are told from a human perspective, contrary to pagan myths in which the gods are the main protagonists. Most biblical stories are not based on supernatural occurrences, but on physically and psychologically possible human events.

The Bible, as the only canon common to all Judaisms, plays a unique role in the creation of national consciousness in Israeli Judaism. Biblical literature is the source of the language spoken and written by the majority of Jewish youth educated in Israel today. From preschool to university, recipients of non-religious

Jewish education in Israel encounter the stories of the bible and its characters.

It is the unprecedented success of turning the words of a 2500-year-old body of literature into a living language – employed in academia and the arts, in day-to-day conversation and the media, in technology and the military – that sets Jewish cultural life in Israel apart from all of the Judaisms of the diaspora.

The ability of twenty first century Jewish children to read manuscripts from the fifth century BCE in the original language is one of the most remarkable phenomena in the cultural history of the world. The language in which we are raised, educated, dream, socialise and create, is the most humanising factor in our lives. In Israel, the Hebrew language and the Bible that is its source, are the bridge between the present and the cultural past. Both consciously and unconsciously, Israelis use biblical expressions absorbed through their acquaintance with the Bible. This kind of bond with classical works of literature that play a central role in the education, socialisation and acculturation of the individual, exists in every national society – from the culture of aboriginal tribes to that of ancient Greece, or educated society in 19th century England, France and Germany.

At a very early age, Jewish Israeli children begin to associate biblical sites with real places they have visited with their families or on school trips. This kind of association also extends to the historical events described in the Bible that constitute one of the elements of Israeli national holidays such as Passover, Sukkot, the 9th of Av, and Shavuot. Jewish Israeli children and adults are exposed monthly or even weekly to radio and television broadcasts on Bible-related topics: archaeological discoveries and debates, scholarship or literature inspired by or relating to the Bible. This ongoing exposure to the works of the Bible, as well as the linguistic bond between the language of the present and that of the Bible, strengthen the spiritual affinity secular Jewish Israelis feel toward the Bible; as opposed to Orthodox Jews who feel a stronger spiritual tie to the works of the Talmud and the Midrash – perceiving the Bible only within its talmudic and midrashic exegetical context.

Chapter Three

Secular Literature in the Bible

The vast majority of works in the Bible are religious, in the sense that belief in the god Yahweh is central to them, and God numbers among the stories' protagonists, influencing the course of events and historical processes they depict. The redactors of the final version of the biblical canon also included examples of secular literature – in the sense of works in which God and faith play only a minor role, or none at all.

The inclusion of such works in the Bible reinforces its importance as a corpus reflecting the entire range of Jewish culture of the period; including the presence of many different religions, as well as literature and other phenomena without any religious significance.

Secular biblical literature comprises both complete works and independent literary units within larger works, such as:

The Life of Joseph – A long tale within the patriarch and matriarch narratives in the book of Genesis, it begins with the story of an ambitious child with dreams of grandeur. The son of his father's favourite wife, Joseph considers himself to be superior to his brothers, who sell him to the Ishmaelites, who in turn sell him to an Egyptian landowner. By his own devices he eventually becomes viceroy of the greatest power on Earth, ruling by force of his personality, intelligence and economic planning; marries the daughter of an Egyptian priest and raises his children as Egyptians to the extent that his father fails to recognise them when they approach his deathbed seeking his blessing. Joseph is the loneliest man in the Bible. The Egyptian courtiers refuse to dine with him because of his Hebrew origins, even when he becomes ruler of the entire kingdom; and he will not dine with his brothers, from whom he conceals his identity, due to his own vindictive nature.

Judah's Monologue – A magnificent example of Jewish rhetoric, in which Judah saves his youngest brother, and thereby spares his father devastating anguish. The monologue provides the intricate story of Joseph and his brothers with a dramatic turning point, at which Joseph raises – for the first time – the possibility that God is behind all they have experienced. The splendid structure of this short monologue brings the reader to believe in the protagonist's ability to change the course of events, melting even the heart of Joseph: the Jew who had become a vindictive and unrelenting Egyptian, who had not only tormented his brothers for all those years, but also his father – hiding his fate and identity from him for so long, although his palace stood only a few days' journey from his father's tents.

Jotham's Parable – Failing to find a king among the good fruit trees, the trees of the forest are compelled to accept the leafless and fruitless bramble – the power of which lies entirely in the fire that can issue from it and devour all the others – as their sovereign. Jotham's parable is an incisive universal metaphor for the failure of every political regime in which the barren trees – those lacking education and expertise – come to power, because all of the educated, talented experts consider ruling over others a waste of time and energy, and therefore refuse "to hold sway over the trees". The dire consequences of the fertile trees' refusal, according to Jotham in the tenth or eleventh century BCE, is that the brambles will seize power in every regime, periodically spewing forth fire and devouring all of the trees of the forest. The author places this monologue in the mouth of Jotham, in the context of a political struggle for the throne toward the end of the first millennium BCE. It's power however, lies in the parable, which offers a moral that is as clear today as it was then.

The story of Tamar, wife of Er, who disguised herself as a prostitute and seduced Judah, in order to compel him to accept his obligations under the law of levirate marriage. In the end, he was forced to admit "she hath been more righteous than I" when he pardoned her, after having condemned her to death by fire for "being with child by whoredom". This is one of the many examples of a biblical author's sympathetic attitude toward his (or her) female protagonist who – only by her own sexual initiative succeeds in overcoming her inferior status and total dependence upon men; even sinners like Onan, who spilled his seed to the ground as he lay with Tamar, his brother's widow, that her sons might not inherit with his.

The story of Ruth the Moabite falls into the same category as that of Tamar: a woman in great distress, widowed and childless, without a man to protect or support her. Here too, Ruth uses sex in order to extricate herself from her predicament, when she follows her mother-in-law's advice and rapes Boaz, master of the estate, coming to his bed when he is in a drunken sleep (like Jacob, who was raped by Leah), causing him to "startle" and lie with her, thereby becoming her husband and retroactively fulfilling the levirate duties that apply to male relatives of a childless widow's husband.

The Rape of Tamar sister of Absalom, by her brother Amnon, is the opening chapter of a central secular narrative within the historical novel of the life of David, in most of which God plays no part. The story of Tamar's rape marks the beginning of the deterioration in relations between David and his favourite son – culminating in Absalom's rebellion against his father, who failed to respond to the abomination perpetrated by Amnon. The author recounts the story of Absalom's revenge, how he chases David out of his capital, publicly lies with the exiled king's wives, and engages him in battle, until Absalom is finally slain, having been caught by the hair in the branches of a tree, and the battle is decided in favour of David's army.

The epilogue affords one of the saddest scenes in all of biblical literature. The father mourns the death of his beloved son, as if taking no pleasure whatsoever in the victory that has suppressed the rebellion. David's cry of anguish over the loss of his son marks a tragic turning point in this historical novel, as a lifetime of escape from every misfortune draws to a close. The aging king abandons affairs of state, and closets himself with his love, Abishag the Shunammite, the maiden who delivered him from the cold he suffered in his final years.

The short political novel Esther, plays a greater role in Jewish cultural life than any of the Bible's other secular works. This novel, dedicated to the thwarting of history's first "final solution" to the Jewish problem: the problem of being different from the peoples among whom they live, as the author explains. The story describes the Jewish diaspora in the lands of the Persian Empire – most of the known world at the time. Mordechai, a Jewish leader and go-between at the gates of the royal court, introduces his young relative, Esther, into the palace. The first Jewish woman in literature to hide her identity, Esther thereby succeeds in entering and winning the international sex competition conducted by the king in order to choose a new queen to add to his harem.

All of the Jews in the world are in danger of physical annihilation, yet the author does not involve God in the story of their deliverance. Mordechai places all of the responsibility upon the shoulders of Esther, who has attained prominence in the palace, pretending to be a non-Jew. Despite her fears and initial hesitation, this Jewish woman takes on the task, and displays amazing skill as she lays a sexual trap, reminiscent of the intrigues that feature many centuries later in literature describing the French royal court.

In a seduction scene that forces the chief minister who had planned the annihilation of the Jews to appear as if he had been trying to make a pass at the queen or rape her, Esther causes him to fall on her bed while the king steps out into the palace garden, thereby effecting the political downfall and execution of the planner of the first final solution, along with all of his sons. Without revealing her Jewish identity, she succeeds in having her Jewish uncle promoted to the position of chief minister of the Persian Empire – the second Jewish minister in the Bible to take control of a great empire.

The author, like all prose authors in the Bible, tries to lend his account a historiographical air. The story moves from the royal court to Jewish victory celebrations, held throughout the diaspora to mark the annulment of the decree of mass destruction issued and promulgated by the royal court. The celebrations turn into pogroms of vengeance perpetrated by the Jews against their neighbours, like the rebellion of diaspora Jewish communities in the Roman Empire of the second century CE.

This bloody episode suddenly connects to the account of events at the palace, helping Esther assume the role it came to play in Jewish cultural life in diaspora communities for two thousand years. Jews, who lived as a persecuted minority throughout Christian and Moslem Asia, Africa and Europe, came to see the story of Esther as realising their inner hopes of penetrating the upper echelons of power and avenging themselves of their persecutors.

Since the story ignores the God of Israel entirely, Esther became a part of carnival celebrations, costume-wearing and general licence from all decent, rational behaviour – including the obligation to drink to the point of being "unable to distinguish between blessed Mordechai and cursed Haman".

The secular (without prohibitions or ritual) holiday of Purim (the "Feast of Lots" and fortune) is celebrated to commemorate the victory of Esther and her successful disguise, as a carnival festival of the kind that can be found in every culture: one day a year free of the normal conventions of propriety, on which people may behave – behind a mask – as if they have indeed changed identity. In Jewish culture, the annual carnival is given added "historical" significance, associated with the story of Esther and the Jewish People's wondrous deliverance from all attempts to destroy it.

Esther and the holiday of Purim have played a decisive role in Jewish dramatic art and culture. From the carnival processions of yeshivah students in the Middle Ages (see Schiffer on the history of Jewish theatre) intended to rival the carnival celebrations of Christian seminarians, to plays written for the holiday (the Purimspiel and renaissance plays such as *A Comedy of Betrothal* by De' Sommi), which constituted an early phase in the history of popular Jewish theatre, from the Haskalah to modern Jewish theatre – developing in many parts of the diaspora and in Eretz Yisrael during the twentieth century.

The secular works of prose in Bible include many stories, like those of Esther, Tamar wife of Er, Ruth, Tamar sister of Amnon, the life of Joseph, Jeremiah's struggle in the court of Zedekiah, the story of Nehemiah, etc.

The Bible's greatest work of secular poetry is a magnificent poem celebrating love between a man and a woman. Precisely because it is a secular work, in which God plays no role and is not even mentioned, the work has been wrapped in midrashic and Kabbalistic interpretation, to the point of concealing its original force and literary merit.

Song of Songs: A Secular Masterpiece Arbitrarily Distorted by Midrashic Interpretation

Even the name Song of Songs reflects the biblical redactors' awareness of the greatness and importance of this lyrical secular work in world literature. We can assume that the redactors of the Bible in the early first millennium CE, knew Aramaic, Greek and Hebrew, and were no less capable of evaluating literary merit than we are. That is perhaps why they insisted that the secular Song of Songs be included in the "Book of Books", despite criticism and opposition. Those who opposed including the Song of Songs in the canon of holy scripture were well aware of its vitality, sensuality, erotic and aesthetic force, and its contribution to understanding the sublime spirituality of physical love.

The redactors attributed the poem to Solomon, whose idealised image was well established by their time. He was reputed to have been a great, successful, rich and wise king; a great lover of the many women in his harem, and of the Queen who had come all the way from Sheba in Africa to seek his company. Attributing the Song of Songs to Solomon added 'secular poet' to the many other accomplishments of this king so beloved in Jewish tradition, despite the religious transgressions he committed in establishing the cults of the gods of neighbouring peoples in temples he built for them in Jerusalem.

The greatness of the Song of Songs as a secular love poem is revealed when it is read by Hebrew-readers, who understand most of its words and expressions without commentary, and experience the poem on an emotional as well as an intellectual level – a response elicited by all great poetry. The cadence of the language, the soliloquies of anguish followed by soliloquies of joy, the passage from dialogue to refrain, from monologue to chorus, the variety of images and styles, the natural metaphors and landscapes of Eretz Yisrael used to express the lovers' feelings.

These devices combine with the poetic setting and the dramatic events portrayed in the poem: A girl's love for a shepherd and her memory of their lovemaking; an enamoured king who offers her all of the treasures of the palace, bewildered to the point that "her soul sets her upon the chariots of her princely people"; she feels as if held captive behind a locked gate, and begins to wander and seek her true love, although she is pursued and beaten by the watchmen; until finally, love triumphs and as she is reunited with her lover and they make wondrous love – urging every beloved woman to rejoice in her happiness, and to leave the king his gold and treasures.

Those who read the Song of Songs in translation, as with all translations of great poetry, read a work diminished in stature and reduced in poetic intensity. Even in translation however, the Song of Songs has won the admiration of connoisseurs of good literature throughout the world. Many of them (from Renan to Pujet and Max Brod) have recognised the dramatic element within the poetry, which shapes the work's characters as well as its plot.

The roles that the Song of Songs has played within Jewish culture have been many and varied, often worlds apart from one another. Those who experience the work as poetry understand its words and expressions in a "simple" fashion, i.e. in keeping with the meaning ascribed to these words in everyday use of the language in which they were written.

This is the essence of "*peshat*" (plain meaning): Literal interpretation of a text, treating the words it comprises in relation to the meaning (function, according to Wittgenstein) we ascribe to them when they are used in various circumstances and situations, beyond the text we are interpreting according to the *peshat* method.

Read in this fashion, the Song of Songs is a sensual poem, celebrating spring and love. In Jewish religious tradition, the Song of Songs has been appended to the Passover Haggadah, and is read by religious Jews (Ashkenazi and Sephardic) on the first eve of Passover, thereby recalling the fact that Passover, in addition to being a historical holiday, is also an ancient festival of spring – predating the exodus from Egypt.

Since the early twentieth century, the poem has played many roles in the secular Jewish culture that has developed in Hebrew in Eretz Yisrael. Many of its verses have been set to music and have become folk songs; the poem has also inspired the songs and music that have accompanied new folk dances; and its characters have been portrayed in works of art.

Recently, the Song of Songs has also begun to return to the secular Passover *Seder* (a dramatic version of the text, written by the French monk Pujet – following the original order of the verses, but dividing them into different voices so they can easily be read as a play – was published in 1965, and reprinted in the "New Israeli Haggadah" that appeared in *Free Judaism* in 1995).

The Song of Songs can elicit the above responses and fulfil the many functions that it does in the majority culture today owing to its *peshat* reading – i.e. one that affords words and expression meanings that readers have learned from experience, having encountered the functions (meanings) of these words and expression in the various circumstances of their lives.

The reader instinctively understands expressions such as: "Behold, thou art fair, my love; behold, thou art fair; thine eyes are as doves"; "Behold, thou art fair, my beloved, yea, pleasant; also our bed is green." … "As an apple-tree among the trees of the wood, so is my beloved among the sons. Under its shadow I delighted to sit, and its fruit was sweet to my taste"; His left hand should be under my head, and his right hand should embrace me"; "I adjure you, O daughters of Jerusalem, that ye stir not up, nor awaken love, until it please".

In understanding the words' plain meaning, the reader also experiences the poetic depth of meaning that charges the lovers' memories and longing with erotic sensuality because s/he knows the expressions that make up these verses, from other contexts in the Hebrew language. Such intuitive understanding forms the basis of the poetic experience and the aesthetic appreciation that explains it. Midrashic interpretation ignores this mode of understanding, clothing the poem in meaning that is alien to the poem's content and spirit, destroying the poetic experience, turning the poem into a puzzle, and engaging the reader in trying to find a solution or in negotiating the solutions offered by other midrashic commentators.

I am inclined toward the opinion of those who suggest that Rabbi Akiva, in the second century CE, may have proposed such a midrashic interpretation in order to save the Song of Songs from being suppressed, as more stringent sages had demanded. He cunningly asserted that the Song of Songs was "holy of holies", and not merely "holy" like the other writings of the Bible. In order to justify this claim, it was necessary to find commentary that would distance the poem from its original meaning, like the midrash that established that the Song of Songs is an expression of the love between God and the Catholic Church or the People of Israel – an interpretation that could sanction the poem's inclusion in the Jewish and Christian scriptures, despite its being a secular work and despite its explicit eroticism.

A similar discrepancy can be found between the plain meaning and midrashic interpretation of all of the works of the Bible, none however so clearly demonstrated as in the case of the Song of Songs. Rashi, one of the greatest mediaeval biblical commentators, frequently offers both the plain, literal meaning, and a midrashic, allegorical interpretation of the text, representing an idea or phenomenon of particular interest to the commentator, albeit absent from the original passage.

For the verse in the Song of Songs beginning "I am black, but comely, O ye daughters of Jerusalem", Rashi suggests the following literal interpretation: "My friends, make not light of me, even if my man has left me for my blackness, for I am black because the sun hath tanned me, but comely in figure. If I am black as the tents of Kedar that blacken from the rain, for they are always pitched in the desert, I am easily washed and made as the curtains of Solomon." There are however, writes Rashi, those who propose the following allegorical interpretation: "I (the People of Israel – Y.M.) am black in my deeds, but comely in the deeds of my fathers, although some of my deeds are also comely. Although I bear the transgression of the golden calf, I also bear the merit of having received the Torah. And the nations are called 'daughters of Jerusalem', as [the city] will one day become a metropolis for all."

When explaining the phrase "thy two breasts" however, Rashi offers only a midrashic interpretation: "The two breasts that nurse you, that is Moses and Aaron". When midrashic commentary relates to the two breasts of the Shulamite as "Moses and Aaron", it becomes apparent just how ludicrous and arbitrary is the very attempt to interpret this love poem as a metaphor for the love between God and the Jewish People.

Midrashic commentary begins to appear socially and politically dangerous when anti-Zionists today read the verse "I adjure you, O daughters of Jerusalem, that ye stir not up, nor awaken love, until it please", and see in it a divine exhortation against Zionism, which fails to await the miraculous messiah but rather, actively pursues redemption, realising the dream of independence and rebirth of the Jewish state in its ancient homeland, as envisioned by prophets, messiahs, and philosophers such as Maimonides and Spinoza.

The danger in such arbitrary interpretation lies in attributing any political idea the midrashist may have to a text held sacred by religious Jews, as if such things had been written in the text itself. The arbitrariness of such interpretation becomes malice when rabbis like Yoel of Satmar accuse Zionists and other secular Jews of having caused the Nazi Holocaust by their sins against God – as implied by the political interpretation given to this piece of love poetry.

The contrast between the plain and allegorical interpretations of the Song of Songs is but one example of the gap that exists between the two most influential approaches to Jewish and Bible studies. There is a fundamental difference between the religious-traditional approach to the Bible, which views Scripture as an integral part of a chain of talmudic and post-talmudic commentary; and the approach that treats each individual piece of biblical literature as an independent work, unrelated to religious commentary. The latter approach sees religious biblical exegesis as a separate branch of Jewish culture, comprising hundreds of contemporary, Haskalah and mediaeval works, as well as Hellenistic-Byzantine works, some of which can be ascribed to the authors of the Talmud – only one of the many literary works associated with the Bible.

The Independent Status of Midrashic Literature

In the diaspora, most young Jews are no longer familiar with the Bible, since it is not part of the curriculum at the non-Jewish schools they attend. Most young secular Jews in the various streams of Judaism in the diaspora are unaware of Judaism's biblical and other foundations, and are gradually breaking away from the Jewish People's common cultural heritage. To effect change, we must re-acquaint Jewish readers with biblical literature, as literary works offering the intelligent reader a poetic and intellectual experience, and an opportunity to discover the foundations of her/his national culture. Non-religious young Jews are turned off by Judaism, when it is presented to them only or mostly as a religion. Similarly, they are turned off by biblical literature, when it is presented to them cloaked in religious midrash and commentary.

The vast body of midrashic literature of course includes works of independent literary worth – like many of the haggadic legends assembled by Bialik, Ravnitzky and others in later literature. The haggadic literature, religious midrash and commentary on the Bible, number among the many literary works created over a period of two thousand years, inspired by the Bible and used retroactively to interpret it. They are however, a category apart from biblical literature. The works of literature that relate to the Bible differ fundamentally from the Bible itself, in almost every possible way: the periods in which they were written, the religious or secular perspectives of their authors, the goals and functions they have served in Jewish and world culture. They should therefore not be appended to the biblical text, as in religious editions of the Bible, in which a few lines of biblical text are surrounded by dozens of lines relating to the original work. While the works of the Bible reflect the lives and views of the biblical era, the works that relate to the Bible the periods in which they were written. In the Hellenistic period for example, Jewish and Christian belief systems began to adopt the concept of life after death, making it one of the pillars of their respective faiths – contrary to the religious outlook of most authors of the Bible and the Prophets.

Many of the midrashic works sought to base new beliefs and

precepts upon Scripture, in order to afford them greater validity and sanctity, as if rooted in the words of Moses and the prophets. The religion of Halakhah, developed in the Oral Law, was a product of the rabbinical (Hazal) reform movement that changed the face of biblical Halakhah and added to it, thereby creating a new Halakhah, with the help of biblical exegesis. The goals and functions of the various works of biblical commentary naturally differ from the goals and functions of the various works of the Bible, which are not all alike, and should not be seen as a single ideological-religious work, as midrashic commentary has sought to portray them.

In order to become acquainted with the literature relating to or inspired by the Bible one would have to select not only from midrashic literature, but from thousands of contemporary and past works of literature, art, scholarship, commentary and philosophy. Such a selection might include works on various levels, such as: Sholem Asch's *"Moses"*, Bialik's *"Dead of the Desert"*, Heim or Heller's *"King David"*, Kafka's *"Description of a Struggle"*, Jacobson's The Rape of Tamar, Tchernichowsky's *"Saul"*, Alterman's Plague Poems, Robert Alter's *"The Art of Biblical Narrative"* and *"The Art of Biblical Poetry"*, and other works of the Bible as literature.

A good introduction to literature relating to the Bible would naturally include works from past eras as well – from the Haskalah, the Middle Ages, and the Hellenistic-Byzantine era. It would of course comprise works from all streams of Judaism past and present. From the Hellenistic-Byzantine period for example, it might include the commentary and exegesis of the creators of the Oral Law and the Midrash, alongside works representing Greek-speaking Jews who lived within the sphere of Hellenic culture – like the works of Philo, Josephus and Ezekiel of Cyrenaica; the frescoes of Dura Europos and synagogue mosaics from Gaza, Tiberias, Sepphoris and Beit Alpha; the Apocrypha and the Pseudepigrapha, the New Testament, the Dead Sea Scrolls, and more.

These authors and artists offered their own interpretations of the works of the Bible. To these we should add the works of scholars – historians, archaeologists, philologists – who have studied the source-materials from which the Bible was created, and compared the works of the Bible to other ancient literature.

A representative sample of the thousands of contemporary and past works relating to and interpreting biblical literature offers a glimpse into the myriad approaches to the biblical text, without marring the enjoyment and experience afforded by the works themselves.

None of these works however, should be appended to the original biblical text or allowed to eclipse it. The works of the Bible should be presented "naked", just as they were heard or read in biblical times, and later translated.

Chapter Four

Individual Interpretation at every Reading
and Peshat as the Common Denominator for All

The naked text reveals itself to the reader who understands its language, knows the different uses of the words of which it is made up, and understands its "plain meaning". This kind of reading is suited to all literature, biblical literature included. Of course, each individual reading is different, but there is a common element we refer to as the *peshat*: interpretation by virtue of the knowledge common to all speakers of the language, who succeed in living and communicating in it, since they know the "literal meaning" of the words, ie the function they fulfil or may fulfil, as Wittgenstein explained in his *Philosophical Investigations*. Since there can be no private language, words and expressions have a meaning known to the speakers of the language in which the work is written. *Peshat* is an expression of the comprehension of the words and expressions that appear in a text, based on a familiarity with their public meaning.

When midrashic and esoteric hermeneutics (*remez, derash and sod*)* replace *peshat*, the literary experience afforded by the original work is lost, since the words' meaning – changed by the commentator – ceases to be public. The words take on meaning in the private language in which the commentator attempts to clothe them (e.g. breasts = Moses and Aaron). The original work disappears beneath the mantle of the other work, which consists of arbitrary meanings invented by the midrashist.

In this sense, there is no difference between religious midrash and modern secular midrash – semiological, deconstructionist, or the like – that sees the text only as a collection of signifiers for the signifieds invented by the deconstructor, without any consideration for the meanings of the public linguistic expressions that make up the text.

Both read into the text things that are not there, and since non-existence is infinite, there is no limit to midrashic interpretation.

Those who read a text cloaked in one of the mantles of midrash, like the one that sees the Song of Songs as a celebration of the love between Yahweh and the Catholic Church or the People of Israel, or an exhortation to fight "redemption-precipitating" Zionism, are not reading "the Song of Songs which is Solomon's" that appears in the Bible, but a different work, one that is not there.

Readers of the original Song of Songs, according to its plain meaning, also suggest different readings of the biblical text, like seeing the poem as a drama comprising many poems around a central narrative, in which the king's love competes with that of the shepherd in the heart and life of the girl who is the play's protagonist. Such individual readings are all based on the literal meaning of the words and expressions that appear in the poem, as they are used in the language in which the work was written. In this sense, such readings afford direct contact with linguistic reality and the human reality it serves.

Bergson said of one such reader of the Song of Songs as drama – the French monk Pujet – "He was a wonderful man. He never let an idea of any kind stand between him and reality".

Peshat in the Hellenistic Era – Greek and Aramaic Translations of the Bible

Peshat interpretation was already the predominant approach to biblical literature in the Hellenistic era, as witnessed by the first translations of biblical works. Many years before the creation of the biblical canon, there began to appear in Greek and Aramaic-speaking communities, translations of works sanctified by tradition, that would later become part of the biblical anthology.

Any translation can be a midrashic interpretation, employing phrases that bear little resemblance to those appearing in the original text. Most of the translations that began to appear in the early Hellenistic-Byzantine period however, closely follow the *peshat*, and employ expressions closely resembling those used in the original texts.

Many of the books later included in the Hebrew Bible, were commonly regarded as scripture as early as the first half of the first millennium BCE. The "Septuagint" – Hebrew to Greek translation – begun in the third century BCE, played a central role in Jewish cultural life and in the culture of other nations, inasmuch as it made the masterpieces of Hebrew literature accessible to the Greek-speakers of the Middle East and southern Europe, thereby introducing to them, the foundations of the monotheism of Moses and the prophets, and the Jewish historical legacy established through these works as the cornerstone of Jewish national consciousness.

The public reading of the Torah in the synagogues in the vernacular developed a Jewish national consciousness intermingled with Jewish religion. In the large, Greek-speaking Jewish communities of Egypt, Cyrenaica and the many Hellenistic cities in Eretz Yisrael and elsewhere in Asia and southern Europe, biblical literature disseminated through these translations was to become a cohesive element, common to all communities and streams of Judaism in the Hellenistic period.

Aramaic translations played a similar role in the Jewish communities of Eretz Yisrael and the eastern diaspora, in which Aramaic was both the vernacular and the literary language.

Owing to their *peshat* method of interpretation, these translations made it possible to disseminate a historical and cultural heritage common to all Jewish communities.

The synagogues, which began to proliferate during the Second Temple period, but especially after the destruction of the temple, played a central role in the educational system – aimed at adults as well as children – that began to develop within the Jewish communities. In religious Judaism of the period, as in secular Judaism today, biblical literature was the cornerstone of Jewish education and constituted the better part of its curriculum.

On the Sabbath and holidays – which were gradually transformed from nature festivals to historical holidays – chapters were read from the books of the Bible, providing seasonal reminders of the literature itself, and of the historical legacy both Jews and non-Jews believed it faithfully represented.

Peshat readings, as reflected in most of the verses of the Greek and Aramaic (Yonatan ben Uziel and Onkelos) translations, were essential to the preservation and development of a historical and cultural legacy common to all Jews: Pharisees and Sadducees, Essenes and members of the Qumran sect, Hellenists and Rabbinical Jews, Karaites, Samaritans, and Christian Jews.

Most of the translations, say experts, employ expressions that would have been understood by readers as common expressions in those languages, familiar from their functions in contexts wholly unrelated to the biblical literature. A reader of one of the translations could thus envision and reflect upon the reality created by and expressed in the original Hebrew.

The exceptions prove this rule. For example, Onkelos translates the humane requirement that a kid not be cooked in its mother's milk, as a prohibition against mixing milk and meat. This odd translation arose from Onkelos' familiarity with the precept invented by the post-biblical halakhic reformers, whereby meat and milk could not be consumed together. Since Onkelos understood the biblical verse in the context of the later prohibition, he interpreted the source in midrashic fashion, as if the biblical author had in fact been referring to the new laws of kashruth. Such midrashic interpretation distorts the original source and its intention, and serves as an indication of the great difference between *peshat* and *derash*.

In the eyes of a reader familiar with biblical literature, Onkelos' translation of this verse is entirely without basis, since there is no biblical injunction against the consumption of milk and meat together. Abram, father of the Jewish nation, was thus able to cook and serve a meal of meat and milk to God, when the latter visited his home in the company of two messengers.

From the Septuagint to the French translations of Edouard Dohrm and the English translations of Robert Alter (based upon a reading of the biblical text as it is understood by those who know and speak the Hebrew language), the *peshat* tradition continues; resumed by the secular Jewish educational system in Palestine in the first half of the twentieth century, following the principle established during the Haskalah, whereby the biblical text should be read naked of midrashic commentary.

The rebirth of Hebrew as a spoken and literary language in late nineteenth century Europe and throughout the twentieth century in Eretz Yisrael, imbued the original biblical text with new life, in the minds of the sons and daughters of Hebrew culture. Children whose mother tongue is Hebrew enjoy the rare privilege of reading works of literature written two to three thousand years ago, as they were written – in a language close to their own vernacular. Those in Israel for whom Hebrew is the language of speech, communication and literature, understand most of the expressions that make up the works of the Bible. Peshat interpretation therefore predominates among Hebrew-readers who are not obligated to append the traditional commentaries common in Orthodox religious Judaism to every biblical text.

When we read the Bible using the peshat method, Jacob once again struggles with God at Peniel, "face to face", as he plainly says, and the angel invented by the commentators disappears from the story.

The Advantages of Reading the Bible as Literature and the Danger of Giving Biblical Criticism Exclusive Rein

The second half of the twentieth century saw the "Bible as literature" approach regain popularity. According to this approach, the various components of the Bible can be read as complete and independent works, based on the peshat method, detached from religious midrashic commentary, and compared to other works of Jewish and world literature in all eras.

Readers of the Bible as literature see the biblical anthology as a selection representing the whole of Jewish literature created during the first millennium BCE – as opposed to those who consider the Bible to be a single monolithic work, conveying a uniform religious message.

The Bible as literature approach also stands in contrast to the approach that views the Bible as a repository of sources to be studied individually, so that each work is broken down into its estimated component parts, precluding the possibility of reading it as a work of literature. Reading the works of the Bible as complete works of literature, does not imply ignoring the theories regarding the various sources that form the whole. The "author" of a given work of biblical literature presumably refers to a group of many authors, as well as the editors who shaped it into a single literary work. Job or the Song of Songs can thus be divided into what scholars believe to be their component parts, as they stood before having been joined together. They can also be read however, as complete literary units, in which the presumed parts have combined to create a poetic, philosophical and emotional experience – alongside or even despite our awareness of the

279

possibility that they are in fact conglomerates of many previously existing units.

Rereading the Bible as an anthology of literary works in which most of the existing genres in western literature are represented, helps renew our bond to the Bible. Those who do not view the Bible as God-given, and do not relate to it as a religious or sacred text, are rediscovering these exciting, enjoyable, thought-provoking works of literature, and identifying with the characters they have shaped.

Reading the Bible in this fashion differs fundamentally from the midrashic reading of religious tradition, as it does from the dissection of biblical works into their "sources" for the purposes of historical and philological research.

Secular readers of the Bible as literature need not ignore the research done in the field of biblical criticism, or the theories it proposes regarding the sources of biblical texts. In order to be able to read the works of the Bible as complete works of literature however, they must "suspend disbelief". The "suspension of disbelief" appeared to Coleridge to be a condition for the enjoyment of any work of fiction. When reading fiction, we are aware of the fact that the work we are reading is indeed fiction and not an account of events as they really happened, but we suspend our disbelief in the historical truth of the events it depicts. The literary experience depends upon the reader's ability to treat the story and events as if they were faithful representations of reality. Thanks to the ability to suspend disbelief in the truthfulness of a work of fiction, readers and audiences can feel suspense, fear, sadness or joy at the events portrayed in a novel or film, identifying with the characters, as if they were living people and not made of words, or roles played by actors.

The same is true of biblical fiction. For example, we agree

with Abram that the judge of all the earth does not act justly when he metes out collective punishment; we are shaken and condemn Abraham when he binds his son on the altar and brings the slaughtering knife to his throat in order to sacrifice him to his God. The poetic experience derived from these stories does not depend upon knowledge of the Yahwist, Elohist, Priestly or Deuteronomist sources – as interesting as they may be.

Many writers have contributed to the renewed interest in reading the works of the Bible as complete literary works. Their own work highlights the elements of the poetic experience, emotional and aesthetic, elicited by the form and content of biblical literature.

In many of the works of the Bible, read as complete works, we find the insight into the human experience that is to be found in great literature. They present the reader with moral dilemmas faced by all human beings. Only when they are read as complete literary units, do we discover their ability to shape the divine and human characters that live in their pages, and as real historical figures in our minds.

Since Auerbach's *Mimesis*, Robert Alter has paved the way for the Bible as literature (although he personally dislikes the term "Bible as literature" because it states the obvious and is therefore meaningless). Through his books on the art of biblical narrative and poetry, his many articles addressing various aspects of the topic, his annotated English translation of Genesis, and The Literary Guide to the Bible edited together with Frank Kermode, Alter has become the most influential literary critic within a broad movement advocating the reading of the Bible as a literary anthology.

Among the many books that have influenced this approach: *The Book of God* by Gabriel Josipovici, Nahum Sarna's *Understanding Genesis* and *On the Book of Psalms*, *The Bible as*

Literature by Samuel Daiches, Robert Gordis' *Koheleth*, Samuel P. Fokkelman's *Narrative Art and Poetry in the Books of Samuel*, Harold Bloom's *The Book of J*, *Poetry in the Bible* by Edouard Dohrm, *Joseph and his Brothers* by Thomas Mann, Martin Buber's *On the Bible*, Yair Hoffman's *A Blemished Perfection*, Yaira Amit's *The Book of Judges – The Art of Editing*, *Biblical Narrative* by Frank Pollack, Yair Zakovitch's *David*, Shlomo Dov Goitein's *The Art of Biblical Narrative*, *The Poetics of Biblical Narrative* by Meir Sternberg, etc.

This renewed interest in the Bible is not only influenced by critical research and other scholarship. The attitude to works of the bible as literature is reflected in the hundreds of works of prose, poetry, music, painting, sculpture, film and theatre they have inspired.

The religious nature of some biblical works – in which God and faith play decisive roles – does not detract from their poetic beauty in the spiritual lives of secular Jews. Religious works of all periods and religions are appreciated as works of art and literature in the cultural lives of secular Jews and non-Jews alike.

Biblical literature is once again becoming a part of secular Jewish education, in conjunction with the study of Jewish and surrounding cultures. Such studies broaden and deepen secular Jewish awareness of our national culture.

The Danger of Appending Semiological Midrash to Biblical Literature Like the Danger of Appending Religious Midrash

The idea of reading biblical works as inspiring literature has saved them from neglect and the obscurity to which they have been relegated by religious midrash, and from pseudo-scientific semiological and psychoanalytic midrash aimed at deconstructing the original texts.

282

Semiological midrash presents every text as concealing and suppressing a "subtext", revealed and interpreted by its liberator, the poststructural analyst. The text is treated as a collection of signifiers, the significance of which lies in their signifieds – hidden from the reader but accessible to the scholarly analyst who knows the text's hidden political, ideological and psychological intentions.

Semiological midrash of all kinds follows in the footsteps of traditional religious midrash, in that it substitutes a new creation for the original work, no longer capable of providing a poetic and emotional experience, or a personal bond with the characters and their creators.

Midrash, both religious and scientific, addresses the signifieds presumed by its creators, and ignores what it considers to be a mere collection of signifiers. This kind of practice neutralises the poetic force of the work and its ability to influence the emotional and cultural lives of its readers.

This approach, which swept through many of the departments of literature and art at universities throughout the world in the 1970s, alienated students from the study of literature, which had disappeared under a mountain of interpretation and semiological analysis, just as biblical text had disappeared under a mountain of religious commentary.

To correct this, the reading of literature should be kept separate from the reading and study of research and analysis that use literary texts as raw material to create other, midrashic works. Some of these midrashic creations – religious and scientific – might be interesting on an intellectual level, or include brilliant hypotheses regarding the authors' political and psychological motives. Even when such works are worthy creations in and of themselves however, they should not be appended to the literary texts to which they relate.

The Role of the Bible in Judaism as Culture,
Past and Present

The works of the Bible have functioned as classical literature in the culture of the Jewish People in all times and places. A national culture's "classics" are works of art and literature that the educational elite and leadership recognise and disseminate as the founding works of the nation's historical and cultural heritage.

Classical literature remains alive and relevant as long as people are exposed to it. It offers readers a poetic experience, and contributes to a conscious awareness of a common historical and cultural legacy. This type of consciousness has existed to varying degrees throughout our history, depending on social stratum and period.

The Bible's literary works began to function in this capacity during the second half of the first millennium BCE, even before the creation of the biblical canon. Works of literature that had been widely disseminated in Jewish culture and had fulfilled the functions of classical national literature were included by the redactors of the biblical anthology, when the canon of Jewish Holy Scripture was completed in the early first millennium CE.

These works played central roles in the cultural lives of Jewish communities in the diaspora and in Eretz Yisrael within the framework of the synagogue, around which Jewish cultural communities had formed. In the synagogues, which served as communal education and cultural centres, the Bible was read publicly on the Sabbath and holidays, in the Hebrew original and in the vernacular. The readings were accompanied by sermons, which further developed Jewish rhetorical literature, rooted in the discourses of the prophets. It was on the basis of these sermons that the Halakhic and Haggadic Midrash literature developed during the Hellenistic period in Palestine and in Babylonia, alongside the exegesis of Hellenistic Jewish writers such as Philo,

Josephus, Ezekiel the dramaturge and others, in the western diaspora.

This tradition of weekly public readings from the Bible and Bible study within the framework of Bible-centred Jewish education established biblical literature as the classical literature of the Jewish People.

The Bible, the "wandering homeland of the Jewish People", as Heine called it, continued to play a central role in Jewish cultural and educational life. Only toward the end of the first millennium CE, following the completion of the Talmuds, did the Oral Law begin to replace the Bible as the main focus of education in rabbinical Judaism. The large Karaite movement, which sought to maintain the primacy of the Bible as the sole "Book of Books" of Jewish culture and Halakhah, remained faithful to the Bible as the main subject of Jewish studies.

The tradition of reading from the Bible on the Sabbath and holidays persisted in all Judaisms, allowing the Bible to continue to exert an influence, as classical literature, upon broad sections of the people, not educated in the talmudic academies. The Bible remained the constant frame of reference in the Talmud, Midrash and Kabbalah literature, which continued to develop throughout the Middle Ages, establishing the Bible as the only basis common to all Jewish social strata, ethnicities and diasporas.

In the Middle Ages and the modern era, educated Jews in Africa, Asia and Europe knew Hebrew, as a result of Bible studies in Jewish educational networks. Most works of mediaeval Jewish art and literature and a large part of such works from the Haskalah period, relate to the works of the Bible as a source of inspiration and point of reference.

In the Orthodox educational systems that developed in the modern era, talmudic and midrashic literature came to dominate the curriculum, marginalising Bible studies. Halakhah became the main subject of study in the Orthodox stream of Judaism. In our times it has ceased to develop, going from a dialogue-based process to a fixed set of laws codified in the Shulhan Arukh.

The pluralism characteristic of biblical literature, continued to develop in the modern era in Judaism's non-Orthodox streams. Mass religious movements such as the Reform and Conservative movements, as well as mass secular Jewish movements, both Zionist and anti-Zionist, returned to the Bible as the backbone of Jewish education. In secular Jewish schools in Eretz Yisrael, talmudic studies were marginalised.

The Jewish culture that is reflected in the Bible – marked by a broad range of beliefs, precepts, God concepts, morality and ritual – is closer to the Jewish culture that developed in Eretz Yisrael in the twentieth century, than the halakhic religious Judaism reflected in the Talmud, in which diverse opinions are expressed, but only within the narrow framework of halakhic discourse.

From the late ninteenth century to the years preceding the Holocaust, a majority of the Jewish People abandoned Orthodoxy, its lifestyle and its educational institutions. In Orthodox communities – both hassidic and mitnagdic – insularism from general culture and from other streams of religious and secular Judaism prevailed. While the Bible had become central once again at most Jewish educational institutions around the world, Orthodox education continued to focus solely or primarily on talmudic studies.

In Israel, the Bible fulfils the functions of classical literature, instilling national consciousness, playing a central role in the education of the secular majority of the Jewish population, and serving as a source of inspiration for many products of Israeli culture – in the fields of poetry, music, art, literature and scholarship.

The tradition of reading from the Bible on the Sabbath and Holidays continues and continues to change in active secular cultural communities. In dozens of secular synagogues throughout the United States for example, biblical texts are read in the course of study or at bar and bat-mitzvahs.

Ever since the first Hebrew radio broadcasts during the times of the British Mandate, and subsequently on Israeli television as well, biblical texts have been a part of daily broadcasts, and have featured in special programmes on the Sabbath and holidays.

In scores of secular synagogues, havurot and other secular communities in the United States and Canada, and at secular cultural centres in Paris and Brussels, chapters from the Bible are the focal point of bat and bar-mitzvah celebrations.

Secular Jewish culture continues to enhance the tradition of reading works of the Bible at specific times. Many have renewed the custom of associating biblical works with the Jewish holidays. This custom enriches the holiday celebrations and reveals new facets in the biblical works themselves, through greater familiarity with them, and comparison to contemporary or past works relating to or inspired by them. Religious tradition has associated masterpieces of biblical literature with all of the important holidays: Genesis with Rosh Hashanah, Jonah with Yom Kippur, Ecclesiastes with Sukkot, Esther with Purim, Song of Songs with Passover, Ruth with Shavuot, Lamentations with the ninth of Av (or Holocaust Remembrance Day). To the above, some add: Maccabees on Hannukah, the life of Jeremiah and selected prophecies on the Fast of Gedaliah or Rabin Memorial Day, selected stories from the life of King David and Kings on Israel Independence Day, and the stories of Joseph and Moses on Passover.

The majority of young people living in Jewish culture in Israel, for whom Hebrew is a spoken language as well as the language of education, scholarship, entertainment and art, share a unique linguistic affinity toward the Bible. This affinity has developed

287

since the revolution of the Hebrew language's rebirth in the early twentieth century. Within a few decades, Hebrew was re-established as the language of the Jewish People living in Israel, and of the millions of Jewish immigrants it absorbed over the course of the second half of the twentieth century.

The rebirth of an ancient tongue, making it a modern language for all purposes and all fields, after not having been spoken popularly for over two thousand years, is an unprecedented phenomenon in the history of world culture. The Bible played a central role in this social and cultural revolution. Biblical Hebrew continues to exert a significant influence on spoken and written language in Israel even as it continues to develop, gaining thousands of new words and expressions that do not appear anywhere in the Bible. Many Hebrew speakers and writers are completely unaware of the biblical origins of the expressions they use. The presence of biblical language in the modern vernacular, and the convergence of the two, is evident in the words and expressions Israelis use on a daily basis, in metaphors and literary references, grammatical forms and orthography.

Biblical characters and subjects have become the themes of new works of Hebrew poetry, prose, painting, sculpture and the performing arts. From pop songs such as "Goliat" and "Beriat Ha'olam" to tragic poetry on the theme of Isaac's binding applied to the present generation of Israeli parents, from plays on biblical themes to turning the biblical text itself into powerful and popular theatre. The long list goes on to include works inspired by the Bible and attuned to contemporary audiences.

The Bible is central not only to Israeli art and culture, but also to social and political life in the Jewish state. Zionism itself and the ideologies of the various political movements in Israel are based upon or use historical and literary references from the Bible in support of their political positions. Opposite those who use biblical literature to support the idea of "Israel as a Jewish state in all of Eretz Yisrael", stand those who assert that most of the Jewish states in biblical times controlled only parts of Eretz Yisrael.

The idea of the Jewish People's return to its homeland is expressed by the biblical prophets, and shared by all streams of Zionism, which asserts the right of the Jewish People, like any other people, to live in its own sovereign state, so that any of its members who wish or need to come to its shores, may do so. The Bible however, also attests to the fact that most of the Jews who left Israel during the first Jewish exile, never returned. Only a small fraction of the Babylonian exiles and their descendants heeded the call of the emperor Cyrus, allowing and even encouraging Jews to return to their land and rebuild it. Most of the Jews residing in the large communities of Babylonia and Egypt ignored Cyrus' appeal, just as a majority of Jews in the twentieth century ignored the Balfour Declaration, and continued to live in all the lands of the diaspora.

The secular and Zionist yishuv that developed in Palestine, beginning in the early twentieth century, saw itself as fulfilling the hopes of the biblical prophets and preparing the ground for the re-establishment of an independent Jewish state in Eretz Yisrael.

The political leadership (particularly Ben Gurion and Dayan) and the educational system, encouraged affinity toward the Bible, the Land of Israel, the landscapes and sites described in the Bible and discovered in archaeological digs and tours throughout the country. Biblical archaeology became news in the daily press before and after the establishment of the state.

Belief in the historical and cultural legacy established by the Bible in the minds and cultures of all Judaisms, has formed the basis of the various religious and secular messianic movements that have been a part of Jewish history ever since the rebellion against Rome and the civil war between the various Jewish factions in Jerusalem, bringing about the destruction of the city and the temple by the Romans in the first century CE. The messianic movements – religious (like the mass movement of Nathan of Gaza and Shabbetai Zevi), and secular (like political Zionism) – also based their ideas on the works of the Bible and the hopes expressed therein, "for the return of the Jewish People to its homeland, to a state that would be an international centre of ethical monotheism, sending forth the message of peace to all peoples". The difficulties these movements experienced in realising their goals and the great discrepancy between utopia and reality, did not weaken the ardour and strength of those who believed in them.

Secular Zionism, that has begun to realise the utopia that was the cornerstone of its ideology, needed the Bible and the words of the prophets in order to make this ideology an integral part of Judaism as the culture of the Jewish People.

As secular Judaism grows throughout the world, as Jews in most diaspora Judaisms grow further away from Jewish studies of all kinds, so the Bible becomes increasingly important, as the only common basis for the study of Judaism as culture in all forms of Jewish education.

Rebellion against God, The Basis of Man's Humanity

Maimonides was the first Jewish thinker to relate to the Genesis stories as human creations, in which the authors used allegory to make God in man's image, that the simple and uneducated masses might believe in a personal God. He devotes most of the first part of the Guide for the Perplexed to God's abstractness: possessing neither shape nor form, beyond every human concept – even that of "existence", in the sense that human discourse ascribes to the word. It was clear to Maimonides that in no real sense could God be described in man's image, as possessing a mouth able to speak and command, or an arm capable of striking and punishing, or the ability to walk about his garden or perform any other human action. The biblical narrative thus ascribes to God all of the physical attributes that, according to Maimonides, cannot be ascribed to him. The godhead, in the opinion of the author of the Guide for the Perplexed, is an entity devoid not only of human substance, but of all human conception. The physical, anthropomorphic, God of the Bible is, according to Maimonides, a product of human literary imagination, which has played a decisive role in the religious history of the Jewish People and of many other peoples as well: enabling those unable to grasp the concept of divinity as the supreme wisdom of the cosmos – comprising, dictating and creating the laws of nature – to believe in God. Maimonides writes as follows:

"The Torah speaks according to the language of man, that is to say, expressions, which can easily be comprehended and understood by all, are applied to the Creator. Hence the description of God by attributes implying corporeality, in order to express His existence: because the multitude of people do not easily conceive existence unless in connection with a body, and that which is not a body nor connected with a body has for them no existence." (Guide for the Perplexed, I,26; translation M. Friedlander, 1904)

There is no doubt that without corporeality, all of the actions ascribed to God as if he were a living being – by the masses accustomed to them from childhood – could not be imagined (ibid.). As a religious thinker who believed in the obligation to observe all of the precepts in the Talmud, as codified in his Mishneh Torah; and believing, as he did, in indisputable "demonstrated proof" of the existence of God; Maimonides was convinced that the biblical authors who created a corporeal anthropomorphic God, had played an essential role in convincing the Jewish masses of the existence of a divinity worthy of belief, as the source of all the religious precepts.

This revolutionary approach to the biblical narratives enabled Maimonides to discuss the behaviour of Elohim (the plural form of God employed in the first chapters of Genesis – tr.) as a literary figure shaped by the Genesis stories, as if they were living human beings, while aware of the fact that they are merely characters in a literary allegory, rather than a reflection of reality.

In chapter 2 of the Guide for the Perplexed, Maimonides cites an unnamed "learned man", who said to him that it was strange that God had given divine understanding, morality and wisdom to Adam who had rebelled against him:

> "It would at first sight ... appear from Scripture that man was originally intended to be perfectly equal to the rest of the animal creation, which is not endowed with intellect, reason, or power of distinguishing between good and evil: but that Adam's disobedience to the command of God procured him that great perfection which is the Peculiarity of man, viz., the power of distinguishing between good and evil the noblest of all the faculties of our nature, the essential characteristic of the human race. It thus appears strange that the punishment for rebelliousness should be the means of elevating man to a pinnacle of perfection to which he had not attained previously." (ibid. I, 2)

Maimonides tries to demonstrate the error of the learned man's words. The very dispute between them however, entailed relating to the literary figures appearing in Genesis 2 as if they were real people, the motivation and justification of whose actions could be discussed. The story of "man's rebellion" against God, as it is termed by Maimonides, exemplifies the power of literature to portray its characters as present and living, while simultaneously casting their narrative as allegory, revealing spiritual truth to its readers, the only beings in the world endowed with understanding and the ability to distinguish between good and evil.

The biblical narrative relates to God as a man: a sculptor who fashioned Adam in his image from the earth, planted a garden in the region of Eden, dug irrigation ditches that were to become the rivers of Mesopotamia, planted trees in his garden, and allowed Adam to eat the fruit of all the tress except that of the tree of knowledge of good and evil. God rescued Adam from his loneliness by performing surgery under general anaesthetic, in which he removed one of his ribs and fashioned a woman from it. When Adam awoke, he discovered that he was no longer alone in the world. Before him stood woman created from man, a "help meet for him".

This concise account immediately brings to light the difference in personality between the man and the woman. The man was satisfied with his life in the garden, like people who lived for thousands of years in ancient rain forests, eating the fruits of the trees, like animals, not needing to work for their livelihood, without ambitions or moral dilemmas, never compelled to choose between good and evil. The first woman, on the other hand, was not satisfied with being satisfied. Upon discovering that among the trees of the garden there was one marvellous tree, the fruit of which was forbidden by law, she became intrigued by that one tree, wanting to discover its secret. She knew that the only law established by the owner of the garden in his world was a blatantly immoral law, proscribing morality itself; and according to its author, any who break it will die.

The first woman, endowed with curiosity and daring, discussed the matter with a wise creature called *nahash* (snake) – perhaps due to his ability to divine (*leNaHeSH*) the future, to foresee consequences. The snake asserted that there was no danger in violating the prohibition against eating from the tree of knowledge of good and evil, and that God had lied when he said that any who would eat of its fruit would die. The snake knew that one cannot die from knowledge. In his opinion, Elohim had made this law for fear that any who would eat of the tree of knowledge would become like them, and Elohim fear nothing as they fear the possibility that man might come to resemble his Gods – as they in fact state explicitly later on in the story.

The woman hesitated, for fear of death, but finally became convinced when she saw how desirable the tree of knowledge of good and evil was "to make one wise". Man's rebellion, as it is called by the learned man in the *Guide of the Perplexed*, began when she ate of the fruit and gave some to her man, that he might eat with her as well. Maimonides does not repeat the nonsense spouted by those who ascribe the rebellion to the woman. According to Maimonides' learned man, the rebellion was of the human race, called "Adam" in Genesis 1, and comprising both male and female. It was a rebellion against the ignorance and psychopathy of all creatures – man included – who could not distinguish between good and evil.

Shame, according to the biblical author, was the first consequence of knowing good and evil; shame that causes man to feel pangs of conscience or regret; shame that revealed to the owner of the garden that the creatures he had fashioned with his own hands had rebelled against him, broken the only law in his world, a law that had made all other laws superfluous. One day, the master of the garden was walking through his garden in the cool of the day, as was apparently his custom. Ordinarily, he would have met the man he had created, along the garden paths. This time however, although he sought him out, the man was nowhere to be found.

God is the protagonist of the story, but he is not omnipotent. When the man and his woman hide from God amongst the trees of the garden, he cannot see them, and seeks to discover the whereabouts of his creations. When the man declares from his hiding-place that he has hidden himself because he was ashamed, because he was naked, God knows that he has eaten from the forbidden tree.

God, it seems, must come to terms with the consequences of the rebellion, because knowledge cannot be returned to the scabbard of ignorance. The snake was right of course. Adam – man and woman – did not die of knowledge. Elohim however, were alarmed by their failure to stop the spread of knowledge among mankind. Elohim in the story said to one another that Adam could now eat from the tree of life as well, and attain immortality. What would be the difference then between man and God? Adam was therefore banished from the garden of Eden, and this departure from the primordial forest marks the beginning of human history and culture. The biblical authors believe that there is no way back: mankind goes forth from Eden not toward it.

God punishes the rebels, and makes them garments to cover their nakedness. Henceforth, their food will no longer be readily available – they will have to eke it from the soil they will till by the sweat of their brows; and the woman will suffer pregnancy and childbirth, and subjugation to the man to whom she is bound by her desire and her love. The banishment from Eden appears in the bible as the beginning of culture and civilisation: the emergence of production and creation, the domestication of animals, and the development of agriculture, art and industry.

Maimonides' "learned man" appears to have been right. As a result of their rebellion, man obtained divine wisdom, allowing them to leave the rain forest and the gatherer phase behind, to enter the age of creation and production; going from hundreds of thousands of years of human stagnation to a few tens of thousands of years of rapidly developing human culture.

Biblical literature has played, and continues to play a broad range of roles in Jewish and world culture, including: the creation of a personal god that lives in readers' hearts and imaginations; cultivating and fostering faith in this god among the uneducated masses; and establishing the foundation of all Jewish cultures for the two thousand years that have elapsed since the redaction of this unique anthology.

Chapter Five

God and Moses

Literary Protagonists that Became Historical Figures, Leaders of the First Struggle for Liberation and Causes of the Suffering it Entailed.

Introduction
God and Moses – Literary Protagonists that Became Historical Figures

In collective Jewish and western memory, God and Moses function as influential symbols and figures in the history of spirituality and the monotheistic religions, in liberation movements throughout the ages, in formulating the principles of national constitutions as social contracts based on universal moral values, and according to Spinoza – in aspiring toward democracy, as evidenced by the fact that Moses: a) Presented himself neither as ruler nor founder of a dynasty of rulers, but as a messenger and constitutional framer on behalf of the divine sovereign; b) Presented the law and moral principles embodied in the commandments as being above any ruler; c) Established the principle of separation of powers; d) Based the constitution upon a social contract – a covenant accepted by the people; e) Barred the priestly class from owning land, making them dependent upon public expenditure (see E. Schweid, "Spinoza", Free Judaism 25, Spring 2002).

Moses, among all of the biblical protagonists, thus gained singular importance, becoming a historical figure, affecting religion, thought, literature and art in western and Jewish culture.

Moses is also credited with the conceptual revolution in the perception of God as an abstract entity constituting all that is, and with all of the religious precepts Jews have observed

297

throughout history, so that even in their everyday lives, religious Jews have remembered Moses. Their scholars and judges have relied upon him as the founding figure and authority behind their rulings and the rules governing their lives.

Moses and Yahweh were created by the biblical historical novel recounting the life of Moses, as political leaders involved in affairs of state and war aimed at achieving the national objective of resettlement in the land in which the nation's forefathers had resided. As political leaders, they had to contend with ten insurrections by Israelites disaffected with their policies and achievements, when they realised that the price of freedom and independence included promises without guarantees, hunger and thirst, as well as constant attacks by the peoples of the desert.

The authors develped the unique personalities of these two literary figures – Yahweh and Moses – through the turning points and clashes in relations between the two, culminating tragically in Moses' realisation that Yahweh will not allow him to enter the Promised Land, that he must die on the verge of fulfilling his lifelong ambition, as recounted in the various accounts that constitute the story of the Life of Moses, including the autobiographical monologue in which Moses, about to die before reaching his goal, takes his leave.

Developing the Character of Moses as a Living and Unique Literary Figure

In four of the five books of the Pentateuch (the first part of the Old Testament anthology), the figures and personalities of Moses and Yahweh are developed through narratives that give them their unique characteristics, establishing their presence as living figures in human imagination.

The story of the Life of Moses begins with his birth into

a family of Hebrew slaves, on the banks of the great river of Egypt, and ends with his death at an unknown location, on a mountain on the eastern bank of the Jordan River, which God did not allow him to cross.

In the story of Moses' life we observe the complex relations he has with God, his wives, his brother and sister, the Egyptian king, and the leaders of the Israelite clans who challenge his authority.

Moses was raised in the royal court as the adopted son of Pharaoh's daughter – one of the 59 daughters of Rameses II, according to Josephus. As an adult, the author recounts, Moses met his God 'face to face', although according to another biblical author Moses believed his God to be a shapeless, faceless entity, like fire and cloud that dissipate as they form.

The crucial turning point in Moses' life was his first flight from Egypt, after having murdered an Egyptian man in a fit of rage, without trial, for having beaten an Israelite. Moses fled to the desert, a fugitive from a royal death sentence, like the Egyptian leader described in the papyruses, who fled to the desert and joined a tribe of nomads.

Moses helps Zipporah, daughter of Jethro – leader of one of these desert peoples, water her sheep, wins her hand, and tends his father-in-law's flocks.

Later in the story, Moses' father-in-law will play an important role in guiding the new leader of the Israelite tribes, in organising his people's legal system, and in preparing them for the wars they will have to fight against the desert peoples, who saw the Israelites as trespassers in their territory.

In the stories of the wars and alliances that won the Israelites safe passage and enabled them to continue their journey toward their final destination (in return for detailed commitments to pay even for the water they will drink from the wells of Edom, for example), Moses is portrayed as the military and political leader of the people, as well as its liberator and framer of its constitution. In the early stages of his life story however, Moses appears as a lone shepherd wandering the desert with his flock, as if having forgotten his past – the child of Hebrew slaves raised in the royal court and forced to flee his country after having killed an Egyptian in a fit of rage, for having beaten one of his brethren.

The story of Moses' life becomes a formative chapter in the historical legacy of the ancient Israelites, and of the Judaism taking shape within it, from the moment the lone shepherd encounters the new and unprecedented god calling himself "I AM THAT I AM".

Narrative Style – Recounting Events that Make up Jewish History

The stories of the Bible are written in a realistic style, reporting events at the time and place of their occurrence. The authors write as eyewitnesses, party to the thoughts, encounters and actions of their characters, even when they appear to be alone.

Moses is portrayed by the authors of his story as the first Jewish writer – the first man to write on tablets of stone, as the ancient Egyptians did in their wall paintings.

The literary work we see before us comprises a number of versions of the same story, concluding with an autobiographical monologue (in the book of Deuteronomy), in which the literary character Moses presents his version of events.

The appearance of numerous versions of the story throughout the four books dedicated to Moses, strengthens their credibility as historical accounts, since reports of actual events tend to differ from one another in the details they present, and wins the readers' confidence as the similarities between them outweigh the differences. Most of the stories about Moses, together constituting a realistic novel, ring true even to the modern reader, although the text we possess is at least 2,500 years old.

The Moses stories include accounts of a number of miracles – displays of supernatural occurrences. These accounts do not alter the character of the work as a whole, since some of them (such as the encounters between Moses and God) take place in the presence of a single witness – like many extraordinary events that occur in dreams, visions or hallucinations – and not as public events we would consider real, were we to find the numerous testimonies to their veracity convincing.

Many fictional works (from Homer to Kafka), portray events that defy natural explanation, without affecting their ability to depict human reality in a credible fashion, perhaps because it is in man's nature to live simultaneously in two worlds: the world of public reality, and that of private dream and vision.

Although not necessarily convinced by the historical (i.e. verifiable) truth of the events portrayed, the reader is won over by their poetic truth as 'a credible composite of events that might have occurred'.

Works that succeed in convincing us of their human and poetic truth are usually representative of historical reality, inasmuch as they represent the social, cultural and spiritual environment in which the author lived.

In this sense, works of fiction can be counted among the historical documents pertaining to a given period. The greater the correlation between the content of fictional works, documents and archaeological findings from the same period, the greater their value as historical documents – as has happened over the past two centuries with regard to many ancient myths, such as Gilgamesh, the Iliad, or the Moses stories.

As with other ancient epics, we do not relate to the events

in the Moses stories as authentic accounts of real occurrences, exactly as they are described, but as evidence of the spiritual response elicited by the historical reality we know from research and archaeological findings.

Moses' Perception of the Divine as Precursor to that of the Philosophers and Atheists

According to the author of the burning bush story, it is in this encounter with Moses that God first appeared as Yahweh. According to other biblical accounts, God is already known as Yahweh in the time of the patriarchs and matriarchs of the book of Genesis. Even the Israelite taskmasters in Egypt, who rebuke Moses for speaking to Pharaoh in their name, thus undermining their relationship with the sovereign, know that their God is Yahweh.

From the perspective of the story itself, it is possible that Moses was the only one who did not know God as Yahweh, since he had lived in the Egyptian and Midianite cultures, unfamiliar with Yahweh. In any event it is clear that the author of the burning bush story attempts, inter alia, to explain this unusual name born by the Israelite God, a name unlike that of any other god, a single word that is an incomplete Hebrew sentence: "He will cause to be …".

The uniqueness of Moses' discovery, as described by the author of the burning bush story, lies in the new definition of God's essence, as expressed in his enigmatic name. Moses' need to define his God by name begins with the practical consideration of his chances of persuading the people he wishes to free from slavery that he has indeed been sent by the God of their fathers:

"And Moses said unto God, Behold when I come unto the Israelites, and shall say to them, The God of your fathers hath sent me unto you; and they shall say to me, What is his name? What shall I say unto them? And God said unto Moses, I AM THAT I AM: and he said, Thus shalt thou say unto the Israelites, I AM hath sent me unto you." The author thus explains for the first time, the meaning of the word 'Yahweh', since God calls himself by the same name, but in the first person: I will be (Ahweh) all that is, and that is why others call me (in the third person, future): 'Yehweh' (He will be).

This all-important utterance ascribed by the author to God, was the beginning of a series of profound revolutions in both religious and atheistic thought.

Already in ancient times, many understood it as an expression of faith in God's being the potential of all existence (termed "the one thing which encompasses us all" by first century author Strabo, in his Geography).

The God of Moses cannot be conceived by sensual experience, nor can any other experience be imagined, whereby he might be conceived. Maimonides therefore claimed that "presence" cannot be ascribed to God, in the sense that we ascribe presence to every other existing thing, thus laying the foundation for every doubt or negation of God's existence.

We therefore cannot ascribe to God, figure or shape, or resemblance to man or any other thing – animate or inanimate – in the universe. Divinity that consists entirely of that which will be, cannot even have a present.

"I will be" ('Ehyeh'), or in the third person future tense, 'Yehweh', is either an ancient form of pi'el (according to Albright), or an ironic statement (following Edouard Dohrm), simply meaning: I am what I am and I shall be what I shall be, and no one can know what I am in myself, just as no one can know any thing in itself (as asserted by Kant).

Since God, according to this approach, does not exist in the world of natural events, he cannot be conceived in terms of the events that occur within the reality in which we live, and everything that is said of him, as possessing an "arm", or being full of "vengeance and wrath", or having a "mouth" that speaks and commands – is merely a parable or a metaphor (according to Maimonides 12th century Guide for the Perplexed), a symbol that serves to explain God to human beings who are incapable of grasping the essence of his divinity. In Maimonides' opinion, even the greatest talmudic scholars cannot enter the palace of the "King" – whose presence is beyond human conception.

"I AM THAT I AM" as a name for a God that cannot be known, but in whose existence in the world of 'things in themselves' one can believe, forms the basis of the new monotheistic religion, fundamentally different from the monotheism of Amenhotep IV (the Egyptian Pharaoh Ikhnaton, who lived in Amarna in the 14th century BCE), who believed in a universal sun-god and his own divinity.

The author of the burning bush story thus provided an abstract conception of God as 'being that brings into being', which served as a point of departure for future changes in rational western thought. Medieval philosophers, influenced by Aristotle and Arab philosophers, perceived divinity as imperceptible to man, as the 'primum mobile' of eternal existence, wisdom above human comprehension, self-enlightening mind, with which wise men can only aspire to converge and conjoin – for that is the only significance of the afterlife according to this approach.

The perception of God as First Cause, or in the words of Moses according to Strabo 'the one thing which encompasses us all', led to the pantheism of Spinoza, which perceived divinity as a characteristic of nature, or to agnosticism – which believes only in the certainty of doubt and rejects all belief in the existence of a supernatural being, or to deism – which recognises the existence of a supreme being , distinct and detached from humanity and the world (a new variation on gnosticism, which distinguished between a divine being isolated from the world, and a creative, satanic 'demiurge', involved in its affairs).

Under the influence of these processes, there developed in the west, in the age of enlightenment – beginning in the 17th and 18th centuries – the atheistic belief in man as the creator of God and morality, committed to his humanity and to that of his fellow man, recognising his commitment to the society that sustains his humanity and to its laws, guided by moral principles, without recourse to divine authority.

Such belief is in many ways heir to the spirit of atheism espoused by the Greek philosophers – before and after Socrates – atheistic Hellenistic poets and authors, and their clandestine successors among the medieval European intelligentsia.

The atheistic beliefs that developed under the above influences in the west (as described in Georges Minois' Histoire de L'atheisme) differ from the prevailing atheistic belief in ancient Buddhism from the middle of the first millennium BCE, but like it, perceive a world without gods.

The God of Moses: Abstract Concept and Personified Literary Protagonist

Moses created a god without figure or shape who may therefore never be represented in idol form, nor may an idol be regarded as a god. In the only public event at which Moses introduced the people to its God, Mount Sinai was enveloped in smoke and fire, accompanied ominous blasts upon the shofar – the greatest 'sound and light show' in all of literature (staged perhaps by Moses friends the Kenites, who were smiths and experts with fire).

The crowd that witnessed the display was frightened by it, and asked Moses to act as a go-between with the terrible deity that had revealed itself to them within a screen of noise, wind and flame.

Moses acceded, becoming the first mediator between the Israelite nation and their God, dictating in his name, the first national social charter based on moral principles (as Rousseau termed Moses' constitution – by virtue of which, he asserts, the liberated masses became a free people). In form, the covenant between God and his people resembles a treaty between an emperor and one of his vassals (the treaty between the Hittite empire and the Phoenician kingdom, for example).

In content, the document presented in the story of Moses includes the commandments – precepts and statutes that express moral values such as the sanctity of human life, property rights, marital fidelity, safeguarding human dignity even in old age, loyalty to a single god, the imperative that one speak the truth when bearing witness. These precepts and statutes together form the nation's founding charter, expressing the moral principles the prophets would later come to see as the essence of the Jewish faith, and to which priests, rabbis and halakhists of all future generations would add ritual precepts and innumerable "fences" – requirements of the religion they were developing, wholly absent from the original charter.

According to the authors, Moses uttered and recorded every word of the covenant directly from the "mouth" of the incorporeal and invisible deity, revealed to Moses alone.

The very same authors however, develop the character of the God Yahweh as a literary protagonist with a unique human personality, albeit devoid of any physical description.

From the very first encounter at the burning bush, Moses met with his God in private – whether atop the mountain or in the Tent of Meeting Moses erected outside the camp following the brief civil war he waged in response to the worship of the golden calf.

The philosophy and ideas that developed among the Israelites, are presented in the Pentateuch and Prophets sections of the Bible, primarily in the form of narratives and orations. In the Writings (Hagiographa) ideas are also presented in treatise, poetry and drama form. In the burning bush story, for the first time, the idea of freedom from slavery is expressed, along with an unprecedented conception of the nature of God. The ideas are presented within the story of a shepherd surprised to see a fire in a bush that was not burned. When he approached to see the marvel, he heard a bodiless voice, as if emanating from the fire itself. The voice, for the first time, expresses the two central ideas of the Mosaic faith: freedom from slavery, and an incorporeal deity as 'being that brings into being'.

Moses learns from the voice that the God of his fathers and his people, his own God, who had done nothing to bring succour to the enslaved Hebrews for four hundred years, had suddenly remembered that they must be freed.

The voice within the fire introduces itself as a new god lacking a personal designation like all the other gods, described rather by a Hebrew phrase, " I AM THAT I AM", intimating its identity as 'being that brings all things into being' – an explanation of the name Yahweh, by which the Israelite God had been known from the time of the Patriarchs up to Moses' own time, without being understood by those who had used it, according to the voice in the fire.

Yahweh once again becomes an active character in the historical novel of the Life of Moses. His human personality is gradually revealed in his actions, reactions, conversations with Moses, disappointments, curses, promises and regrets.

The story of the Life of Moses is interrupted from time to time – throughout the four books of the Bible over which it is told – with laws and religious precepts. Despite these interruptions, the story of Moses' life, from infancy to adulthood in Egypt to old age and death on the threshold of the Promised Land, unfolds before the reader.

Setting the laws within the narrative of Moses' life afforded them unique authority and sanctity, as an integral part of the story in which the characters of Yahweh and Moses, the conflicts between them, and the conflicts that arose between them and the Israelites, were formed.

Yahweh: Source of Morality and Violator of its Principles, Liberator and Would-be Destroyer of His People

Yahweh possesses rhetorical abilities, expresses strong emotions, is able to write on stone tablets, and when these are broken by Moses, dictates them once again, stressing his demand that the faithful worship Yahweh alone, and ignore other gods and their idols.

God sends Moses to free the Israelites from slavery, but when wandering in the desert, they complain of hunger and thirst, Yahweh is offended by their ingratitude. This approach is apparent from the very outset. When they reach the shores of the Red Sea and the Egyptian army is fast approaching, the author has the people pose the following sarcastic question: Does Moses not think that there are enough graves in Egypt, that he has brought us to die in this place?

As the complaints and protests concerning conditions in the desert increased – even after the splitting of the sea that had enabled the Israelites to pass through safely and drowned the Egyptian army – Yahweh's disappointment grew. Being quick of temper and action, he suggested to Moses that he would destroy the People of Israel, replacing them with another people, consisting entirely of Moses' descendants, and equally obedient.

Moses was so close to Yahweh that, according to the author, he was the only one to have seen not only the face of God, but his back as well. Upon hearing Yahweh's diabolical proposal, Moses attempted to convince him that destroying the People of Israel at that point would only harm his good name. 'What will they say in Egypt?' he asks Yahweh. 'Will they not say that you took this people out of Egypt only to destroy them in the desert?'

God is convinced by this threat to his reputation in the eyes of the nations, and changes his mind regarding the second final solution mentioned in the Bible (the first was devised by Pharaoh, who decreed that all sons born to Hebrew women be killed).

The Israelites were given a new lease on life, to wander and complain and rebel. God has no choice but to come to terms with all of this. Yahweh's lack of consistency contributes to his human image. Like all great literary figures – representing living human beings – Yahweh is also fickle by nature.

Unlike other gods, who 'specialise' in a given area – fertility, the sun, rain, death, love, etc. – Yahweh has no specific role, being God of all things. The author also incorporates him in historical and political events.

When Moses asks Pharaoh to allow his people to go out into the desert to celebrate the sacrificial feast (apparently much more ancient than the feast of the paschal sacrifice), Yahweh torments Pharaoh, causes him to refuse all of Moses' requests, and for each refusal (caused by Yahweh himself), strikes the Egyptian people with a plague or horrifying natural disaster: all of the water in Egypt turns to blood, light disappears from its skies leaving a cloak of darkness so thick that it could be 'felt', locusts and an assortment of wild beasts attack its towns and villages.

Despite being the source of the universal principle "thou shalt not kill" according to these stories, Yahweh kills all of the Egyptian firstborn children, after having struck Egypt with nine chilling plagues. (In keeping with the tradition that apparently preserved in popular memory the series of disasters that befell Egypt at the end of the third millennium BCE, according to modern historical research).

The author offsets these immoral acts with the great human achievement of liberation of an enslaved people. Like all revolutions for national or other liberation however, it entailed tragedies and horrifying acts of violence.

The liberation of the people of slaves – Israelites and a mixed multitude from other nations that joined them (without conversion) in their flight from Egypt – became one of the symbols of the desire for freedom in all western cultures, as described by Michael Walzer in his book Exodus and Revolution. Leaders and poets of the African-American liberation movement have drawn upon the story of Moses as if it had been part of their own historical heritage, and its echoes can be heard in the works of Jewish songwriters such as the Gershwin brothers, while figures such as Calvin and Cromwell and the leaders of the American Revolutionary War saw Moses and the exodus from Egypt as a model and symbol for their revolutions.

A Literary Work Describing the Process of God's Invention

The editors of the biblical anthology inserted the story of Moses and dated the historical events in which he took part, after the stories of the patriarchs and before the stories of the colonisation of the land of the Canaanite peoples. This dating – about 300 years before David – places Moses and the Exodus in the 13th century BCE, toward the end of the reign of Rameses and during the period of unrest and war that followed his death.

Moses' God, invented about a century after Ikhnaton's universal sun-god, was an unprecedented development in religious history.

Men who create (give form to) gods, usually see them as members of a family of gods, relatives of other gods of their time. Each god has a particular shape and form, which can be represented in images or idols.

The God of Moses is unique in that he is incorporeal and alone in the world, without mother or father or other relatives – human or divine. The introduction of Yahweh was in itself the negation of the divinity of all other gods.

Moses is described by the biblical authors as the agent of a revolution in human belief in the divine and in religion (an integrated system of ritual laws and mores).

The Hellenistic historian Strabo, who saw Moses as the founder of the belief in the 'God of all things', explains that this belief excludes all other beliefs – those held by the Egyptians, Libyans and Greeks – whereby the gods have animal or human forms.

Once a god is fashioned and assumes a specific conceptive or perceptive form, it becomes an entity in its own right, ostensibly independent of its creators. They believe in it as if it were their creator. They fear the god they have created, worship it pray, extol, sacrifice, fast, perform rituals, and sometimes copulate in its name, whether to ensure the fertility of the fertility goddess or the successful coupling of Yahweh and his consort, according to one kabbalistic belief.

The process of creating a god and turning it into an independent and awe-inspiring entity is described in the story of the golden calf. First the people approached Aaron, the priest, demanding: "Up, make us a god". Next, they contributed their golden earrings, and Aaron fashioned Yahweh in the form of a golden calf, similar to gods such as the Egyptian Apis (as suggested by Philo).

Once the new god had been fashioned, the author tells us, Aaron began to revere it, and declared a sacrificial feast day to the new calf-Yahweh, which they henceforth believed had brought them out of Egypt – just as Jeroboam would do only a few centuries later, repeating Aaron's action and declaring the calf-god he had made to be the god that had taken Israel out of Egypt.

The author of the burning bush story believed Moses' discovery to be original, and that the patriarchs of the Israelite nation had not known their God as Yahweh.

The prophets of Yahweh, and subsequently Maimonides, deduced from the Pentateuch (the Books of Moses) that the entire attitude to religious cult worship must also be changed, since the essence of the covenant with Yahweh is ethical behaviour (according to a universal morality), which is to be preferred over sacrifice and prayer to a God that has no need or desire for them.

It is eminently clear that the God of Moses in no way resembles the God that had required a father to bind his son upon the altar, slaughter and sacrifice him as a burnt offering – as in the case of Abraham, and that of the many Israelites who slaughtered their sons and daughters on the altars of Jerusalem, according Jeremiah.

In Judaism, as in other cultures, many continued to believe in an anthropomorphic god, like the one created by the authors of the patriarch stories or the accounts of Jesus son of God – who in the eyes of many Christian believers became an independent deity whose images and idols must be venerated. In Jewish mystical literature contemporaneous with the Talmud, the authors of the Shiur Komah (literally "Measure of the Body", i.e. the body of

God) fashioned a god in the form of a giant man, many times the size of the universe, the precise measurements of whose body and indeed each nostril or finger were known to the author who created him. In the the Zohar, written in13th century, other Jewish authors created a Yahweh with a family, and a consort with whom he has sexual intercourse.

God was therefore afforded various forms in the beliefs and works of believers. Ever since the creation of Moses' Yahweh by the biblical authors, there have been two opposing approaches within Judaism and other monotheistic religions: incorporeal Yahweh as 'being that brings into being', and tangible Yahweh as calf or man (despite the explicit statement by the author of Genesis 1 that God created both male and female in his own image, indicating that God too is both male and female).

The precepts of Halakhah, presented as expressions of God's will, spoken, written or dictated by him, represent a belief system that created an anthropomorphic god possessing a mouth and the power of speech, the desire and ability to regulate all matters pertaining to ritual and human behaviour, food taboos or sex; the power to punish or reward, inscribe individuals in the Book of Life or in the Book of Death, issue decrees and verdicts; and other characteristics and abilities associated with an anthropomorphic god. Such a god naturally arouses reverence and fear, as well as a desire to satisfy him and cause him to deal mercifully with us, forgiving all of our sins.

Such a god runs contrary to the deity created within the context of Moses' faith, in the literary work that described it as an indefinable entity, devoid of human shape or form, which consequently cannot possess human will or be credited with precepts devised by men presuming to speak in its name.

The unique moral-monotheistic belief system attributed to

Moses, and the accompanying religion of precepts, aroused sharp resistance at first, both among the Israelites and among other nations.

The Religion of Israel as Opposed to the Israelite Religions of the Biblical Period, and their Convergence in the Hellenistic Era

According to the authors of the Pentateuch, there were ten insurrections against the religion and leadership of Moses during the period of the Israelites' wanderings in the desert. In the national memory, these stories became the beginning of the distinction between the religion of Moses and Israel, and the religion of the majority of the Israelites.

According to the prophets and historians of the remaining books of the Bible, the deviation from the religion of Moses spread throughout the culture of most of the Israelites in both kingdoms, with a majority of Jews worshiping Canaanite gods and believing in Yahweh as a golden calf.

Two statues depicting Yahweh as a golden calf were erected in temples of the kingdom of ten of the twelve tribes, and were declared by the founder of that kingdom to be temples to the God who had taken them out of Egypt – faithful to the formula uttered by Aaron, the first high priest, who had created Yahweh as a golden calf.

In Jerusalem, King Solomon built temples to all of the gods, alongside the temple he built to Yahweh. According to Jeremiah and others, Jews continued to sacrifice their sons and daughters on the altars of Moloch in Jerusalem on the eve of its destruction, like other ancient peoples, and intimated in the story of Abraham's binding of Isaac.

Scholarly scepticism regarding the credibility of these biblical

314

sources is illogical. It is clear that the editors of the Bible, its historians and prophets, remained faithful to Yahweh as the one and only God, opposing the existence of other religions and any deviation from the religion of Moses. Their staunch opposition to what they believed to be a sin, lends credibility to their testimonies that this was in fact the prevailing culture among Israelites of all classes, both during the period of colonisation (as described in the book of Judges), and in the era of the first two kingdoms (as described in the books of Samuel and Kings).

In the libretto of Schoenberg's opera Moses und Aron, Aaron explains to Moses that human beings cannot believe in something entirely abstract, that they need a god who is a specific object and not merely a concept. In other words, the religious cannot be required to give up their accessible god, one that can be imagined as palpable and in need of votive offerings. Human beings need a god capable of inspiring awe, and hope that he will answer their petitions and prayers, and not only arouse thoughts, study and scholarship, whereby Maimonides hoped man could approach his God.

The religion of Moses and Yahweh as sole deity developed during the Hellenistic-Byzantine period, becoming the national faith of the Jewish People – a single common religion for all Jewish streams and sects.

It was after the destruction of the first two Jewish kingdoms and their temples, during the Babylonian exile and third Jewish kingdom (Hasmonean) and the period of the second temple to Yahweh in Jerusalem (following the destruction of Yahweh temples in Upper Egypt and near Cairo) that the religion of Moses developed as an exclusive national faith.

The Religion of Israel converged with the religions of the Jews. Jewish national identity converged with Jewish religious identity. Jews were henceforth not only members of the Jewish People, but also people whose lives were governed by the rules and precepts of the Jewish religion, in the version deemed most faithful to the religion of Moses, whether Sadducee or Karaite, Pharisee or Rabbinic, Hellenist, Samaritan, Christian, Essene, or other.

This national religious culture made Judaism all the more unique, as multi-national religions such as Greek paganism and Christianity spread throughout the Hellenistic-Byzantine world.

The Jewish people – on all three continents of its diaspora – was the only people in the Roman Empire to express its national-religious identity also in the form of a tax to its one and only temple, dedicated to the one and only Yahweh, in Jerusalem.

A common historical legacy, as compiled in the Pentateuch and other books of the Bible (centuries before its canonisation in the 1st century CE), served as the basis for Jewish national consciousness among Hebrew, Greek and Aramaic-speaking Jews.

Hellenistic writers and philosophers, Jews and non-Jews, including some who vilified Jews as a people of lepers banished from Egypt, recognised Moses as a historical figure and the religion of Moses as characteristic of all Jews. Jews were distinguished from the peoples among whom they resided, as a result of their different lifestyle – dictated by the precepts of their religion, such as the Sabbath, festivals, dietary laws, circumcision, etc..

Anti-Semitism in the Hellenistic Era - A Reaction to Jewish Profession of the Mosaic Religion as a Unique National Faith

The unique lifestyle practised by Jews, prevented them from assimilating into the Hellenistic communities that emerged throughout the Ptolemaic, Seleucid and subsequent Roman Empires. Consequently, a sense of hostility developed toward the Jewish People in the Hellenistic era. Josephus, in Against Apion, documents these early expressions of anti-Semitism that appeared mainly in places where large Jewish communities flourished amid non-Jewish populations, such as the million-strong Jewish community of Egypt in Philo's day.

The author of the book of Esther was aware of the existence of Jews who, like Esther, concealed their Jewish identity, particularly when seeking to attain high positions in society or at the royal court, or in order to participate in the international copulation contest featuring in his story – to which Esther, as the victor, owed her accession to the throne.

The author cites the diversity of the Jews' lifestyle as justification for the Persian Imperial government's plan to annihilate all of the Jews in the Empire, in accordance with the "final solution" laws attributed to the character of Haman (in fact the third "final solution to the Jewish problem" to be devised – preceded by Pharaoh's attempt to kill all of the male children born to the Israelites, and Yahweh's proposal to destroy the entire Israelite nation).

In a global society and economy based on slavery, the Mosaic religion aroused strong opposition, primarily due to the egalitarian Sabbath laws, laws requiring the release of slaves or otherwise restricting the behaviour of slave-owners, laws ensuring human and civil rights for strangers, the duty to provide for those without means, such as orphans and widows, and the constant resort to the memory of the revolution led by Moses for liberation from slavery, as justification for all of these laws.

In pagan culture, religious precepts were distinct from the laws of the state, thus enabling polytheistic religion to be international, and believers in its numerous variations to develop a sense of tolerance toward worshipers of gods ostensibly different from the local deities. Eventually, believers in the polytheistic religions of Hellenistic times discovered that the gods in other lands were essentially the same as theirs, only bearing different names, like Jupiter and Zeus, or Ashtoreth, Aphrodite and Venus.

Jews and Christians were considered by pagan believers to be atheistic, since they denied the divinity of the gods of all of the other religions.

Monotheism in its various forms, based first on the Mosaic religion, was characterised by a lack of tolerance toward the polytheistic religions and toward all monotheistic cults other than its own.

This fundamental difference between polytheism that created and recognised many gods, and monotheism that believed in principle only in one God, fostered mutual intolerance and hostility toward Jewish adherents to the Mosaic religion, both among believers in the Greek gods, and among Christians who had developed a new form of Jewish monotheism and broken away from the Mosaic religion.

Intolerance also characterised the Jewish religion that developed in Babylonian exile and in the Kingdom of Israel during the Second Temple period, manifested most extremely in the sectarian policies of Ezra and Nehemiah among the community of returnees to Zion.

The ideological and often violent clashes between the different sects of the Second Temple period reflected the development of the intolerance typical of Jewish religious and cultural factions to this day. Jews of one faction view those who belong to another religious faction as 'heretics' and 'apostates', and the struggle against them as war of the sons of light against the sons of darkness..

Members of the different monotheistic sects ascribe their own exclusive truths to Moses and his God . There is a talmudic story tinged with irony, regarding the widespread use of Moses' name by those who would seek to reinforce their own views by presenting them as his: Moses heard God sing the praises of Rabbi Akiva, and wished to attend one of his lectures. He descended to Akiva's study hall, sat in the eighteenth row (a detail included by the narrator in order to lend greater credence to his story), listened to Rabbi Akiva, and failed to understand a word he had said. When one of the students asked the teacher to explain, Akiva simply resorted to the all-purpose cliche: "It is a law that was given to Moses at Sinai." Moses got up, left Rabbi Akiva's lecture and returned to his place in heaven.

Insurrections against Moses and the Cost of Freedom in Light of a Reasonable Account of Historical Events

For four hundred years, according to the Bible's authors, the Israelites lived in the Land of Goshen: a fertile region, fed by numerous rivers - like that of the eastern Nile delta. In their labour taxes the Israelites participated in the construction of large cities, such as "Raamses" – that is Avaris, the ancient capital of the Kingdom of the Hyksos, destroyed by the liberator of Egypt, Ahmose I, in the middle of the second millennium BCE. After the expulsion of the Hyksos – Semitic invaders who had ruled Egypt for over three centuries – power was restored to Egyptian kings such as Rameses II, who in the 13th century ruled for 70 years and rebuilt Avaris, which was renamed "Raamses".

This historical background, discovered by 20th century historians and archaeologists, is reflected in the biblical narrative from the first millennium BCE, explaining the immense disappointment and protest felt and voiced by the Israelites, whose liberation from Egyptian servitude had placed them in the desert, and radically altered their lifestyle. People who had been accustomed to living in a three-thousand-year-old civilisation, in a land of rivers and flourishing agriculture, in which they could enjoy a cheap and varied diet – an abundance of fish they could catch for free, meat and vegetables of all kinds – suddenly found themselves in a state of constant thirst and hunger, subsisting on the monotonous diet of desert nomads.

As the adversity experienced by the liberated Israelites grew, they began to wonder whether they had not paid too dearly for their freedom and liberation from the labour tax – imposed upon all residents of Egypt, but apparently with greater severity upon the Semitic tribes allowed to settle on its eastern frontier, even after the expulsion of the Semitic rulers of the dynasty of Hyksos (whose memory is perhaps echoed in the stories of Joseph who nationalised Egypt's private farms, making them – through non-violent economic revolution – the personal property of the king).

Historical and geographical details appear incidentally throughout the story of the Life of Moses, thereby reinforcing its claim to be a report of events constituting a national historical legacy.

The story's credibility in the eyes of readers is strengthened by the fact that it details not only Moses' accomplishments and endeavours, but also the ten popular insurrections against him, and the widespread dissatisfaction with his entire liberation and exodus venture.

In the stories that describe the liberated Israelites' disappointment and protests, the term "land flowing with milk and honey" first appears not as a designation for the Promised Land, but in reference to the land they had departed, under Moses' leadership. The authors thus present the universal dilemma of the cost of freedom and independence:

Are freedom and independence really worth the trials and tribulations of the kind experienced by the Israelites and their families? Is it worth leaving lands of plenty, rich in fish, meat and vegetables, even if one has lived there as a member of a tolerated or persecuted minority, in order to gain independence at the cost of living in desert lands, fighting desert tribes, struggling for water and food, even if it is done under independent national leadership rather than foreign rule?

These specific questions are followed by a more general one, associated with every war of liberation in history: Should people come to terms with a successful revolutionary leadership that quickly becomes a repressive regime, pursuing its goals by brutally suppressing all opposition, criticism or protest against its own behaviour?

The Dramatic Conflict between the Victims of Liberation and the Liberators - Moses and his God

This dramatic conflict between the people, its leader and its God, is central to the Exodus story.

The conflict begins at the very outset of Moses' and Aaron's political careers, when they call on Pharaoh and try to convince him to allow the Israelites to celebrate a sacrificial feast in the desert. Not only do they meet with refusal on Pharaoh's part, but with the anger of Israelite leaders as well – Hebrew officers set over the Israelites and responsible for their output, did not look favourably upon the interference of this Jewish-Egyptian intellectual in their affairs:

"And the officers of the Israelites did see that they were in evil case ... And they met Moses and Aaron, who stood in the way, as they came forth from Pharaoh: And they said unto them, The Lord look upon you, and judge; because ye have made our savour to be abhorred in the eyes of Pharaoh, and in the eyes of his servants, to put a sword in their hand to slay us."

After liberation, this early opposition turned into protests and complaints over the dangers and adversities that accompanied the revolution, beginning with a sarcastic remark upon reaching the sea ("Because there were no graves in Egypt ...") and intensifying after the crossing of the sea, when the escaped Israelites began to suffer thirst and hunger, and the monotony of the desert fare they were given: manna and the meagre flesh of the quail.

Yahweh views such rebellion and protests against hunger, thirst and war, as ingratitude on the part of the Israelites.

"And when the people complained ... and the Israelites also wept again, and said, Who shall give us flesh to eat? We remember the fish, which we did eat in Egypt freely; the cucumbers, and the melons, and the leeks, and the onions, and the garlick ... Then Moses heard the people weep throughout their families ..."

The itemisation of the diet to which the Israelites had been accustomed when enslaved in Egypt, illustrates and amplifies the sense of distress experienced by the Israelite families, as they remembered their meals from the good old days, when they lived in Egypt, before liberation and independence. The gravity of the situation – as experienced by the complaining, weeping people – is impressed upon the reader.

Moses, like other revolutionary leaders throughout history, sees only his vision and the goal he was striving to achieve – ignoring the cost in human suffering along the way.

The story of the clash between the liberated people and their leaders reveals a great deal about of the personalities of the two main protagonists: Moses and Yahweh.

Yahweh – both cosmic and national God – appears to be easily offended, insensitive to the suffering of others, incapable of understanding the protests and disappointment of the masses, one who takes every political reaction as a personal affront, desperate and volatile in the face of ingratitude, quick to suggest the annihilation and supplanting of his people.

Moses too had a quick temper. In his rage over the golden calf revelries, he broke the tablets of the law, the only tablets written by the finger of God, tincture upon stone.

Compared to Yahweh, Moses appears the very model of a cool-headed and considerate leader, judging by overall results rather than impulsive reactions. Moses' leadership style is tough and uncompromising, he imposes his political and religious control by military means, training his soldiers to act without mercy, even when it is members of their own families who have strayed from his religious path.

Moses' response to the celebration held by the Israelites to consecrate the calf Yahweh – the god that Aaron had made for them by their demand – was to slaughter 3,000 of the participants. Following the killing and victory, he ground the calf into gold dust, which he cast into the water.

When political opposition arises , against his rule and that of his family – which had assumed all of the profitable positions in the priesthood – Moses cracks down on the dissenters and buries them alive, leaders and followers alike.

Moses however, also understands the limits of power, knows how to come to terms with things he cannot change, opposes annihilation of the people, compromises with the religious proclivities of the masses, and approves the erection of a tabernacle with graven images of cherubs in the holy of holies and a sacrificial cult resembling that of other gods.

Maimonides explains that God, in his "cunning", understood that sacrificial practices borrowed from idolatry must be allowed initially, since human beings are slaves of habit and cannot go suddenly from one extreme to the other. The Israelites were therefore permitted to continue practising ritual sacrifice, from which they were weaned gradually, until the custom eventually disappeared after the destruction of the Second Temple.

Following his victory in the civil war, and the killing of the three thousand adherents of Yahweh the calf, Moses can no longer live within the Israelites' camp. He pitches a tent of his own beyond the confines of the camp – a "tent of meeting" in which he may commune with his God, without recourse to cult practices borrowed from other cultures.

Moses saw himself as the people's natural leader, and like many subsequent revolutionary leaders, took upon himself both the military and judicial leadership, rejecting the protests of "two hundred and fifty princes of the assembly, famous in the congregation, men of renown", who objected to Moses' "lifting" himself above them in Yahweh's name. "And they gathered themselves together against Moses and against Aaron, and said unto them, Ye take too much upon you, seeing all the congregation are holy, every one of them, and the Lord is among them: wherefore then lift ye up yourselves above the congregation of the Lord?"

When Moses heard these complaints, he resorted to the sorcery at which he had excelled alongside the Egyptian magicians in the first stories of the cycle, punishing the participants in this protest by burying them en masse, causing the ground to "cleave asunder" and swallow all who stood there:

"And when Moses heard it, he fell upon his face ... And the earth opened her mouth, and swallowed them up, and their houses, and all the men that appertained unto Korah, and all their goods. They, and all that appertained to them, went down alive into the pit."

Moses' repression of religious and political insurrection, and Yahweh's proposal to annihilate the people, reveal a horrifying facet of the respective personalities of these two leaders – divine and human alike. Through them, the texts pose the moral dilemma of leadership, the permitted limits of power assumed by leaders convinced that only they can bring the people's goals to fruition.

The Unique Personalities of Moses and Yahweh as Revealed in their Biographies and in Descriptions of the Roles they Played in Historical Events

Like all literary works, the "Life of Moses" was influenced by other works. The "baby in a basket on the water" motif is common to many myths of the ancient Near East – like the story of the infant King Sargon, whose mother was a high priestess and therefore not allowed to conceive a child. She left him in a basket on the river, where he was found by a poor fisherman, and eventually grew up to be king.

A living character cannot be described in abstract terms, but only by means of a unique, representative and characteristic life story. The biblical "Life of Moses" presents the unique personalities of its protagonists Moses and Yahweh. Unlike other versions of the baby in the basket motif, Moses appears not as the son of kings or the nobility, but as the child of Hebrew slaves, whose murder – along with that of all Jewish male children – had been ordered by the king.

The little slave-child was adopted by an Egyptian princess, and given the common Egyptian name "Mushah" (similar to "Ra-Musah", meaning "the god is born") – which the Hebrews interpreted as deriving from the Hebrew root "MSh"H", or "to draw out".

Moses grew up at the royal court as an Egyptian prince, educated in a three-thousand-year-old culture. According to Josephus, Moses was one of the Egyptian military commanders who participated in the conquest of Ethiopia, which was annexed to the kingdom of his step-father, Rameses the Great, who extended the borders of Egypt but had to sign a non-aggression pact with the Hittites at Kadesh, since he was unable to defeat them.

Moses' unique character is revealed through a series of events, actions and reactions that, from a literary perspective, give remarkable expression to his personality.

The religious revelation ascribed to Moses by the author, makes him one of the leading figures in the history of faith and thought – of the Jewish People and the world. Strabo sees Moses not only as the originator of the 'God of all things' concept, but as the founder of a new national community, who "persuaded a large body of right-minded persons to accompany him to the place where Jerusalem now stands". Strabo presents Moses as a legislator who established "no ordinary kind of government" in Jerusalem, which was so excellent that "all the nations around willingly united themselves to him, allured by his discourses and promises".

Yahweh too, plays an active role in political history and relations between peoples. Through his involvement in historical events, the authors fashion Yahweh as a unique personality as well.

Yahweh is an active figure in linear history, that is one-time events, rather than the repetitive cycles associated with the lives of other gods or natural processes. Each of these events has implications for the future, and thus becomes part of Jewish historical tradition, in which the character of Yahweh plays a central role.

The portions of the story dealing with Moses' family life are also charged with dramatic conflict. The worst of these conflicts is not the public debate over Aaron's having forged the Yahweh-calf image. Moses ignores his brother's sin when he represses the popular rebellion.

When Moses marries a Kushite woman however (perhaps from the lands he conquered as an Egyptian general, postulate extra-biblical sources), the family dispute flares up. Aaron and Miriam try to dissuade him from marrying the Kushite woman, and Moses afflicts his sister Miriam with leprosy. Miriam, the renowned popular poet, the woman who looked after Moses when he was an infant floating on the Nile, is now terminally ill because she opposed the marriage of the nation's leader to a black foreign woman.

"And Miriam and Aaron spake against Moses because of the Kushite woman whom he had married: for he had married a Kushite woman. And they said, Hath the Lord indeed spoken only by Moses? hath he not spoken also by us? ... And the Lord came down in the pillar of the cloud, and stood in the door of the tent ...And the cloud departed from off the tent; and behold, Miriam became leprous, white as snow."

As a leper, Miriam lived outside the camp, and died a short time later.

Once again, Moses appears as a wrathful and pitiless man, like his God, and the author incidentally raises a problems that will later plague Jewish leaders, from Ezra and Nehemiah to the present day – that of intermarriage between Jewish men and women of other nations, something for which Moses provided a precedent and which he defended against all his detractors.

Correlation between the Exodus Story and the Historical Background that Arises from Scientific Research

It is increasingly fashionable nowadays to reject the historical evidence appearing in the works of the Bible – following the development of biblical criticism in the 19th century, and particularly the advent, in the 20th century, of the "Bible deniers" movement and its approach to the existence of the People of Israel in ancient times. Even if all of the books of the Bible are works of fiction however, this approach ignores the fact that they – like all fiction – represent a social and cultural reality.

Writers do not invent reality. They discover it, respond to it in their works, creating a new, autonomous reality. Literature at its best succeeds in creating living characters, in such a fashion as to reflect spiritual, cultural and social reality, by redefining humanity in each and every generation.

The cultural reality in which writers work includes written and oral traditions, stories, and figures from the far past who have made a lasting impression on life in their own times. Tradition comprises stories passed down from generation to generation, finally becoming the raw materials from which writers create literature.

All literature is historical documentation – the more so when dealing with works we know to have been written at least two thousand five hundred years ago: a rare archaeological find, already recognised as such by its Greek translators, shortly after the conquests of Alexander the Great and the establishment of the centres of Hellenistic Jewish culture in Egypt.

The traditions method is thus an appropriate one, examining the historical processes addressed in the literary works of the Bible, alongside research according to the sources method, which hypothesises regarding the various strata and sources of biblical works.

Using the traditions method, many researchers have discovered an amazing correlation between the details revealed through historical and archaeological research, and the background information provided by the biblical stories, with regard to daily life, economy, military affairs, religion, political structure, social organisation and migration. Archaeological finds and ancient manuscripts discovered in the Near East strengthen the view that such a correlation exists. The anachronisms that appear in the Moses stories are minimal, compared to the wealth of detail corresponding to the historical background provided by scientific research.

The popular traditions reflected in the writings of the biblical anthology represent the collective memory. The correlation between story and historiography is thus better explained by the premise that the stories are based on earlier traditions – oral and written – than by postulating that they were "invented in the middle of the first millennium BCE, in order to afford a national mythology to groups of Canaanite slaves who had rebelled against their masters and wished to create a new people for themselves".

Authors in the first half of the first millennium BCE were unlikely to have had the tools or documents necessary for studying the past. They were unlikely to have had the ability to reconstruct the historical conditions described in the Moses stories – centuries before their own time.

Ancient manuscripts and archaeological finds indicate a migration of western Semites (Amorite peoples) in the southern part of the Fertile Crescent – from Ur in south Mesopotamia to Haran in the north, and southward via Syria and the Lebanon to Egypt. That is what transpired in the clan of the literary figure Abraham, his son, grandson and great-grandson.

Documents in the archives of Mari and Nuzi confirm these findings, as do letters discovered in the archives of Ikhnaton IV at Tel Amarna (14th century BCE), in which Canaanite kings and rulers complain to the Egyptian king, of "Hapiru" or "A'piru" (or "A'biru") tribes that had invaded their territories and attempted to settle there. Information about the Hurrians was found in the archives of Haran and Tel Adana in Asia Minor, where 450 Akkadian tablets dating from the 18th to the 15th century BCE were discovered.

The 20th century witnessed the discovery at Ras Shamra of Ugaritic texts dating from the early second millennium BCE – written in a language and script very close to Hebrew. We thus learn that there was a spoken and written language among the Hebrew tribes, long before the period of the Israelite monarchy (early first millennium BCE), raising the possibility that some of the traditions that preserved ancient tales from the dawn of Israelite history, may have been committed not only to memory but to writing as well.

David Daiches, in his book on Moses, writes that scholarship has no clear-cut answer to the question of whether the "Hebrews" were "Hapiru" or "A'piru" (the dusty ones, nomads) – apparently a general term for a variety of nomadic tribes (like the term "Beduin").

Despite the lack of proof, it is a reasonable assumption to identify the one with the other. The Egyptians, who called some of the nomadic tribes that had arrived in their region "Hapiru" (written "'pr" in a letter dating from the reign of Rameses II, concerning the construction of a gateway in the city of Raamses) may have been referring to members of western Semitic nomadic tribes, also depicted in Egyptian reliefs from this period.

During the process of settlement, nomadic tribes combine with one another within the confines of specific territories, to form peoples. With the settlement of the Israelite tribes in the land of the numerous Canaanite peoples, the name "Hebrew" disappears, replaced by the name "Israel", as inscribed upon the 1207 BCE stele of Pharaoh Merneptah, listing his victories over various peoples.

Of course, none of this proves the veracity of the Exodus stories. It is clear however, that biblical literature, like all fiction in all places at all times, reflects historical reality and historical processes, even if the narratives themselves are fictional.

Bibliography:

Israel Abrams, **Jewish Life In The Middle Ages**, Meridian Books, 1958

Gedayah Alon, **The Jews In Their Land In The Talmudic Age,** Harvard University Press, 1984

Robert Alter; Frank Kermode, (Eds), **The Literary Guide To The Bible**, Harvard, Cambridge, University Press, 1986

Robert Alter, **The World Of Bible As Literature**, Basic Books, 1991

Robert Alter, **The Art Of The Biblical Narrative**, Basic Books, 1981

Erich Auerbuch, **Mimesis**, Princeton University Press, 1953

Salo W. Baron, **The Social And Religious History Of The Jews**, Columbia University Press, 1969

David Biale, (Ed.), **The Cultures Of The Jews**, Shocken Books, 2002

Harold Bloom, David Rosenberg, **The Book Of J.**, Grove, Widenfeld, 1990

Martin Buber, **On The Bible**, Introduction, Harold Bloom, Shocken Books, 1982

Arthur R.Cohen; Paul Mendes Flohr, (Ed), **Contemporary Jewish Religious Thought**, The Free Press Macmillan Publishers, 1987

Louis H. Feldman, **Jews And Gentiles In The Ancient World,** Princeton University Press, 1993

Louis Finkelstein (Ed.), **The Jews - Their Religion And Culture,** Shocken Books, 1971

Harold Fisch, **Poetry With A Purpose - Biblical Poetics And Interpretation**, Indiana University Press, 1988

J. P. Fokkelman, **Narrative Art And Poetry In The Books Of Samuel**, Wang, 1986

Richard Elliot Friedman, **The Hidden Face Of God**, Harper San Francisco, 1995

Erwin Goodenough, **Jewish Symbols In The Greco-Roman Period** (Abridged By Jacob Neusner), Princeton University Press, 1988

Robert Gordis, **Koheleth, The Man And His World**, Shocken, 1968

Erich S Gruen, Diaspora, **Jews Amongst Greeks And Romans,** Harvard University Press, 2002

Herman Gunkel, **The Legends Of Genesis**, Shocken Books, 1964 (First Published: 1901)

Arthur Herzberg, **The French Enlightenment And The Jews,** Columbia University Press, 1968

Dan Jacobson, **The Story Of Stories**, Secker and Warburg, 1982

Harold M. Kallen, **The Book Of Job As A Greek Tragedy**, Hill And Wang, 1959

Mordechai Kaplan, **Judaism As Civilization**, The Jewish Publication Society Of America, 1981

Renee Kogel, Zeev Katz, (Ed.), **Judaism In A Secular Age - An Anthology Of Secular Humanistic Jewish Thought**, Milan Press, 1995

James I. Kugel, **The Ideas Of Biblical Poetry**, Yale University Press, 1981

Saul Lieberman, **Hellenism In Jewish Palestine**, The Jewish Theological Seminary Of America, 1950

Raphael Mahler, **The History Of Modern Jewry**, Shocken Books, 1971

Yaakov Malkin, **What Do Secular Jews Believe**, Milan Press, 1994

Yaakov Malkin, (Ed.), **Free Judaism And Religion In Israel - An Anthlogy Of Contemporary Secular Jewish Israeli Thought**, Milan Press, 1996

Yudel Mark, **The Yiddish Language - Its Cultural Impact,** American Jewish Historical Quarterly, 1969

Paul R. Mendes Flohr, Yehuda Reinharz, **Jews In The Modern Age - A Documentary History**, Oxford University Press, 1980

Raphael Patai, **The Jewish Mind**, Charles Scribner's Sons, 1977

Raphael Patai, **Israel Between East And West**, Jewish Publication Society, 1953

Raphael Patai, **The Hebrew Goddess**, Wayne State University Press, 1978

Raphael Patai, **Sex And Family In The Bible And The Middle East**, Doubleday, 1959

David Rosenberg, (Ed.), **Congregation - Contemporary Writers Read The Jewish Bible**, Including: Bashevis Singer, Harold Bloom, Leon Wieseltier, Mordecai Richler, Robert Pinsky, Elie Wiesel, Leslie Fiedler, Cynthia Ozick, Anne Roiphe Harcourt Brace Jovanovich, 1987

Samuel Samnel, **The Enjoyment Of Scriptures**, Oxford University Press, 1974

Nahum M. Sarna, **On The Book Of Psalms**, Shocken Books, 1995

Nahum M. Sarna, **Understanding Genesis**, Shocken Books, 1970

Nahum M. Sarna, **Exploring Exodus - The Heritage Of Biblical Israel**, Shocken Books, 1987

Hayim Schauss, **The Jewish Festivals - History And Observance**, Shocken Books, 1938

Gershom Scholem, **Major Trends In Jewish Mysticism**, Shocken Books, 1961

Meir Sternberg, **The Poetics Of Biblical Narrative**, Indiana University Press, 1985

Victor Tchericover, **Hellenistic Civilization And The Jews**, Atheneum, 1970

Michael Walzer, **Exodus And Revolution**, Basic Books, 1984

Sherwin T Wine, **Judaism Beyond God**, Milan Press, 1970

Gabriel Yossipovici, **The Book Of God**, Yale University Press, 1988

אלון ארי, **עלמא די**, שדמות, 1990

אליאור רחל, **חירות על הלוחות–המחשבה החסידית ומקורותיה המיסטיים**, הוצאת משרד הביטחון, סדרת האוניברסיטה המשודרת, 2002

אמית יאירה, **ספר שופטים – אמנות העריכה**, מוסד ביאליק, 1992

אמית יאירה, **היסטוריה ואידיאולוגיה במקרא**, משרד הבטחון/אוניברסיטה משודרת, 1988

בובר מרטין, **נתיבות באוטופיה**, עם עובד, 1983

בובר מרטין, **תעודה ויעוד**, הספריה הציונית, תשכ"א

ברדיצ'בסקי מ.י, **על הקשר בין אתיקה ואסתטיקה**, הקבוץ המאוחד/ספרית פועלים, 1986

ברינקר מנחם, **עד הסימטה הטבריינית - סיפור ומחשבה ביצירת ברנר**, עם עובד, 1990

ברנביא אלי (עורך), **אטלס תולדות ישראל**, משכל, 1999

גוברין נורית, **מאורע ברנר, המאבק על חופש הביטוי**, יד בן־צבי, תשמ"ה

גירץ קליפורד, **פרשנות של תרבויות**, כתר, 1990

דובנוב שמעון, **מכתבים על היהדות הישנה והחדשה**, דביר, תרצ"ז

הופמן יאיר, **שלמות פגומה**, מוסד ביאליק/אוניברסיטת תל-אביב, 1995

הרצל תיאודור, **אלטנוילנד**, בבל, 1997

טל אוריאל, **מיתוס ותבונה ביהדות ימינו**, ספרית פועלים, 1987

יהושע א.ב, **בזכות הנורמליות**, שוקן, 1980

יצחקי ידידיה, **בראש גלוי**, אוניברסיטת חיפה/זמורה-ביתן, 2000

ירון קלמן ומנדס-פלור פול, **מרטין בובר במבחן הזמן**, מאגנס, 1992

כהן חיים, **זכויות אדם במקרא ובתלמוד**, משרד הבטחון/אוניברסיטה משודרת, 1988

כהנוב עזר, **זהות לאומית לעומת זהות דתית ביהדות הספרדית**, המכללה האקדמית "אחוה" ו"יהדות חופשית", 2002

כץ יעקב, **היציאה מהגטו**, עם עובד, 1985

כץ יעקב, **מסורת ומשבר**, מוסד ביאליק, תשמ"ה

מלכין יעקב, **במה מאמינים יהודים חילונים**, ספרית פועלים, 2000

מנדס-פלור פול, **חכמת ישראל**, מרכז זלמן שזר, 1979

פיינר שמואל, **מהפכת הנאורות-תנועת ההשכלה היהודית במאה ה-18**, מרכז זלמן שזר, תשס"ב

צוקר דדי (עורך), **אנו היהודים החילונים - מהי זהות יהודית חילונית?**, ידיעות אחרונות, 1999

ציפרשטיין סטיבן, **נביא חמקמק, אחד-העם ומקורות הציונות**, עם עובד, ספרית אפקים, 1993

קויפמן יחזקאל, **גולה ונכר**, דביר, תשי"ד-תשכ"א

קנוהל ישראל, **ריבוי פנים באמנות הייחוד - זרמים ותפיסות ביהדות בעת העתיקה**, משרד הבטחון/אוניברסיטה משודרת, 1987

קפלן מרדכי, **דת הלאומיות המוסרית, תרומת ישראל לשלום העולם**, מסדה, 1975

רוטנשטרייך נתן, **תרבות והומניזם**, מאגנס, תשכ"ד

רוטנשטרייך נתן, **המחשבה היהודית בעת החדשה**, עם עובד, 1987

רות סביל ונרקיס, בצלאל, **תולדות האמנות היהודית**, מסדה, 1996

רש יהושע (עורך), **כזה ראה וחדש - היהודי החפשי ומורשתו**, ספרית פועלים, 1986

שאנן אביגדור (עורך), **אותו האיש – יהודים מספרים על ישו**, ידיעות אחרונות, 2001
שביד אליעזר, **לקראת תרבות יהודית מודרנית**, עם עובד, 1995
שביד אליעזר, **תולדות ההגות היהודית בזמן החדש**, כתר/הקיבוץ המאוחד, תשל"ח
שלום גרשום, **דברים בגו**, עם עובד, 1975

"אלוהים?"... – אסופת מאמרים בגליון של "יהדות חופשית" בין המחברים:
יצחק אורפז, ארי אלון, רחל אליאור, יאירה אמית, אברהם בורג, אלי ברנביא, ראובן גרבר, ציונה גרוסמרק, יוסף דן, אלוף הראבן, שולמית הראבן, אברהם וולפנזון, ידידיה יצחקי, בנימין כהן, חיים כהן, יעקב כהן, ירון לונדון, יעקב מלכין, צופיה מלר, עמוס עוז.

מאמרים:
ברדיצ'בסקי מ.י, "על אם הדרך"/"סיני וגריזים"/"להערצת החסידות", בתוך: כתבים, דביר, תש"ך
ברנר יוסף חיים, בעתונות ובספרות – "הגורם ל'מאורע ברנר'"/"לבירור העניין"/ "להערכת עצמנו בשלושת הכרכים" (בעקבות מנדלי מוכר ספרים), כתבים, הקבוץ המאוחד וספרית פועלים, תשמ"ה
יציב גדי, "חילוניות יהודית", הלקסיקון למדעי החברה, המכללה למנהל
מלכין יעקב, **הומניזם ולאומיות, חוברת הרצאה**, הוצאת יהדות חופשית
שמרוק חונא, "ספרות יידית", **האנציקלופדיה העברית**, כרך י"ט

מאמרים בכתב העת "יהדות חופשית": כרכים 1995-2003, 1-4
אלוני שולמית, (ראיון), **אני ויהדותי**, גליון 19
אריאלי יהושע, **היות יהודי חילוני בישראל, 'תחילה'**, גליון 5
באואר יהודה, **אמונה ומיסטיקה**, גליון 2
באואר יהודה, **היכן היה אלוהים בשואה?**, גליון 23
באואר יהודה, **חיוניות האופוזיציה החילונית ליהדות אמריקה**, גליון 5
באר חיים, **האם אלוהים נותר אילם?**, גליון 26
בן גוריון אריה, **אני מאמין של היהודי החילוני**, גליון 5

וולפנזון אברהם, **המשיחיות הדתית והחילונית**, גליון 4

וילר גרשון, **המאבק בין תרבות חילונית למסורת דתית**, גליון 4

יגיל גדי, **השיטה המדעית והשיטה הדתית – ניגוד או השלמה?**, גליון 13

יהושע א.ב., **המהפכה הציונית היש לה המשך?**, גליון 26

יהושע א.ב., **זהות ישראלית בעידן השלום**, גליון 4

יזהר ס., **עז להיות יהודי חילוני**, גליון 20

יזהר ס., **האי רציונלי הולך אתנו כל הזמן**, גליון 20

יצחקי ידידיה, **זאב ז'בוטינסקי**, גליון 25

יצחקי רינה, **צא ולמד – תכניות לימודים ליהדות כתרבות**, גליון 22

כהן חיים, **שחרור האמנות מכבלי ההלכה**, גליון 6

כהן חיים, **מי הוא יהודי**, גליון 4 וגליון 26

כשר אסא; צבן, יאיר; ליבמן, ישעיהו; פירון, ש, **רב שיח, יהדות ודמוקרטיה – תואם או ניגוד?**, גליון 13

מלכין יעקב, **הכמיהה לרוחניות בקרב חילוניים**, גליון 23

מלכין יעקב, **בית המקדש, עבר זמנו משבטל קרבנו**, גליון 23

מלכין יעקב, **פרומתאוס וחוה – סמלי ההומניזם וחטאו הקדמון של אלוהים**, גליון 14

מלכין יעקב, **ראשית ההפרדה בין זהות לאומית לדתית ביהדות התנ"ך**, גליון 25

מלר צופיה, **היחס לחילונים בספורי האבות**, גליון 19

מלר צופיה, **הנביא ירמיהו בין מינוי לשליחות**, גליון 22

עוז עמוס, **עגלה מלאה ועגלה ריקה**, גליון 11

עינם שניאור, **שלושה מעגלי זהות: יהודי הומניסטי ציוני**, גליון 4

פוזן פליקס, **החילוניות ביהדות – הגדול והזנוח בנושאי המחקר וההוראה**, גליון 22

פוזן פליקס, **ייחוד החילוניות כזרם ביהדות**, גליון 16

פוזן פליקס, **החילוניות – הגדול והזנוח בנושאי המחקר וההוראה**, גליון 22

צבן יאיר, **התרבות העברית החדשה – תשתית הזהות היהודית החילונית**, גליון 1

קליינברג אביעד, **על מוסר חילוני ותרבות יהודית**, גליון 26

שבייד אליעזר, **שפינוזה והזהות היהודית הלאומית**, גליון 25

שבייד אליעזר, **זהות יהודית הומניסטית**, גליון 4

336